D0731102

Z E N
M I N D
Z E N
H O R S E

ZEN MIND ZEN HORSE

...

The Science and Spirituality of
Working with Horses

ALLAN J. HAMILTON, MD

Storey Publishing

To my wonderful Opa,
who gave me a love of horses and of life.

"I'm gonna walk with my granddaddy, and he'll match me step for step
And I'll tell him how I've missed him, every minute since he left.
Then I'll hug his neck."

"When I Get Where I'm Going" by George Teren and Rivers Rutherford

■ ■ ■

The mission of Storey Publishing is to serve our customers by
publishing practical information that encourages
personal independence in harmony with the environment.

Edited by Deborah Burns
Art direction and book design by
 Dan O. Williams
Text production by Jennifer Jepson Smith

Cover illustration by Yoshijiro Urushibara
Interior photography credits
 appear on page 300
Author photo by Daniel Snyder
Illustrations by © Elayne Sears

Indexed by Samantha Miller

© 2011 by Allan J. Hamilton

All rights reserved. No part of this book may
be reproduced without written permission from
the publisher, except by a reviewer who may
quote brief passages or reproduce illustrations
in a review with appropriate credits; nor may
any part of this book be reproduced, stored in a
retrieval system, or transmitted in any form or
by any means — electronic, mechanical, photo-
copying, recording, or other — without written
permission from the publisher.

The information in this book is true and complete to the best of our knowledge. All recom-
mendations are made without guarantee on the
part of the author or Storey Publishing. The
author and publisher disclaim any liability in
connection with the use of this information.

Storey books are available for special premium
and promotional uses and for customized edi-
tions. For further information, please call
1-800-793-9396.

Storey Publishing
210 MASS MoCA Way
North Adams, MA 01247
www.storey.com

Printed in China by R.R. Donnelley
10 9 8 7 6 5 4 3 2 1

Library of Congress
Cataloging-in-Publication Data
Hamilton, Allan J.
 Zen mind, zen horse : the science and
 spirituality of working with horses /
 Allan J. Hamilton.
 p. cm.
 Includes index.
 ISBN 978-1-60342-565-0 (pbk.)
 1. Horses—Behavior. 2. Horses—
 Psychology. 3. Horses—Training.
 4. Human-animal communication.
 5. Zen Buddhism. I. Title.
SF281.H36 2011
636.1'0835—dc22
                    2011012946

On the cover: Yoshijiro (Mokuchu) Urushibara
(1889–1953) was a woodblock print craftsman
who helped introduce Japanese art to the world
in the early twentieth century. His renderings of
horses were especially celebrated for their fluid
beauty and grace.

CONTENTS

FOREWORD

I N RECENT YEARS there has been a wealth of books written about what has become recognizable to horse lovers as Natural Horsemanship, and what these authors seem to regard as the path to understanding the mind of *Equus*. Most equestrians learn their horsemanship hands on. They are observers of behavior and architects of harmony. Some of these authors even address what I call the "language of *Equus*." It isn't often, however, that they fully understand how the mind of the horse functions.

Most people recognize that body language is the primal form of communication. *Equus* has survived for millions of years through his communication system made up almost entirely of a silent language of gestures. This system allows the herd to cohabit successfully with predators. My years of observing and working with horses of all kinds have allowed me to put together an expansive lexicon of gestures and postures that has given me insight into the "language of *Equus*."

Zen Mind, Zen Horse explores the depth of understanding and transforms the foundation of my work and concepts into a more probing exploration of the mind of the horse. In this comprehensive essay, we can gain valuable insight into the reasoning behind the horse's reactions to the intentions we humans communicate through our thoughts and actions. We discover that *Equus* is brilliant in his simplicity of reasoning.

As enlightened horsemen and horsewomen, we learn that it is our responsibility to create an environment in which the horse can learn. The round pen is a wonderful classroom in which to use the silent language of *Equus*. Using the lexicon of body language and gestures, we communicate to the horse our desire to form a partnership based on mutual respect and trust within this safe enviroment.

In *Zen Mind, Zen Horse*, the author has generously given the reader the tools to appreciate how we can better understand the mind of *Equus*. This in itself can energize us to have a fresh outlook or approach to life, not just with horses, but with fellow humans as well. This wonderful animal called the horse is helping heal our wounded warriors who suffer from PTSD and is changing the lives of autistic and challenged children and adults in therapeutic riding academies.

We are just scratching the surface of the evolution of equine training by what is termed Natural Horsemanship. Thankfully, open-minded people have come to recognize how much further we can go to gain optimal performance by taking violence out of the lives of our animals through kinder and gentler techniques. This book is a wonderful tribute to all the horsemen who have dedicated their lives and are sharing their concepts with other horsemen the world over.

MONTY ROBERTS, trainer and author, *The Man Who Listens to Horses* and other books

■ ■ ■

I WAS ASKED to do this Foreword because, after a lifetime of effort, I am now considered an expert on equine behavior. How I wish Dr. Hamilton had written this book in 1949. I was twenty-two years of age and had just decided that the conventional methods of horsemanship with which I was familiar were not the best ways of communicating with horses.

Reading books written in past centuries and experimenting with horses allowed me, in the subsequent half century, to learn some of the information available in this book, but by no means all. I am grateful for this opportunity.

Read on and you will learn far more than the author's very interesting autobiography. I studied some neurology when I was in veterinary school more than a half century ago. The neuroscience presented in this book, however, was a revelation to me and helped me understand so much more of why and how both humans and horses functioned.

The information on what we consider to be primitive societies is makes us reevaluate their intellectual capabilities. There have always been reasoning, curious individuals. The voluminous, well-illustrated chapters on handling and training horses, on the scientifically confirmed facts about equine behavior, make reading this book a privilege to all who work with horses. The sections on the power of intention, the relationship that can be established during routine grooming, the all-important virtue of patience, and the psychology of learning are invaluable.

Half of the book is devoted to the art and science of Natural Horsemanship, a method that is sweeping the world and replacing and improving traditional methods, so much of which was and is unnecessarily coercive. For people already skilled in and familiar with this revolution in horsemanship, the book will justify and explain their devotion. Those unfamiliar with this revolutionary concept will, hopefully, be motivated to come on board, not only for their own benefit, but for the horses.

ROBERT M. MILLER, DVM, author, *Imprint Training of the Newborn Foal* and other books

Horses seem to have special abilities to connect emotionally with humans.

INTRODUCTION

...

A CHILLING THOUGHT OCCURRED TO ME: could Lillian be trying to kill herself, hoping my 1,200-pound stallion might stomp her to death? Was this how she intended to commit suicide? Weak, frail, and eroded by the torrents of chemotherapy she'd endured during the last few months, Lillian had recently learned that her doctors had given her less than three months to live. Her brain tumor was growing too fast to be stopped. A novice around horses, she was now asking — begging — me to let her enter the round pen and work with my stallion Romeo.

Her experience with horses was nil: she had been on a few pony rides as a little girl, nothing more. Romeo, on the other hand, was not a horse to take lightly. As a stallion he could be a handful — a potentially lethal one — even for a professional trainer. Stallions, in that sense, are a bit like grenades. Play catch with them if you choose, but just be sure the pin always stays in place. To make matters worse, Romeo was in the full throes of breeding season, half crazed with testosterone, and stoked with desire by the nearby mares in heat. His stallion's drive to demonstrate his explosive strength and physical dominance in front of the mares seemed barely constrained by the steel railings of the round pen itself.

Next to Romeo, Lillian appeared puny and inconsequential, a weakling, with matchstick limbs hanging from her diminutive, skeletal frame. She was virtually paralyzed on one half of her body. I could see the groove in the sand where she had been dragging her weak leg behind her to get positioned in the center of the round pen. I was afraid this might turn into less of a training exercise and more of a sacrifice. Still there was something about her request that seemed compelling. She looked like a pilgrim, searching for an answer. She was going into the round pen to confront something substantive, something to which Romeo held the key.

Normally I would never agree to put an inexperienced person in with a stud horse, but my gut told me there was more to this. It had a solemnity to it, like a deathbed promise. So I nodded my consent against every fiber of caution.

Lillian opened the gate. I braced my hands on the top railing, readying myself to jump in and pull the horse away from her if things turned violent. But it wasn't required. In the face of that charging, snorting horse, Lillian simply closed her eyes and began to breathe. After a few moments, she gently and patiently focused her gaze on Romeo. At first the stallion thundered around the pen, but soon he began to slow down, growing visibly quieter and calmer with each revolution.

After five minutes, Lillian seemed to have drained all the force and fury out of him. Romeo drew closer to her, in tighter and tighter circles, until he came to stand next to her. He stopped there, almost at attention. Then he sighed and hung his head down next to her. She turned and buried her face into his huge, muscular neck. From outside the round pen, I could see her shoulders shake as she wrapped her arms around him and sobbed. After a few minutes, she walked over to me and said apologetically, "I felt like I had to be strong enough to calm this horse down or I wouldn't be able to fight this cancer any longer. I needed to know I could make myself that strong to keep on living. That's why it had to be Romeo."

Lillian did have the strength to keep living — a whole extra year. Her ashes are buried in the center of the round pen on my ranch. That was her final request. Every morning, I go out there and greet her spirit and pay tribute to the demonstration of spiritual strength Lillian shared with me that day many years ago. Her presence makes my round pen a sacred place.

■ ■ ■

IT'S HUMAN NATURE to want to improve ourselves: physically, financially, emotionally. And as we age and mature, our efforts seem to focus naturally on spiritual growth as well. But that requires new insights and skills we must learn and practice. We need to build up karmic muscle to turn the breakdowns in our lives into breakthroughs. We must turn into warriors who take up the discipline of spiritual pursuit in earnest. But how?

How do we train for a journey of spiritual transformation alone? The truth is that we need a spiritual coach, a *sensei,* to teach us — to show us how to focus our intention and to demonstrate how to live in the present and how to achieve Zen-like tranquility. We need a teacher to show us how to see ourselves — not just with heightened objectivity but also with greater forgiveness. For that job, there *is* a master: a sage who can teach any willing student the way. That sage is the horse.

This animal has been considered among humanity's most revered and sacred companions across many great civilizations. To the Egyptians, horses were *htr* (pronounced "heter"). Their hieroglyphic depiction for the horse was a symbol for the bond between human and animal: a simple, intertwined rope (*see figure 1.1*).

Horse was *hippos* to the Greeks, whose mythological gods lived among equally immortal steeds. And the Latin *Equus* became almost emblematic of Rome's imperial power. Why has the horse evoked such deep, emotional and spiritual sentiments? Because he can carry us physically and spiritually into unchartered territory, beyond our everyday worries and distractions. The horse is a symbol of transcendence.

For most of us, the overarching problem in our lives is time itself. Our schedules no longer seem to belong to us. Our waking hours (and many sleeping ones, too) seem allocated to issues other than our own deep personal needs and values. Happiness and tranquility do not receive high priority in our daily regimens. Instead, they drift out of sight in the fog of daily routine.

Our internal voices seem to be constantly yelling at us to pull harder at the oars, to go after more. They suggest that we're losing out or giving in or being passed over. These voices become like a broken record, endlessly droning on about regrets in the past and worries in the future. We know listening to our ego's exhortations is not how we are meant to live. We admit our lifestyle isn't working for us, but how can we change it?

There is one single key, one secret, to undertaking transformational change. It is the same in every great meditative discipline or self-improvement practice. *Get that inner voice to shut up!* Until we create inner silence — literally, peace of mind — we are unable to transform our lives into more peaceful and purposeful ones.

Why are our inner voices so ubiquitous and incessant? Think about this: at the very moment we are reading these words on the page, we are also hearing them echo inside our heads. When we think, we hear a voice. Our thoughts take shape as words. To the extent that we even exist, this voice seems to occur in the context of what Dr. Antonio Damasio has termed "the autobiographical self." This entity — *our* identity — is constantly thinking "aloud," inside our head. Later I will discuss in detail why this autobiographical self is a unique and necessary byproduct of our left cerebral dominance. But for now, it suffices to say that this self emerges from our own species' unique dependence on language.

The Power of Gesture and Glance

...

THE REASON THE HORSE can become such a gifted teacher for us is because he does not need an inner voice. He doesn't think in words at all. He feels. He experiences the simple energy of his emotional state of being. More than thirty million years of evolutionary pressure have turned the horse into the quintessential prey animal. Rather than using words or vocalizations to communicate — sounds that help a predator pinpoint its prey — horses learned instead how *not* to talk, how not to make sounds, and how to make sense from being, *not* thinking.

Horses infuse emotional meaning into every body movement. They pour this vital, emotional energy — *chi* — into every gesture and glance, lending them the nuances of tone, accent, and value. By sensitizing themselves to chi, horses can not only convey the meaning of what they want to share with other members of the herd but can also feel the palpably sharp energy emitted by a stalking predator, eyes locked intently on its prey (*see figure 1.2*). Evolution has driven equids to the farthest limits of nonverbal, right-sided brain function.

1.2 Zebras on savanna being stalked by lioness in foreground. Evolutionary pressures exerted by constant predation over millions of years put a premium on equids' development of nonverbal communication skills that allowed them to avoid detection.

Evolution of the Super-Predator

■■■

THE HUMAN SPECIES WENT in the opposite direction. Selective biological pressures, coupled with a rapid increase in cranial capacity (*see figure 1.3*), permitted hominids to leave behind an arboreal existence and take to the savannas. Our ancestors became foragers and, eventually, keen predators. *Homo sapiens* sharpened the skills housed within the brain's left hemisphere. We flourished as a species, using language to coordinate our movements as pack hunters. And we became storytellers, sharing tales about the game species we sought, creating mythologies, building cultures, and even establishing empires. In the process, we became a new kind of super-predator, an unimaginably successful killer species, playful with our wits and lethal with our intellects, but, eventually no longer in touch with the secrets deep within our own hearts.

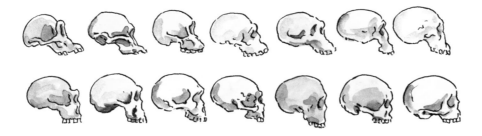

1.3 The evolution of hominids was marked by the most rapid growth of skull size ever seen in any archeological record. This set of skulls covers a remarkably short span of only a few hundred thousand years. It is hypothesized that the rapid development in language and speech function may have required dramatic expansion of brain size.

The Rise of the "I"
and the Fall of the "We"

■■■

THE SUCCESS HUMANS DERIVED from left-hemispheric dominance came at a price. Just as the horse surrendered its vocal abilities to gain herd identity, the human species forfeited its intuitive powers for the benefits of language. We became outcasts from the natural world, because raising the function of speech to its highest level of expression required the emergence of a separate consciousness. Speech demanded a "me" to be the inner

Carl Jung, the father of modern psychoanalysis

voice. The expression of language gave rise to the autobiographical self, an identity separate from the world at large.

Carl Jung, the father of modern psychoanalysis, wrote:

The source of numerous psychic disturbances and difficulties occasioned by man's progressive alienation from his instinctual foundation, i.e., by his uprootedness and identification with his conscious knowledge of himself, by his concern with consciousness at the expense of the unconscious. . . . he forgets himself in the process, losing sight of his instinctual nature and putting his own conception of himself in place of his real being.

— Carl Gustav Jung, *The Undiscovered Self*, 1957

So an "I" was born in each of us, conceived from the neuroanatomical development of our species. And it owns us lock, stock, and barrel, because once it emerges, it seizes control of vast territories of brain function, of our very self-perception and self-awareness. There is an intracerebral coup, and the existence of a singular, internalized identity is the party line we are told to accept. But our left hemisphere, armed with its overwhelming power of speech, remains wary of its reticent, emotive, and mute counterpart on the right. The left brain demands absolute loyalty. It zealously safeguards the supremacy of its creation: namely, our ego.

The left knows that if an uprising were to start, it would be sparked by the right half of our brain. Though this side has no voice, it has the power to remind us silently of the union we once enjoyed with all life around us. The right hemisphere offers us the hope that a sense of unification might be more important to our spiritual well-being than a sense of identification. Inevitably, the hemispheric struggle becomes a battle of consciousness, of a solitary, monolithic *me* implacably opposed to the notion of a communal, interconnected *we*.

We need opportunities to lead with our right hemispheres. We need to practice *being* connected without worrying about an explanation of why we are connected. Our innate longing for connectivity — and the profound warmth, peace, and happiness that we derive from it — requires us to rely on our right hemisphere.

For most of us, that right-sided function has atrophied. It's weak, feeble, shaky. We're unaccustomed to what the right side feels like because of the overbearing presence of the left. To hear the silence of the right, we must strengthen our intuitive, nonverbal powers.

Partnering with Equus

■ ■ ■

INTERACTING WITH HORSES does just that. We glimpse nature from a radically different perspective: a view of the world drawn by the right brain. Relating to horses provides us a unique opportunity to mute our left hemisphere. To force it into silence. Horses provide us with a respite from thinking about ourselves, a chance to escape from the prison of *being ourselves by ourselves.*

Because horses function from the premise of a herd identity, they see relationships as partnerships. They struggle to include us in their concept of a herd — a huge leap considering they are the ultimate prey species and we the *über* predators.

As humans, it is almost inconceivable to us how dramatically different the equine perspective of inclusivity really is. For illustrative purposes, however, imagine waking up on Christmas morning. As you sit down to open your presents, you suddenly discover an 800-pound Bengal tiger seated next to you on the living room sofa. And your response? You are scared out of your wits; you want to scream, run, and scramble for the nearest rifle or tree limb.

Imagine instead you strive to *include* that tiger in a communal context. Rather than flee, you rack your brain to figure out how to hang a stocking on the hearth to make the tiger feel at home, a part of your family. This gives us an inkling of the enormous emotional achievement horses accomplish each day to include us, human predators, as an integral part of their daily working (and emotional) lives. It's a remarkable spiritual statement about the capacity of the equine heart and soul.

As horses derive their very essence from inclusion in a herd, so they struggle to extend that relationship to us as shared *being.* When a horse is with us, we become a part of his herd. As far as time is concerned, horses live only in the moment. There are no expectations for the future or disappointments from the past to cloud their relationships with us. Without such agendas, horses don't know how to lie, cheat, or deceive. Horses thus offer us a unique opportunity to see ourselves in "divine mirrors," reflecting back the chi we give off in our own emotions, to show ourselves *in the moment.* Horses react to what lies in our hearts, not in our heads. They are not confused by the words we use to lie to ourselves or hide from others.

Horses awaken the dormant right half of the human brain. Because the output of our right hemisphere has been largely suppressed since early childhood, it takes time to feel comfortable as a right-sided "we" instead of a left-sided "me." Eliminating the voice of our egos creates a silence that is at first frightening, but later, we learn, also enthralling. With that silence comes breathtaking power and clarity of thought. As Obi-Wan-Kanobi in *Star Wars* encourages Luke Skywalker to trust "the Force," so horses exhort us to trust our intuitive right-brain abilities.

Working with horses gives us the opportunity to return to a primal, nonverbal state of awareness. Without the interference of language, we reconnect with the energy shared among all life forms. The connection is palpable and immediate. We learn how to find it, focus it, and let it fly. We explore how to apply chi for the purposes of asking our horses to move naturally, effortlessly, and respectfully wherever we wish them to go. We discover by direct, personal interaction with the horse that we are equal parts body and spirit: half chi, half DNA. Theologist John O'Donahue wrote: "Beyond the veils of language and the noise of activity, the most profound events of our lives take place in those fleeting moments where something else shines through, something that can never be fixed in language, something given as quietly as the gift of your next breath."

Horsemanship as a Spiritual Path

■ ■ ■

TRAINING HORSES WITH EMOTIONAL energy, with chi, is an evolution of the concepts of pressure and release used in natural horsemanship. All of us who work with horses owe a debt of gratitude to the pioneers of this discipline. Because of their contributions, we gain a better vantage point, from which we can see that horsemanship can lead us deep into the realm of self-awareness.

In this book, I have relied, in part, on concepts borrowed from different cultures, religions, and philosophies that have inspired me. These teachings or symbols offer beautiful ways to conceptualize and integrate the personal impact of training horses. I have included inspirational writings and scholarly interpretations from such diverse sources as Confucianism, Taoism, Zen Buddhism, Hinduism, Native American folklore, and Yaqui shamanism.

But nothing about training or interacting with horses using chi is meant to be esoteric or academic. The methodology in this book can be used by anyone, with or without prior equine or scholarly experience. Novice or expert, we can all find a comfortable setting in which to be around horses, to play with them, and, most importantly, to learn from them. I have taught individuals ranging from nine years old to ninety, from national-caliber athletes to the disabled, from the CEOs of Fortune 500 companies to hardened criminals. What I teach here is not magic. I am no magician; only the horses possess magical powers. By sharing their nonverbal abilities with us, they show us how to amplify our inner strengths, values, and energies.

First and foremost, this book is for those individuals who feel a certain mystical curiosity. The spiritual itch. It describes an approach to the training of horses that gives us a new way of seeing. Wayne Dyer, the popular psychologist, says, "If you change the way you look at things, the things you look at change." By altering how we visualize our relationships with horses, we discern a pathway leading to self-improvement, fulfillment, and awareness. Horses connect with our souls — the part of us that links us to everything. Horses help us find those bonds. The connections become as real as the ground we walk on. I hope my book will be an equine atlas, showing us another way to find ourselves.

Crossing the Threshold

∎ ∎ ∎

TRAINING HORSES, however, is a path, not a destination. Becoming a horseman or a horsewoman is not some elevated summit to reach but a journey to be undertaken. The way of the horse is a prescription for engaging the Universe. It serves as an algorithm for finding a more fulfilling life; maybe even a shot at peace and happiness, too. Ray Hunt, one of the great sages of natural horsemanship, summed it up:

1.5

Ray Hunt

> *My goal with the horses is not to beat someone; it's to win within myself. To do the best job I can do and tomorrow to try to do better. You'll be working on yourself to accomplish this, not your horse.*

Every time you step into the round pen with a horse, remind yourself that today you may stand on the threshold of a great new personal discovery. Each horse, in his own way, is ready to coach you. And when your resolution to change — to work on the person you want to become — becomes heartfelt and sincere, then the horse will reveal his next great secret, his next great gift, to you.

Horses are like a band of legendary Zen masters. They are perfect teachers because they uncover your real motivation. They tell you when you're wholeheartedly committed or faking it, when you're making a sacred vow or just paying lip service. Horses see what's holding you back. And when you find the courage to confront those shortcomings, horses will always reward you with a way to overcome them. Just as Romeo did for Lillian.

If all this begins to make horsemanship sound like a religious experience, I can accept that analogy. Describing how to work with horses as a way to access spiritual lessons is one of the goals of this book. I hope to encourage people — especially novices — not to feel intimidated by a lack of experience. None is required. Working with horses on the ground is a simple, easy, and safe way to *see* and *feel* spiritual concepts at work. I also want to elucidate a new method for training horses based on the Asian concepts of manipulating chi. I hope the language and writing style are accessible to horsemen and novices from every walk of life and style of riding.

Finally, I pray this book can help convey the power of what horses can teach us about the nature of spirituality. French literary figure Anatole France wrote: "Until one has loved an animal, a part of one's soul remains unawakened."

Horsemanship is another way, another vehicle, to achieve awakening. What is spiritually and developmentally significant in that pursuit is different for each of us. An automobile can take you and me to different locations, yet the method of driving and rules of the road for cars remain universally applicable. Mastering horsemanship is no different. A common set of skills is required before we are ready to seek our own destination.

Happy trails!

NOTE: The term *horsemanship* is unfortunately not entirely gender neutral. This is regrettable in the modern world of horses, where so many of the individuals fiercely dedicated to improving the lives of horses are women. I employ the term, with its historical constraints, to signify the pursuit of furthering the knowledge and understanding of the skills of riding, managing, and training horses, and gaining insight into equine behavior.

CHAPTER ONE

DAYS OF THUNDER

The youth walks up to the white horse, to put its halter on
and the horse looks at him in silence.
They are so silent, they are in another world.

■ ■ ■

D.H. LAWRENCE, *The White Horse*

LIFE SEEMED BARELY ABLE to contain my grandfather, who threatened at every turn to burst it at the seams. Blessed with an epic personality, he could charm, stir, or inspire every man, woman, child, or animal who crossed his path. He had fought with great distinction in two world wars, pioneered oil exploration in the Middle East and the ocean floor, and was an early leader in the Pan-European movement, a precursor of today's European Union. His friends inhabited the upper circles of society and influence: from Queen Victoria's granddaughter, the Queen of Spain, to Konrad Adenauer, the first chancellor of postwar Germany; from oceanographer Jacques Cousteau to inspirational architect Richard Neutra.

All of that meant nothing to me as a child. He was just my grandfather who, I was convinced, had magical powers.

When I was about six, he took me to visit the German Olympic Equestrian facility. He was known as a superb horseman, and one of his friends was the team's dressage coach. We drove through an ornate gated archway, passing manicured lawns and rows of barns. Horses were everywhere, trotting on paths, strolling out of breezeways, coursing over jumps. My grandfather instructed me to wait in the car.

Minutes later he came back astride a massive Thoroughbred. I could not have imagined a loftier human being than my grandfather at that moment. He called me to get out of the car and then swooped down and lifted me off the ground. Plopping me down in the saddle in front of him he wrapped a huge arm around me.

He leaned over and whispered in my ear: "Are you ready?"

"Yes," I answered breathlessly.

Letting out a whoop, he put his spurs to the horse and we exploded like a rocket. The Thoroughbred soared over the ground, huge clumps of grass and earth flying out from his hooves. There was no end to his power and vigor. I heard his breathing get deeper and louder and faster, while the drumbeat of his hooves grew more urgent, more insistent.

Suddenly we turned in a wide circle until a jump appeared before us. My grandfather seemed possessed, unflinchingly urging the horse faster and faster. With each stride his arm tightened around my waist like a giant boa constrictor.

And then we simply leapt free from the earth. We were aloft. I felt as if I were being held in the air by the arms of Zeus himself. And this creature that bore us on his back? Surely, this could only be a creature for the gods.

That was my very first memory of a horse. It seemed to sear my soul. The next time a horse would carry me away, it would save me from desperate disgrace.

...

How do animals seem to know exactly when we need them most, when we're hurting so badly we're about to crumble? How do they know the precise moment to come over to us, put their head next to ours, and nuzzle in close? Just as our tears are ready to come, they sigh. Or they rub against us or insert themselves under our hand for a pet. They offer a thousand different ways and gestures, all with the same message: "I'm here. With you. And, yes, I know why you're hurting inside."

There's a scientifically valid explanation for why our sophisticated human central nervous system developed to allow a four-legged, 1,000-pound herbivore ungulate to plug right into the heart of our deepest emotions. There's a reason why horses are able to connect so intimately with us, to instantly plumb the depths of our most personal feelings. And, yes, there's a solid, potent explanation for why these gifted animals know when we need to be saved.

The Presence of Horses

•••

That horses could inspire me was improbable, because I grew up where there were none: well, practically none. I grew up in Manhattan. But it was not the absence of horses I felt as a child, but rather the power of their presence, no matter how remote. Even a trace was enough. I was born under their spell.

For some kids, it's monster trucks or great ball players. For me, it was always horses. When it came to Saturday morning TV westerns, I was never concerned about Roy Rogers getting shot; it was Trigger I worried about. What if they missed Roy and Trigger took a bullet?

1.1 Roy Rogers and his famous Palomino, Trigger. Both were icons of the Saturday matinee cinema and, later, television.

Horse and carriage
lined up along
Central Park West
next to Plaza Hotel

My obsession with horses drove the rest of my family crazy. Whenever we strolled down a street, my mom stayed on the lookout, eyes peeled. If she saw a horse-drawn carriage or mounted policeman up ahead, she'd instantly reverse course and pray I hadn't yet spotted the horse.

If I had, she'd grab me by the collar so I wouldn't dart blindly out into traffic. And pity the poor driver who parked his hack outside the Plaza Hotel when I walked by. I'd jerk free, Mom yelling after me to remember to be polite. "Ask permission before petting the horse. Watch for cars."

I'd bombard the driver with questions. "Why's the horse have blinders?" To keep him from getting nervous about the cars. "Doesn't he need to be able to see the traffic?" Sometimes. "Can I feed the horse?" No. "How often do you change horseshoes?" Every six weeks. "Can I drive the carriage?" Hell, no.

I was such a pest, some drivers would rather giddyup out of there and lose a fare. They'd snap the reins and trot off just to be rid of me. Mounted riders in Central Park would politely excuse themselves, spurring their mounts down the bridle path, to avoid me. And the poor mounted police — I just could not stop pestering them. "Do you keep them next to your patrol car?" "Do you have to poop scoop?" "Can you tie them up to a parking meter?"

Deep in the DNA

···

I WAS DRAWN TO HORSES as if they were magnets. It was in my blood. I must have inherited from my grandfather a genetic proclivity toward the equine species. Perhaps there's a quirk in the DNA that makes horse people different from everyone else, that instantly divides humanity into those who love horses and the others, who simply don't know.

To be content, horse people need only a horse or, lacking that, someone else who loves horses with whom they can talk. It was always that way with my grandfather. He took me places just so we could *see* horses, be near them. We went to the circus and the rodeo at Madison Square Garden. We watched parades down Fifth Avenue. Finding a horse, real or imagined, was like finding a dab of magic potion that enlivened us both. Sometimes I'd tell my grandfather about all the horses in my elaborate dreams. He'd lean over, smile, and assure me that, one day, I'd have one for real. And if my grandfather, my Opa, told me something was going to come true, it always did.

In school, I mutated every homework assignment into an opportunity to write about or draw horses. In third grade, Mrs. Wainwright asked the

1.3 Washington's horse, "Dynamite," waiting for him on the opposite riverbank, as drawn by the author at age ten

class to draw a picture of George Washington crossing the Delaware River. Twenty-nine heroic depictions of the father of our country were turned in, showing him standing up in the bow of a rowboat. But not mine.

I drew a picture of Washington's horse waiting for him on the opposite riverbank. Washington was a general. Of course, he had a horse — a fierce stallion, no doubt. The only reason he would have made such a perilous crossing, I imagined, was to get to his steed. I nicknamed him "Dynamite."

In Mrs. Gross's fifth-grade class, we were asked to make a poster depicting a contemporary world leader. It was 1960, and internationally prominent figures no longer seemed to have the itch to ride around on horseback. A pity. The nineteenth century valued a heroic profile astride a mount — proof was the imposing figure of Teddy Roosevelt.

But I was faced with immortalizing Mr. Dag Hammarskjöld, the newly appointed secretary general of the United Nations. This would be my Waterloo, my moment of utter defeat. Would I be stumped and surrender my equine obsession? No; I refused to yield. I submitted my homework, handing in a poster that focused on my beloved mounted police, atop their trusty mounts, holding a surging crowd behind traffic barriers as the

1.4 This oil painting hangs over my desk; it is my favorite depiction of Theodore Roosevelt on horseback as a colonel in the Rough Riders. It was faithfully reproduced from the original by Tade Styka, which today hangs in the Roosevelt Room in the West Wing of the White House.

secretary general pulled up to the entrance of the United Nations. He, his limousine, and the UN building were far off in the distance, incidental and barely visible. My grade? An F.

A Door Opens

■■■

HORSES SEEMED DESTINED to thrive only in my imagination. That changed the following summer, however, when I was packed off to sleep-away camp. I had never been away from home, not for even a single night at a friend's house. When it came time to climb aboard the train taking me from Grand Central to the heart of the Adirondacks, I was glued to the platform with fear.

Pete, the camp director, strode up to me, wearing a big smile and holding out a large open hand. I quivered. I looked at the ground. That morning, my mother had strapped brand-new, absurdly oversized hiking boots onto my feet. Where was I being exiled, I wondered, that I would need boots the size of nuclear attack submarines, sealed with waffled soles capable of stripping the very crust off the planet? Where were they sending me?

"Say hello, Allan," my mother said, nudging me forward. "Go on. Be polite. Take Pete's hand. Introduce yourself." She nodded me in his direction.

I didn't move a muscle. Pete was, in my eyes, the warden of the prison where I was being sent, perhaps never to be heard from again. Eight weeks was a life sentence.

"He's shy," Mom explained. "Withdrawn," she added, with an almost clinical wince. "He's likely to keep to himself, if you let him. That's one thing you should keep in mind."

My mother had a ready word of advice for everyone. For Pete: "You and your staff should try to draw him out. Get him involved in activities, engaged. Take him by the hand. Frankly," she added ominously, "you may have to drag him."

Pete's irrepressible smile seemed to wither a bit. He nodded and rubbed my buzz-cut. "Don't worry," he reassured my mother. "We'll take good care of him."

Political prisoners, headed to the gulag, have summoned more enthusiasm than I did climbing aboard that train. We sped through the Bronx, passing constrained backyards, and rolled into the unfamiliar, expansive farmscapes of upstate New York. A few hours later, beyond Albany, we chugged past lakes and streams, going deeper into the alien, evergreen heart of the Adirondacks.

We finally disembarked at a little hole in the forest called Keeseville. The train hissed to a standstill in front of a bleached wooden building. The whole depot sagged, its porch leaning over on its columns, ready to swoon onto the tracks.

A caravan of trucks and vans pulled up. Kids and duffle bags were stuffed into them like soldiers headed to the front. The convoy headed down a twisting road, into the shadowy gullet of the forest. Panic was shredding bits and pieces of me with every mile of the journey and as we rolled into camp, there was nothing left. I felt stripped naked, for all to see and ridicule.

Things only got worse at lights-out. Alone and afraid in my bed, I felt nighttime seeping into me. I couldn't sleep. I hid under the covers, where my flashlight staved off the gloom outside. By its light, I prayed to God to take me home, and finally, I drifted off to sleep.

■ ■ ■

THE NEXT MORNING the sun did shine, and substantially brighter than expected. It was Sunday. We went to the main lodge and sat down to a hearty breakfast of pancakes and cherry fritters. Since it was the first day at camp, everyone was free to explore the various activity centers: boathouse, archery, nature hut, woodshop, and so on. The camp was spread out over 30 acres of woodland, stretching down to blue lakefront. All the kids left the dining room, scattering across the grounds and greeting old friends. Most had a mission: sign up for baseball practice; look at the new sailboats; watch the archery demonstration.

I had a plan of my own. In many of those Saturday morning TV westerns, the hero kept some sugar cubes handy for his favorite horse. So I stuffed my pockets with a fistful of sweet, tasty treats and struck out in search of what I had heard was a barn "filled with horses to ride." I knew instinctively a barn should be located on flat terrain, not a hillside sloping down to a lake.

I headed uphill until I struck a dirt road leading out of camp and followed it a ways. It became more substantial and turned into asphalt. Great stacks of hay in an open field eventually appeared, and then the unmistakable smell of horses filled the air. I let my nose lead me. Sure enough, there they were.

1.5

Black and white pinto

Eight or nine horses milled around in a small corral. One in particular caught my eye: a black and white horse, what I now call a Pinto. Later, I learned his name was Thunder, but I saw nothing tempestuous in his nature. He seemed friendly enough and came up to the fence. I pulled out my first sugar cube, and he munched away on it contentedly. He stood patiently by the fence while I fed him another. And another. How tantalizingly close he was! *It would be an easy matter to clamber up the railing*, I thought. *Couldn't I just lower myself onto the horse's back?*

Suddenly, there I was, sitting astride Thunder's withers. He didn't even flinch. He walked slowly away from the fence, disappointed, maybe, that I was no longer feeding him sugar cubes. He mingled with the rest of the herd. And me? Well, I was in heaven, a million miles away from home, but just where I knew I should be: on horseback. The view from atop Thunder, looking out over the fields as he mingled with his fellow horses, was surreal. A dream. For hours, I rode wherever Thunder wanted to go. Naturally, there was no way for me to steer him, but I felt as free and unfettered as the Indians in my favorite TV westerns.

Then a nagging thought occurred to me. Yes, I was up on Thunder's back. The plan had worked flawlessly to this point. But there was one catch: I was six or seven feet off the ground, with no way to get down! The horse walked around ceaselessly, never moving close enough to the fence that I dared jump off. It dawned on me: I was stuck there, holding

1.6 The horseback-riding program at North Country Camps, located near Keeseville, New York, where the author first learned to ride. (Photo courtesy of Camp Lincoln, North Country Camps)

tightly to the horse's mane, and I had to stay that way until, somehow, help arrived. I hadn't planned for the dismount. And with Thunder constantly roaming about, disembarking appeared a daunting task. Surely someone would come eventually, to put the horses in the stable or to feed them.

Back at camp, lunch came and went. Dinner, too. My absence caused alarm. My mother's words about my shy nature now echoed with foreboding in Pete's head. Could I have actually walked off, or felt the need to hide, or, worse, wandered off into the fathomless Adirondack forest?

Staff members fanned out across camp, searching for me. Daylight died behind the mountain range beyond the lake. By then, I was alone in the dark, holding onto the massive shoulders and bones rolling beneath me. My legs throbbed. My crotch was squashed against Thunder's backbone. I tried to reach down to relieve the pressure on my groin but then stopped, afraid I'd lose my balance. I imagined falling and being trampled in the pitch black.

I noticed pinpoint stars. Headlights bobbed on the faraway interstate. My shoulders sagged wearily, and my thighs burned from hours on Thunder's back. I obsessed about becoming too sleepy and my grip giving out. Then I saw something down toward the lake.

It was a light, darting among the trees like a confused firefly, a haphazard dance in the distance. But then it progressed through the forest, oscillating wildly at first. Eventually, it consolidated just about where I guessed the road became asphalt. It was a flashlight! I started hollering at the top of my lungs.

The light suddenly jerked, steadied, and then surged madly toward me. I heard my name shouted. It was Will! He came at a dead run across the fields and leaped over the fence. The horses snorted uneasily and scattered as he dropped into their midst, next to Thunder. Will wrapped his arms around the horse's neck. "Whoa, boy. Whoa there!"

"Will! Will, I'm sorry. I just got stuck up here and couldn't get down," I stammered.

He grabbed me by the waist and lowered me to the ground. My legs immediately gave way, and I crumpled to my knees. My crotch burned. He yanked me up to my feet, holding me upright by the waist, and moved me toward the road. The van soon arrived. A counselor got out and helped Will lay me on the back seat. Will climbed behind the wheel. Our tires squealed, and the vehicle lurched back onto the asphalt.

I was preparing myself for a real dressing-down. *Maybe even a whipping*, I thought. But we walked into the dining hall, where all the staff regarded me. Will pointed at a plate of food set out on the table, the last supper for the prisoner.

Pete walked in. I could only imagine how mad he must have been. Instead, he grinned from ear to ear. "So much for someone having to take your hand," he said, rubbing my head. Some of the staff guffawed in the background. Will smiled. He already knew: this summer, I was going to be fine.

The next day, when I stepped into the dining hall to grab breakfast, all the kids stared. There was not a sound. It was not contempt or derision in their eyes, but something else entirely. It was awe! Respect! Overnight, I had become a hero. As I walked to my table, I could hear someone mutter: "That's the kid. The junior from Will's cabin who rode Thunder bareback all day. Without even a bridle!"

■ ■ ■

AFTER THE INCIDENT with Thunder, I became one of the ridingest fools the camp had ever seen. I signed up for horseback riding every week that summer. I made Lance, the riding counselor, take me on every trail ride I could qualify for. I rode in sunlight, in downpours, through deep woods, up winding mountain trails, across streams. I rode through swamps where the mosquitoes were so thick, I worried their bites might swell the horses' eyes shut.

In the barn, I helped the farrier. I volunteered to clean tack. I mucked out stalls. I hung flypaper. It didn't matter what I was doing so long as it kept me near horses.

I had found my tribe: a herd of magical, four-legged relatives. The mythical animals who for so long had occupied my imagination now lived in my heart, no longer a fantasy; they were real, between my legs, beneath my hands.

The narrow streets of New York City had opened to broader vistas. The Adirondacks were no longer a dark, endless territory. From my vantage point on horseback, there were now miles of streams to follow and trails to climb. I was an explorer, a heroic figure astride his horse.

Nearly 50 years have passed. Thunder is long gone. I am 60 — getting older and more cautious. But that ride was the mystical, transformational experience of my lifetime. The grandchildren of my bunkmates now go to that camp every summer. The story of my first day has evolved into a kind of legend: part lie, part folklore. It gets recounted and embellished when the kids are told not to wander off. Then Thunder and I ride again, as our story is retold.

1.7 The author today with his black and white gelding Mahto, who looks similar to Thunder, the first horse he rode nearly 50 years ago

CHAPTER TWO

THE TWO SIDES OF ME

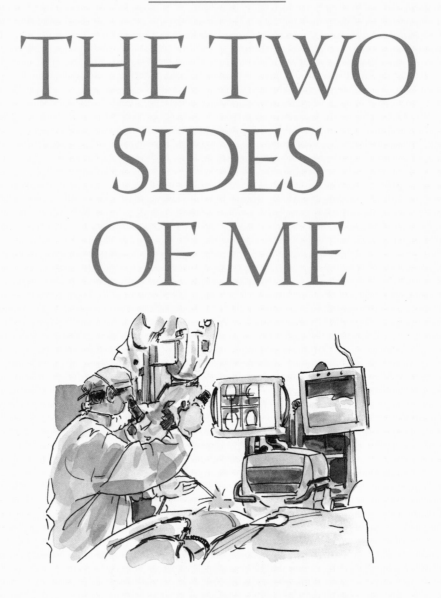

The education system and modern society generally (with its very heavy emphasis on communication and on early training in the three Rs) discriminates against one whole half of the brain.

▪ ▪ ▪

Dr. Roger Sperry,
Winner of the Nobel Prize for his work on right- and left-hemispheric brain function

M Y OWN LIFE has developed along two divergent themes. The first is my profession as a brain surgeon; the second, my avocation as a horse trainer. For four decades I have pursued these two seemingly contradictory callings. The first finds me in an operating theater dominated by stainless steel and digital monitors. The second places me in wide open spaces, in the embrace of earth and sky (*see figure 2.1*). One, all sutures and antiseptics, belongs to science; the other, with its dust and sweat, to nature.

It might seem as though there's an irreconcilable tension between the two. Neurosurgery requires a surreal ability to maintain focus, what Sir William Osler, a nineteenth-century physician, called "…coolness and presence of mind under all circumstances, calmness amid storm, clearness of judgment in moments of grave peril…." For brain surgeons to reach the heights of their technical abilities, they must learn to suppress any interference from their own emotions.

Horsemanship, on the other hand, relies primarily on personal insight and intuitive assessment. Its practitioners must plumb their own emotional depths. And mastery does not come from personal sublimation but rather through intimate transformation.

OUT OF MY RIGHT MIND   This schism that runs through my life represents more than a mere opposition of profession and hobby. It contrasts two different approaches to being me. One way, by imposing an unwavering dedication to technique, requires suppression of the

2.1 The high-tech neurosurgical operating room (opposite) depends largely on cognitive, logical, and mathematical left-hemispheric functions. Working with horses in the round pen (above) depends largely on empathetic, emotional functions housed in the right hemisphere of the human brain.

ego in order to perfect surgical method until it becomes its own form of expression.

The other approach is epitomized by Joseph Campbell's motto: "Follow your bliss." This method requires that we surrender ourselves to our passion until we cross a blistering threshold where the gravitational pull of the ego is simply insufficient to restrain us. It loses its grip and our spirit soars into an orbit of transcendence.

There might seem to be a paradoxical friction between these two different approaches to self-consciousness, but it reflects how differently the two halves of our own brain perceive the world and our relationship to it. This is the result of the struggle between our own right and left hemispheres. Like cerebral siblings, they are forever pinching, shoving, and jostling each other as they vie for our attention, as if to say, "Choose me. Choose my way of seeing the world around you."

In my own case, the left hemisphere provides me with logical, scientific content. Tidy statistical analyses and careful equations let me understand the world, predict its outcomes, and model its results. While my right hemisphere simply jumps to conclusions or reacts with moody impressions, the left has the skills of the preacher, the orator, or even the snake oil salesman. It can cast a spell over me if I let my guard down. But the right hemisphere, the one that relates to horse training, asserts itself like an artist. It has no words at its disposal, but it can play music. It can't write a word, but it can draw impressions. It can color my judgment and stir my imagination. It can lift me toward transcendence with its imagery.

The left brain is like a politician on a never-ending political stomp. It can grab my attention. It can voice my reactions and persuade me, counsel me. It is in the business of giving speeches, at any time, on any topic. And it fills spaces, internal and external, with its words, with its voice — the voice of my ego. But the right hemisphere holds an undeniable attraction. It is where my emotional responses arise, where my gut instincts and intuitions spring forth. Without a voice, the right may not "say" anything to me, but it still has much to show me. In the stillness of the right hemisphere is a seductive invitation to join in the hush of universal awe.

The Awakening

■ ■ ■

EVERY MORNING YOU and I wake up. We rub our eyes, blink like owls, and try to read the time on the face of the alarm clock. Until we can make it out, we dwell in a state of confusion, struggling to find our bearings, to find the answer to our question: where are we now, in time and space?

Wherever we were during sleep, it wasn't the real, physical world that we know. While we were dreaming, our feelings and emotions were spun into stories, magical, mystical, fueled by the powerful symbol-generating engine of our right hemisphere. It may be helpful to think of dreaming as a right-hemisphere construct, an emotional state of mind, whereas wakefulness, or consciousness, in the medical sense of the word, is largely a left-hemispheric version of life.

In the first minutes of awakening, we are certainly not home yet. We're still caught in the night's dreamy eddies and currents, struggling to reach shore and to pull ourselves to the safety of the familiar world.

Our arms stretch out to our sides; then our toes slither down to grab our slippers, and we shuffle off to the bathroom. We flick on the light, shielding ourselves from the glare. Then, in that spotlight, the moment finally comes: without it, no day in our lives would ever truly begin.

Because everything — going to work, closing a deal, or falling in love — hinges on the next split second. Without it, we're not sure we even exist. That flash of existential confirmation occurs when we look in the bathroom mirror and see our own face gazing back at us. Without a sense of "the autobiographical self," we have no perception or awareness.

There is an area of specialized brain tissue known as the *fusiform gyrus* (*see figure 2.2*). Billions of facial images are stored there. The job of this region of the cerebral cortex is to recognize faces and flip through an unimaginably vast, eclectic library of visages. Every face we have ever seen is faithfully recorded, preserved, and catalogued. Even amidst these billions of visages, one image is the focus of this neural library, our cerebral curator's obsession, the centerpiece of the anthology: ourselves. Or, more precisely, our selves.

GREETING YOUR SELF   From within the inexhaustible archives in our brain, answers now unfold with lightning speed, like magnetized pieces snapping together. Soon an image assembles. *We recognize the face in the mirror as our own!* It's almost as if our own sidekick, like Johnny Carson's famous Ed McMahon, suddenly crows: "And...here's m-e-e-e-e!"

2.2

The *fusiform gyrus,* marked in blue, and the visual association area, marked in red, have been identified as specific regions of the human cortex dedicated to facial recognition.

There is a sense of transcendence that surges inward as we recognize ourselves. An instant before, our brains were clutched by uncertainty. Like swimmers, tumbling in a moment of dreadful doubt, we hold our breath, and then a wave of reassurance carries us back to safety. We gasp with relief as we see that we are once again who we always thought we were. We slip back into the familiar waters of self-obsession. It is easy to take that intimate moment — when we strip our reflection off the mirror — for granted. But it is in that flash of recognition we clearly distinguish between "self" and "non-self."

Once we recognize that we are again who we always thought we were, we are free to return to our full-time obsession of analyzing and interpreting everything as either "self" or "nonself." It is easy to take that reassuring moment of self-recognition for granted. But, to put it in perspective, imagine for a moment the shock you would experience if you walked over to the mirror and saw the face of a complete stranger. Say you fell asleep as a chubby, stubbled, 50-year-old man, but when you turned on the lights, you saw a 14-year-old girl staring back at you from the mirror. You would touch your chin, your ears, your hair. Then you would touch the mirror to make sure it was real. Then you'd touch your face again. You wouldn't know which version was accurate or valid, whether to believe what your senses see in the mirror or what your identity inside is telling you.

Seeing yourself, reaffirming you are still who you thought you were, thus allows the boundaries between your ego and the rest of the Universe to be safely re-established. The gates close and lock shut. You are once again serenely entombed within your self.

But even when you see yourself in the mirror, when you breathe a sigh of relief that you didn't wake up a rhino or a housefly, one threat still lurks deep within you. It can profoundly challenge your sense of identity, but it is not resolved with just a look in the mirror. This is a menace you cannot dismiss, because it is your own right-brain version of yourself.

The Mute Threat

∎ ∎ ∎

MOST OF US, most of the time, are happy to put the left side of our brains in command, our ego large and in charge. We want it to run the show. We feel secure and content when we live in a physical world we can interpret through our own individual awareness. For the majority of us, this may be the only world we'll ever know. But is this the only condition we can inhabit? What if there is an alternate world view we can access?

Our ego's control is so forceful and pervasive that we may not even ask ourselves the question. Sometimes, however, our right hemisphere interrupts us and invites us to imagine what music we might hear if only our inner voice could be silenced. The right side tempts us not only to observe the Universe but even to join with it.

Such notions of a shared existence, of being part of something greater than our own existence, make the ego quake in its boots. *What is going to happen to little old Me?* The sense of separation wilts. The ego's force shield begins to fail. And we begin to get the first taste of an infinite community. We might find the alternative perspective appealing. *Just maybe, I am less convinced that my ego has all the answers.*

Putting Your Self on the Line

∎ ∎ ∎

I AM AS MUCH (or maybe more) wedded to my ego as the average individual, but I also know any one of us can learn to reliably connect to the Universe by working with horses, and this is not something we have to wait for until our next reincarnation. It can happen right now, just as we are, and as quickly as we are willing to let it to happen. There is only one prerequisite.

We have to be prepared to put our *selves*, our egos, on the line. This is far from trivial. This is the most tightly held belief we have: that the world can be grasped only as a personal, private experience. Ground work with horses refutes that egocentric perspective.

Horses help us put our hands around the handle of the ego ejection seat; when we're ready, we yank back on it. With a *swush*, we're shot beyond the canopy of our own singularity. Suddenly, we have the opportunity to move beyond the experience of our solitary ego to feel unity with nature. We become swimmers in the midst of all creation. It flows with us, in us.

JUMPING OFF THE CLIFF Leaving behind the world that feels real and right to us is an ambitious goal. But there's a Universe out there. If we want to become a part of it, we have to use a new paradigm of jointly shared consciousness. We need to experience it in order to believe in it. To do that, we need to eliminate our egos, at least for a few moments. A tall order.

When patterns of the brain's hemispheric dominance emerge in the first years of life, the left side exerts a wonderful capability: it speaks. As we develop, our language function improves dramatically, and the left brain explores how to name, label, and even make demands. It discovers the capacity not only to interact with others but also to influence and even direct them. Somewhere along this intoxicating path of cognitive development, we come to a threshold, a point of no return. The duality of subject and object takes root.

Like a radio, language requires a transmitter and receiver, a *me* and a *you*, a speaker and a listener. Language stems from identity, but it also creates separation. As infants, we all experience the prototypical communal bond of mother and child. We are born into a true state of oneness, of shared being. But as we grow through childhood, this innocent, primal state is first weakened and, later, forever shattered by speech. As we learn to communicate our needs, we also learn that these appetites and wants are ours alone. These desires are what we perceive from within, and there's a world beyond us that must be manipulated to satisfy them.

We all readily submit to the internalized autocracy imposed by the left hemisphere's language function. For most of us, the left's supremacy is absolute. We scarcely have any suspicion that one entire half of our brain, an alternate awareness, has been almost completely suppressed and hidden from our conscious accessibility. But this is precisely what's happened. It's why, for so much of our lives, we rarely get beyond our own egos.

The Severed Psyche

∎ ∎ ∎

IN THE EARLY NINETEENTH CENTURY, British physician Arthur Ladbroke Wigans had an acquaintance who died rather unexpectedly. Because of the sudden nature of the man's demise, Wigans offered to perform the autopsy to see if he could discover the cause of death. When he opened the skull, Wigans was astounded to find there was no right cerebral hemisphere within the cranium. The absence was all the more surprising because Wigans had had the opportunity to talk with this gentleman, who had, in Wigans' words, "...conversed rationally and even written verses within a few days of his death."

The deceased had impressed Wigans as being perfectly rational and functional, but how could that be, with an entire side of his brain missing? Over the next two decades, Wigans collected a handful of similar autopsy findings. In 1844, he published his work: *On the Duality of the Mind: A New View of Insanity (see figure 2.4)*. In it he wrote: "If, for example, as I have so often stated, and now again repeat, one brain...be capable of all the emotion, sentiments, and faculties, which we call in the aggregate, mind — then it necessarily follows that man must have two minds with two brains: and however intimate and perfect their unison in their natural state, they must occasionally be discrepant."

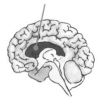

2.3   CORPUS CALLOSUM

The *corpus callosum* is an important bundle of white matter that allows the right and left hemispheres of the brain to communicate. When this bundle is severed surgically, the hemispheres function almost like independent brains.

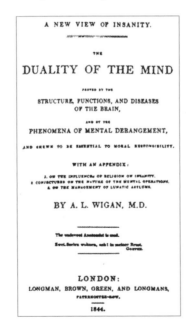

A NEW VIEW OF INSANITY.

THE

DUALITY OF THE MIND

PROVED BY THE

STRUCTURE, FUNCTIONS, AND DISEASES
OF THE BRAIN,

AND BY THE

PHENOMENA OF MENTAL DERANGEMENT,

AND SHEWN TO BE ESSENTIAL TO MORAL RESPONSIBILITY.

WITH AN APPENDIX:

1. ON THE INFLUENCES OF RELIGION ON INSANITY,
2. CONJECTURES ON THE NATURE OF THE MENTAL OPERATIONS,
3. ON THE MANAGEMENT OF LUNATIC ASYLUMS.

BY A. L. WIGAN, M.D.

LONDON:
LONGMAN, BROWN, GREEN, AND LONGMANS,
PATERNOSTER-ROW.

1844.

2.4   Frontispiece of *The Duality of the Mind*, by Dr. Arthur Ladbroke Wigan, published in 1844

He added: "Each individual must be made up of two complete and perfect halves, and with…no more central and common machinery… than is just sufficient to unite the two in one sentient being." Wigans realized the right hemisphere's input had to be so subtle, maybe subconscious, that a human being could appear to be perfectly normal, even to a physician like himself, while the right hemisphere was completely absent (*see figure 2.5*).

As strange as it sounded, Wigan's hypothesis would be borne out by experiments carried out by Richard Sperry more than 150 years later. Sperry and his colleagues studied patients who had undergone a surgical severing of the connections between the left and right cerebral hemispheres to halt the spread of epileptic seizures. The procedure, called a *corpus callosotomy*, allowed the silent right brain to be disconnected from its dominant verbal sibling. Since it housed no language functions, there was no way to engage the right hemisphere with written or verbal stimuli. Saying "stick out your tongue" brought no response. But holding up a photo of someone sticking out his tongue would bring a chuckle. The right side could be accessed, it turned out, with nonverbal stimuli.

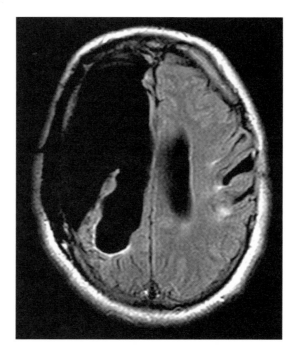

2.5 Magnetic resonance scan of brain after surgical removal of the entire right cerebral hemisphere (visible on left). The individual remained fluently bilingual without substantial deficits. The striking finding is the apparent subtlety of impact on overt human behavior from the right hemisphere's resection — until it was studied in great detail.

Sperry's team discovered the right hemisphere was vibrantly alive, living submerged unless it was freed from the left hemisphere. The right side loved to draw. It was moved by photographs — not by what it could identify or label within them but rather by the emotions the images triggered. The right side of the brain sought to feel, whereas the left wanted to know. One thrived on the flow of words and the sparkle of speech, while the other set sail on a sea of feelings, swept by emotion.

The right hemisphere, Sperry discovered, could express its experiences only through the left hemisphere. For example, an experimental situation could be created with patients who have undergone severing of the corpus callosum. Because the wiring to the brain is "crossed," the left hand delivers sensation to the right side of the brain and the right hand to the left side of the brain. If a rose is placed in the left hand, then only the right hemisphere has the sensory "experience" of the rose. The right hand, however, is empty, so the left hemisphere has no sensory information about the flower. If asked, the individual would deny the presence of any rose. The left hemisphere's experience dictates what is articulated.

At first glance, without the left hemisphere to translate sounds and words, the right appears to be unaware. It isn't. It simply has no voice to express its "hemispheric" experience. Exactly how these two hemispheres actually dance together in a singular consciousness is unclear, because the two sides are not complementary. They act like different brains belonging to different species.

Another difference between right and left hemisphere function is revealed in figure 2.6.

RED
GREEN
BLUE

2.6 A right-versus-left brain experiment: try to say the color of the letters in the word rather than read the color that is being spelled out. Since the left hemisphere commands language function, we find it easy to read the word. The right hemisphere, which interprets the color, has to struggle to override the left hemisphere's dominance.

SPELLBOUND   Sperry's studies demonstrated that we live under the substantial, deep spell cast by the left hemisphere. The left likes flying solo, shaping our cognitive processes unopposed. We live willingly under its hypnotic, egocentric enchantment. But as the Jesuit priest Anthony de Mello wrote, "Spirituality means waking up. Most people, even though they don't know it, are asleep. They're born asleep, they live asleep, they marry in their sleep, they breed children in their sleep, they die in their sleep without ever waking up. They never understand the loveliness and the beauty of this thing we call human existence."

We cannot feel transcendent if we cannot awaken ourselves.

The Plains of Great Bliss

■ ■ ■

SO HOW DO WE set about doing this? By developing new capabilities and strengths that downplay, even downright undermine, our ego. And we can ask horses to help us accomplish this goal because, over millions of years of evolution, they have learned the secret of communication without speech. Their left hemispheres are just as silent as their right. And, as we will see later, the horse's brain functions largely as two disconnected, mute hemispheres. This unique capability allows the equine species to guide us unerringly to the intuitive, spiritual core within the right side of our own brains.

A Tibetan poet, Jetsun Milarepa, wrote: "The horse which is my mind flies like the wind. He gallops on the plains of great bliss." That is the place we want our horses to carry us. While we may not be able to hear our right hemisphere, we can learn to feel its unmistakable presence.

CHAPTER THREE

CHI & EQUUS

We shall not cease from exploration
And the end of all our exploring
Will be to arrive where we started
And know the place for the first time.

■ ■ ■

T. S. Eliot, *Four Quartets*

Mastery requires lots of hours. It's about work and patience, about developing a dedication to your field of endeavor that can transport you out of everyday experience. You discover the struggle was never to master anything but yourself. The true goal was always the journey. Fortunately, some small measure of discovery and adventure always remains. You rejoice there's still time left to learn. As Tennyson wrote in his heroic poem, *Ulysses*:

> *Yet all experience is an arch where through*
> *Gleams that untravelled world, whose margin fades*
> *For ever and for ever when I move.*
> *How dull it is to pause, to make an end,*
> *To rust unburnished, not to shine in use!*

3.1 Japanese print of a samurai warrior on horseback

The Japanese Horse Master

···

THERE'S A WONDERFUL STORY about a Japanese horse master who had lived to be one hundred years old and lay on his deathbed, expressing regret that the end was near. His oldest, most dutiful son was at his side, attending to him.

Suddenly the old man sighed and said, "What a pity that I must die now, at this time."

The son looked back at his father with disbelief and said, "Father, how can you have regrets about dying now? You are one hundred years old. No one in our village is older, wiser, or more revered than you are. You are the most celebrated horseman in Japan. Could anyone ask for more? Why despair about dying?"

"Because," said the old man, "it was just last week that I began to truly understand what horsemanship is about. It's such a pity to die now. I was off to a good start!"

Michelangelo, the creator of the Sistine Chapel, echoed the same sentiments when he said at the end of his life, "I am dying just as I begin to learn the alphabet of my profession."

Without a Second Mind

···

THE ALPHABET OF CONNECTING with horses is composed of life energy, or *chi*. I use the terms synonymously. I will discuss the traditional Chinese concepts in the next section, but each one of us has our own intuitive grasp of chi in action.

For example, you're at a party. You get the impression someone is staring at you. The hairs on the back of your neck stick up. You turn around and…there it is, a pair of eyes locked on you! Just where you thought they were. That's chi.

For another example, you're on the subway. An unsavory character walks through the hissing doors. He steps into the car, looking right and left. He's obviously searching for trouble, seeking out a victim. You can feel it. You can sense a dark purpose. You look down. You know *not* to lock eyes with this person. The slightest visual challenge could be seen as an affront, an excuse for violence. That's chi too.

Understanding horses is about feeling that connective energy, the chi, flowing between our horse and us. Alan Watts, the American Zen sage, described it as "a state of wholeness in which the mind functions freely and easily, without the sensation of a second mind or ego standing over it with a club." Shakti Gawain suggests the process calls for "tuning in as deeply as you can to the energy you feel, following that energy moment to moment, trusting that it will lead you where you want to go and bring you everything you desire."

Chi: The Life Force

• • •

ALTHOUGH CHI AND ENERGY can be used interchangeably, the tem *chi* is more inclusive and descriptive. From Chinese, it translates to "the all-encompassing universal life force." We lose a great many subtleties in the translation. Chi has many other attributes besides simple energy. It also conveys a notion of flow, of directionality. It relates to the vitality of breathing and implies a concept of fundamental vigor, potency, or energetic activity. At the same time, it carries undertones of personal willpower and determination.

3.2

The symbol for
yin and yang

The original Chinese character for chi was meant not only to allude to the quality of steam rising from boiling rice but also to depict the wavy quality of the vapor given off by breath on a cold morning. In Japanese, the equivalent word or character *ki* has more than ten thousand applications or inclusions that lend meaning to such concepts as mind, heart, courage, and emotion.

THE TWO ENERGIES OF CHI   Chi also imparts properties of polarity, much the way atomic particles interact through positive or negative charges. In Chinese tradition, these poles of energy are assigned gender-related attributes, labeled as *yin*, the female force, and *yang*, the male counterpart.

Yin and yang describe two primal, equal, complementary forces found in all matter. Yin is the darker, feminine, passive, nurturing force and is traditionally depicted in the black tones of a nighttime sky. Yang is the brighter male component, reflecting an active, pervasive force symbolized by the white color of bright daylight. Yin is imbued with the properties of water: quenching, life-giving, flowing, and slowly erosive. Yang is symbolized by fire. It is the power of illumination, consumption, activation, and, at times, explosive destruction. Yin and yang are not opposing forces but complementary; each is unable to come into existence without the other.

We know this is also how the whole Universe functions: duality brings forth existence. In Genesis we are told, "And God said, 'Let there be light,' and there was light. God saw that the light was good, and He separated the light from the darkness." The light distinguishes the darkness, but it is also true that darkness delineates what is illuminated.

The interplay between yin and yang fuels the universal engine. For example, in hydroelectric plants, the energy (yang) expended from water (yin) falling from a great height is converted into electricity (yang). One form of energy transforms into the other. The exchange between yin and yang is paralleled in the world of the atom, which Werner Heisenberg, a Nobel Prize winner in quantum mechanics, described as "...a complicated tissue of events, in which connections of different kinds alternate or overlap or combine and thereby determine the texture of the whole."

The Language of the Horse

■ ■ ■

HORSES USE CHI as their primary language, with unimaginable eloquence and elegance. They possess an expansive lexicon of body gestures and postures to shape and emit it. Monty Roberts calls this the language of *Equus* (Latin for horse). Equids are members of the larger family or genus of *Equus* that includes the modern-day domesticated horse (subspecies *Equus caballus*) and nine other horselike subspecies, from jackass to zebra.

Over fifty million years of evolution (several orders of magnitude longer than the human species has inhabited Earth), equids developed a nonverbal vocabulary of body language that could be transmitted accurately across great, sometimes astounding, distances. Vocalization is a terrible method of communication for prey species: in fact, the use of sound — vocalization, and its highest expression, language — is the hallmark of predators.

PREDATOR AND PREY Wolves, for example, have a complex language of calls for coordinating the pack. They also use an extensive vocabulary to maintain and reinforce pack hierarchy. To the extent that social and hunting lives increase in complexity and richness, language is the stamp of a predator's biological success.

The hunted, however, simply cannot afford the luxury of speech. A successful prey animal aims to eliminate noise. Its life depends on being a great silent listener. What better way than to use a soundless language, based on the transmission of chi that is encoded into their body language? Especially if, over millions of years, the species can fine-tune that ability until a mere twitch of the ears, a change in the slope of the shoulders, or a shift of the hips is enough to send ripples of energy throughout all members of the herd. And what if that ability can be linked to an energized network of members, actively charged and augmented by each member?

3.3

Wolves have a complex vocabulary of calls.

3.4 Monty Roberts with his mustang Shy Boy. Monty went to the amazing lengths of inviting a *Q.E.D.* (BBC television series) film crew along to document the process of transforming Shy Boy from a pure, wild, untouched mustang off the plains to a saddle horse he could ride. It is unquestionably one of the greatest and most humbling displays of horsemanship ever witnessed.

To best conceptualize this, look at safari footage of zebras nervously sipping at the edge of a watering hole. Some zebras' heads dip while others rise. Ears perk up, swinging back and forth. Eyes widen. Heads swivel. Nostrils test the wind. And then they *sense* the predator. They feel the lioness crouching low in the grass. They experience the intensity of her hungry stare, the tension encircling her whole body. Even the nervous twitch of her tail is palpable to the zebras. A live zebra intuitively *feels* all that. The dead zebra is the one who waited to be sure.

Prey animals further confound those that hunt them through cooperation among species. In Africa, wildebeest and zebra intermingle with gazelle and antelope. They can function as an interspecies system, throbbing with connectivity: one that allows prey animals to thrive, surrounded by overlapping detection systems that deny access to all but the most stealthiest predators.

AWARENESS THROUGH GROUND WORK   One of the best ways for humans to dramatically enhance their awareness of energetic, non-verbal communication is to practice ground work with horses. Body language is vital to human communication, but it is a woefully neglected and understudied aspect of communication, outside of the advertising, legal, and entertainment industries. Human communication follows the 70-20-10 rule (*see figure 3.5*).

Advertising, legal decisions (jury selection), and entertainment (acting) all depend upon understanding the intricate and profound effect of body language in deciphering a human being's motivations and responses. For all of the attention we lavish on speech-writing, debating, and public speaking, only 10 percent relates to the actual words themselves. In our highly socialized and urban world, we ignore nonverbal communication at our own peril. Consider this statistic: a nonverbal ten-second decision about a job applicant is as accurate as a detailed assessment based on a forty-minute, multivariable inventory of questions.

READING ENERGY   How can a visceral reaction be as sensitive as statistical evaluation? Because we reach intuitive decisions by reading the energy emitted by people. The chi in a job candidate's body position, posture, and facial expression registers instantly in our right hemisphere. Interestingly, we refer to such intuitive snap decisions as "gut reactions," to differentiate them from the logical deliberations of the dominant left hemisphere. The left is the realm of analysis; the right, intuition. Businessman Donald Trump has commented, "Experience taught me a few things. One is to listen to your gut, no matter how good something sounds on paper."

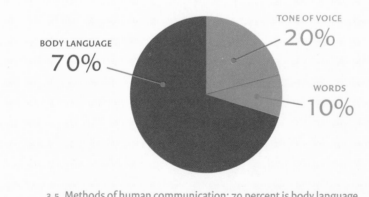

3.5 Methods of human communication: 70 percent is body language (i.e., nonverbal), 20 percent is tone of voice, and the actual words we use make up a lowly 10 percent of communication.

THE SEVEN CHAKRAS

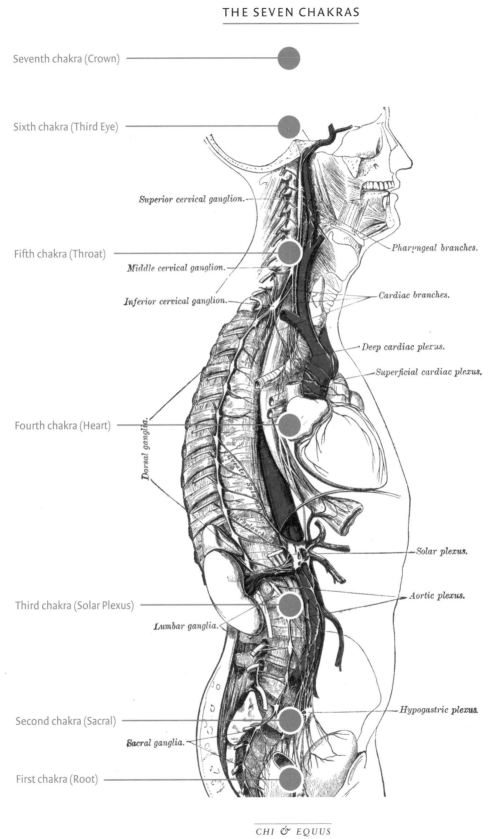

Seventh chakra (Crown)

Sixth chakra (Third Eye)

Superior cervical ganglion.

Pharyngeal branches.

Fifth chakra (Throat)

Middle cervical ganglion.

Inferior cervical ganglion.

Cardiac branches.

Deep cardiac plexus.

Superficial cardiac plexus.

Dorsal ganglia.

Fourth chakra (Heart)

Solar plexus.

Third chakra (Solar Plexus)

Aortic plexus.

Lumbar ganglia.

Hypogastric plexus.

Second chakra (Sacral)

Sacral ganglia.

First chakra (Root)

The ability to communicate clearly, quickly, and silently is vital to a prey animal's survival. It is why horses are virtuosos at reading the energy given off by another horse — or a person, for that matter. Horsemanship is based on the energetic interaction between horse and trainer. So to become adept with horses we must change our sensitivity to chi, turn up the gain.

Chi and Chakras

■ ■ ■

THE TERM *CHAKRA* is a Sanskrit term that literally means "wheel" or "spinning center." Similar terms are found in Hindu, Tibetan, and Chinese writings to refer to the ancient medical concept of chakras, or energetic spots or vortices, aligned along the axis of the human body in seven *loci*: specific centers that generate sustained, spinning energetic output.

Interestingly, many, but not all, of these represent important *plexi*, or networks of nerve pathways (*see figure 3.6*), in the body. Traditional Asian concepts of illness and disease focus on *meridians*, elaborate pathways by which chi flows through the body. They serve as the underlying anatomical and physiological principles of a 5,000-year-old system of medicine that has given us interventions such as acupuncture.

3.7 Indian print depicting the seven chakras along the axis of the human body

Shifting Focus

■ ■ ■

OCCASIONALLY WE EXPERIENCE a sudden, intuitive shift in our understanding. There's a visceral shudder, as if the ground beneath us is shaking from an earthquake. We have all experienced this at one time or another. Falling from a height — a ladder, a tree, a diving platform, even a parachute jump — we may experience time suddenly slowing down during the course of our descent. David Eagleman of Baylor College of Medicine has researched this phenomenon and concluded that while time itself is not altered, the density of our memory *is* radically accelerated while we fall. It is as if we have a faster computer suddenly capable of downloading more bytes of information in a shorter amount of time. We record more information during every moment and we feel as if each moment must be longer. There's a dramatic, intuitive shift in our focus, and reality changes.

It need not be so dramatic — or potentially traumatic. We may be gazing at the stars, seemingly points of lights in flat patterns on the dark vault overhead, when with a jolt we realize they are not just twinkling dots: they are suns and planets suspended deep in the cosmos. We are looking at the heart of the Universe. Or perhaps you walk with a camera over your shoulder. The camera's presence changes how you see the landscape. A professional newspaper photographer once confessed to me: "Sometimes I bring my camera just because it allows me to see the true light in things. I can see them shimmer. Without the camera, I go blind."

Anthropologist and writer Carlos Castañeda wrote about the Yaqui shamans, or *naguals,* who claimed they could change reality by changing how they focused their personal energy. The point of their focus was called the *assemblage point.* By shifting that assemblage point they changed their awareness and, therefore, the reality they perceived.

Working with horses can produce a dramatic shift in our assemblage point. We see a different landscape, one that is accessible through our right hemisphere but not our left. Castañeda admonishes us:

3.8

The Andromeda
Galaxy

> *The greatest flaw of human beings is to remain glued to the inventory of reason. Reason doesn't deal with man as energy… we are organisms that create energy. We are bubbles of energy.*

Horses immerse us into an energetic context, beyond reason but within the reach of emotion. They provide us with detailed feedback about how adept (or clumsy) we are at feeling energy and moving it. We learn from our equine partners how to clear our minds. We silence the incessant reminders our brain is producing about our personal needs, appetites, and anxieties.

When we do, our energetic output suddenly surges. Castañeda refers to this as the silence that "gives rise to intent." Our ability to sense and manipulate chi sharpens. As we acquire the ability to concentrate and focus chi at will, our goals begin to clarify themselves effortlessly.

Along with this budding clarity of thought emerges the property of impeccability. Impeccability, "to be without fault," is derived from the Latin *in-* (without) and *-peccare* (sin). When we clear our minds, we free ourselves of the collective flaws that fill up our daily lives and befoul our thinking. This helps us further amplify our own energy. As we do so, our horse begins to respond with greater ease and willingness.

The Power of Intention

■ ■ ■

THE LAST ELEMENT we learn from horses is the power of energetic will, or intention. Intention is the process by which we focus our energy by visualizing the end result before we begin. A simple example is how downhill skiers close their eyes and picture themselves speeding through the gates and curves on the course before they even step up to the starting gate. When we can empty our minds, they can become impeccably clear. We can see the goal, the desired objective, as being accomplished and finished before we begin.

An equivalent exercise with the horse can be something as simple as visualizing the horse propelling himself over a jump at liberty. Our first efforts will be clumsy, like a student driver surging forward on the gas pedal and then jerking to a stop with the brake. The horse may tentatively move toward the jump and then balk and walk sideways around it. But slowly, as we visualize him stepping smoothly toward the jump, lifting himself effortlessly to arch over it, the horse begins to reflect our intention, gaining an even, consistent flow.

Results from our training begin to unroll without conscious effort. Our goals become manifest. At such moments (and we will practice hard to make them reproducible), the horse will ease seamlessly into whatever task we envision. Intention makes chi pour out of us like a beautiful stream, enabling our horse to finish the task we set for him before he even starts. We have to do nothing but wish the horse's actions into being. Suddenly, the energetic world surges through us, as it comes into being.

Believe me when I tell you that working with horses can be exciting — practically intoxicating at times — because you are learning to play with magic.

Impeccability and Chi

■ ■ ■

AT FIRST, THESE STATES where intention sparks into being will be evanescent. Like flashes of lightning, they barely last an instant. We learn to recognize the physical sensation, a peculiar visceral impulse, when an impeccable state is created within us. It is like the sinking sensation in the solar plexus we experience when we peer over a precipice from a great height. When we can recreate that assemblage point shift, then we can practice sustaining a steady state of concentrated chi for increasingly longer durations.

We might ask ourselves how such a condition of highly organized, aligned chi can be maintained. Such a state might describe the enlightened condition of a powerful sorcerer or enlightened sensei. I think some of us may come close to such a feeling in so-called *flow states* (the name is telling in relation to our discussion of chi). These states were described by psychologist Mihaly Csikszantmihalyi in his book, *Flow: The Psychology of Optimal Experience:* "It is what the sailor holding a tight course feels when the wind whips through her hair....It is what a painter feels when the colors...begin to set up a magnetic tension with each other, a new thing, a living form, takes shape...."

3.9 Michael Jordan going up for one of his impossible shots: a perfect example of a flow state where the outcome seems preordained and the athlete seems to be in an effortless state of grace

These heightened states of awareness occur because our focus appears effortlessly lucid and clear (*see figure 3.9*). Time seems to stand still. We are flooded with a sense of total concentration and, at the same time, the most soothing sense of tranquility.

BECOME THE FENCE POST   A final word on impeccability. For me, the fence post is the perfect symbol of impeccability because the post never gets angry or impatient. Many horsemen have pointed out that a fence post exerts pressure only when the horse exerts pressure upon it. It pulls back with precisely the amount of force the horse applies. If the horse relents the slightest bit — pulls a fraction of a gram less — the post "responds" and releases. It rewards the horse for his slightest attempt.

In its responses, the fence post represents total clarity, perfection, and detachment. The simple fence post (*see figure 3.10*) will therefore serve as our inspirational symbol of an impeccable teacher. The post's responses are merely natural reflections of the horse's actions. So, in a Zen-like fashion, we should endeavor to become fence posts and challenge ourselves to be as quiet, detached, and proficient as they are.

3.10 The perfect symbol of impeccable timing: a fence post

GROOMING AS A TEA CEREMONY

The principles of knighthood include washing your hands and feet and bathing morning and night, keeping your body clean, shaving and dressing your hair every morning, dressing formally according to the seasons and circumstances and always keeping your fan in your belt not to mention your long and your short swords.

■ ■ ■

Code of the Samurai

T HE PATH OF OUR spiritual development with horses lies in ground work. The tasks and exercises we will study, evaluate, and practice are not difficult to assimilate, but they aren't always easy to master either. I'm reminded of the scene in the movie *The Karate Kid* (1984), where Mr. Miyagi, the old karate mentor, has a difficult time making his impetuous young student understand how the menial job of applying wax to a car and then polishing it off can serve as a foundation for a martial arts discipline.

In the same spirit, we'll explore grooming as the first building block in developing the spiritual meaning of human-equine interactions. No other activity focuses us so quickly on attending to our horse's needs over our own. Grooming makes him comfortable, healthy, and clean. It is one of the more altruistic acts we can initiate for our horse, and it provides a physical connection between our body and his.

Grooming should have no agenda but tending to the hygienic needs of the horse. Like so many things with horses, grooming involves technical components that acquire spiritual significance.

CHOP WOOD, CARRY WATER In a famous Zen story, a pupil approaches a great teacher and asks what activities he should undertake in order to reach *satori*, or enlightenment.

The old Zen master answers: "Chop wood and carry water."

After ten years of faithfully carrying out these duties, the frustrated pupil returns and tells his master, "I've done as you asked. I have chopped wood and carried water for ten years, but still I have not attained enlightenment! What should I do now, O Sage One?"

The master answers, "Continue to chop wood and carry water, my son."

The pupil faithfully returns to his duties. Another ten years pass. During that decade, the student matures and reaches satori. He returns to see his old master wearing a simple smile on his face.

"Master," he says, "I have reached satori, and now I am an enlightened being. What should I do now?"

The master answers, "Continue to chop wood and carry water then, O Enlightened One." The pupil bows deeply and retires to his wood and water.

By the same logic, what activity should we undertake to become the best horseman or horsewoman possible? Whatever makes us think most like a horse. For me, it is grooming: a perfect blend of service and insight.

Grooming as Ritual

...

AT FIRST GLANCE, chopping wood and carrying water might seem to be menial, mindless chores. But when they are undertaken with heightened awareness, they become transformational experiences. Grooming can also be seen as a burdensome duty, but when it is carried out with full attentiveness, it takes on profound meaning as a ritual. Pouring tea can be the simple filling of a cup or an elegant and articulate ceremony. Grooming is no different.

THE GARDEN OF GROOMING   We need to focus on grooming long before we touch our horse with the first stroke of a brush. First, have we selected a suitable location? Is it peaceful, or is there commotion nearby? Is it shady or sunny? Is the footing solid or precarious?

We need a tranquil spot, away from clutter and traffic. The horse needs room to move around if necessary. The grooming spot should be near a source of water, such as a hose, for bathing and washing. And we want a place close enough to the barn so cleaning supplies, tack, and/or medications are handy. Choose a grooming site with careful consideration, meaning that you have assessed the site through the eyes of your horse.

The purpose of ritual is to transpose our thinking from the physical to the symbolic. It allows the participant to experience a metaphor. A vivid

SONNY'S SPOT

The thoughtful selection of a grooming site must not be made unilaterally; the individual personality and biases of each horse should be considered. For example, Sonny, one of my Quarter Horses, is a great character. He exhibits a decided preference for one of two apparently identical hitching posts on the north side of my horse barn. One post faces east, with a panoramic view of the nearby Rincon Mountains in the Saguaro National Monu-

ment East. Twenty yards away is a grand old cottonwood tree that towers over the barn. It's home to a raucous pair of Gila woodpeckers. This is where Sonny likes to hang out.

The hitching post on the other side of the breezeway has a nice view of the statelier Santa Catalina mountain range. If he were ever concerned about foodstuffs, Sonny could feel reassured standing by the western post because from there he could see the hay barn, stacked

tall with bales of Bermuda hay. At the far corner, there's a barn owl, shy by day, gazing out over the pastures for a glimpse of a foolhardy ground squirrel. A stock tank of fresh cool water is parked in the shadows, a feature the east side cannot rival. Still, tie Sonny up on the west side and he gets an uneasy, sullen look in his eye. East side? He's a happy camper. He has always made his choice of hitching spots clear.

example occurred to me when I visited the American Cemetery in Normandy, France. I was curious why the grave markers did not face the road or walkways so the names on the individual markers buried there would be more visible. One of the guides explained that all the markers were facing west, across the Atlantic, looking toward the United States, the home they had defended and for which they died.

I suddenly felt a visceral tug, as if I were experiencing the collective yearning for home and family those fallen heroes experienced. The power of the ritual placement of the grave markers shifted my assemblage point. Reality changed; it took on a different meaning.

A WORTHY SITE   When we consider the small, sometimes trivial, details of our grooming site, we must evaluate them with a ritualistic eye. We are not just asking if it's safe to groom there. We pose a different question: is it fitting? We seek a spot worthy of the relationship we wish to honor with the ritual cleansing ceremony called "grooming." The imposition of ritual transforms any task, no matter how mundane, into an exercise in spiritual awareness.

The Singularity of the Halter

∎∎∎

EVERY DETAIL MATTERS. The halter you choose must fit properly. If a halter is fitted for another horse, there's a good chance it does not fit yours. If you share halters among horses, you increase the risk of spreading infections, such as dermatitis or conjunctivitis. The issue, however, goes beyond hygiene.

CUSTOMIZING A HALTER   Learn to customize your horse's halter because, as your appreciation for its function deepens, you'll become aware that its attributes are worthy of attention. There's something to be learned about the fit, the brass fittings (buckles, clips, and so on), and the amount of space between the poll and the crownpiece. Halters can be too loose, too tight, or just right.

Most commercially available, flat nylon web halters are sold as "adjustable," but it is surprising how many fit poorly. Measure your horse, and then, if necessary, carefully adjust the halter so it is perfectly customized. Once the halter is right for your horse, put his name on it so everyone knows which halter goes with which horse.

HALTER BASICS

This halter is far too large for this horse.

This halter is too tight. The brass buckles are jammed tightly against the horse's cheekbones and the space under the throat, the jugular notch.

Here is a well-fitted halter. Note that the brow strap is set for quick release. The halter fits well onto the jugular notch. The noseband is in good position, halfway up the nasal bones. The halter does not hang down where it can get snagged. I am an advocate of securing these halters so they can be quickly released. My preferred method is to tuck the strap into the ring as shown.

A well-tied rope halter. Rope halters are my favorite kind of halter because they can be customized to each horse. They do need to be correctly tied, however, so the free end of the halter rope will not inadvertently hit the horse in the eye.

A rope halter with rolled rawhide nosepiece.

If you choose a leather halter, carefully measure your horse to get the best possible fit, remembering that there may not be room to punch an extra hole or two.

THE VIRTUES OF THE ROPE HALTER   I advocate the simplest and cheapest of all halters: rope. First, because it is secured with a knot, a rope halter is infinitely adjustable, so it fits a horse properly and snugly (*see figure 4.1*). It can accommodate changes in the thickness of horse's coat from season to season. The knots in a rope halter also make it easier to apply pressure to a horse's brow and cheek through a lead rope. A thinner halter makes it easier for the handler to make his intentions clear. (I do not favor heavy or abrasive nosebands.) Rope halters are also easy to store and inexpensive to replace. The simple rope halter allows for the greatest freedom of expression.

Lead Rope, Lead On

■■■

THE LEAD, WITH THE HALTER at one end and our hand at the other, is the physical connection between our horse and us. When it hangs over a hook or rail, it is an inanimate collection of rope, brass, and knots. But it jumps to life when we touch it. Much of how we connect comes down to the simple technical details of fabrication, fit, and feel. A lead should almost buzz with chi when you pick it up. Your state of awareness brings heightened energetic tension to it.

John Lyons, one of America's most popular horse trainers, has likened the lead rope to a telephone line. You pick up the phone. There's a dial tone, or the line is dead. With a horse, your state of mind makes the difference between being simply tethered to the animal and being connected.

A lead rope is also like a writing pen. It can be an exquisitely fabricated, finely tuned instrument, like a Mont Blanc Meisterstuck, or a forgettable, utilitarian, throwaway number. Both write, but one provides an experience and the other is merely a tool.

At first glance, a lead is just a piece of rope, connecting you and your horse, but I contend it represents the essence of communication between you. You will learn to use its nuances skillfully and elegantly. It can provide an experience or it can remain merely a tool.

THE RIGHT ROPE   Most commercial leads are too stiff in the hand and too abrasive to the touch. Such materials can spell disaster when the rope is suddenly jerked out of the trainer's hands.

LIVE AND LEARN

I once chose a braided nylon lead (my first mistake) because it looked showy. It had several brightly colored strands woven into a diamondback pattern. I was working a horse in the round pen, and he suddenly spooked and ran off.

I attempted to jerk back on his lead with my left hand as I hit the dirt — my second mistake, and a poorly considered, reflexive action. A good horseman or horsewoman practices overcoming such reflexes.

The roughly woven lead ripped through my hands, tearing more than 2½ inches of skin from my thumb, index, and middle fingers. It took eight weeks for the epidermis to grow back.

Cheap materials and shoddy craftsmanship come back to haunt us when we least expect it. Whenever purchasing an item, but especially when there are safety implications, try to envision potential consequences under dire emergency conditions, rather than just routine requirements. Like most things in life, you will usually get what you pay for. In this case, if you spend a little more money you will also have purchased peace of mind.

Here are what I consider some of the key features of lead ropes.

FEEL   By far the most important characteristic of a good lead rope is its feel. Texture is everything. The ideal lead rope should have mass — a dense, heavy quality — but be very flexible.

The "stack test" is an easy way to assess lead ropes. Just pick up the lead rope and lower the end to the ground. Start feeding the rope onto the ground. If the rope begins to pile up, loop atop loop, like soft ice cream on top of a cone, it has the correct weight. If the loops resist stacking and the rope lays out in long, flat lengths, leave it on the shelf.

The best leads are made from marine, or yacht, rope. They have the correct weight, can be fashioned into various lengths, and are practically impermeable to weather, rot, or wear. Marine rope (usually ½-inch diameter) also has a smooth outer texture that is easy on the hands.

LENGTH   For lead length, I like 14 feet. Some trainers prefer 12, but to me that shorter length requires me to get too close to some horses. I've found that 14 feet allows me to apply pressure on the horse's hindquarters quickly without having my hands full of rope coils. Sometimes, in fact, with a wild horse or a troublesome stallion on the other end, a 20-foot length gives the handler a safer working distance. It pays to practice working with the longer lead lengths, because it can take time to grow accustomed to longer, heavier loops of lead and seamlessly feeding out and reeling in the additional length.

Earlier I pointed out that quick-release devices are not appropriate for lead ropes, but I believe they do have a place with hitching posts. For example, if there is a place where horses are tied regularly for grooming or saddling, then attaching the halter to a short-length quick-release device is just as safe as a slip knot.

It is important, however, to familiarize yourself with the operation of the panic snap before an emergency occurs. If a horse is thrashing around in a trailer, risking life and limb (not to mention the integrity of the trailer), that's not the time for studying diagrams about how to work a quick-release snap!

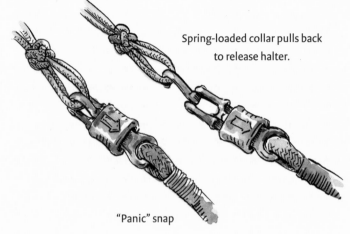

Spring-loaded collar pulls back to release halter.

"Panic" snap

HARDWARE Brass is the best choice for fixtures at the end of a lead rope that attach to the halter. It's lighter than stainless steel and easier to manipulate with gloves or fingers.

I am not a fan of spring-loaded clips. Although the mechanism to open and close the sliding clip is more intuitive than are swivel or release collars, it does not hold up to the elements. The metal thumb tab fatigues; the spring gradually loses its power; and the slide itself bogs down with grit.

Release collars have the same spring-related drawbacks, and they also are too heavy. They have enough mass that an inadvertent swing or overly vigorous shake of the lead could deliver quite a wallop.

Finally, fixtures only work well if one understands how they are designed to work. Make sure you are completely familiar with securing and opening fixtures on the end of the lead.

All fixtures should be spliced into the lead rope. At the store you will find dozens of leads that have the rope looped through the fixture and then clamped back upon itself with a pressure fitting. Bad idea. The extra loop and the metal clamp make the lead very bulky. The metal band itself is dangerous; it can not only hurt the horse but also cut your hand — a deal breaker, as far as I am concerned.

KNOTS AND POPPERS   Many leads come with leather poppers at the tail end. Small poppers assist us in getting a horse's attention with a snapping sound. Large poppers may make more noise but are more dangerous because of their weight. This latter problem is further aggravated when decorative rawhide pineapple knots are used to anchor the large poppers in place. Not only can the rough surface of the knot drag through the handler's hands with devastating results, but the knot and popper can hurt a horse with a misplaced swipe near the horse's head.

Hitching: The High Slip

■ ■ ■

BEFORE YOU ATTACH your lead rope to your horse, you must acquire certain skills. One is learning how to tie a slipknot flawlessly (*figures 4.2 and 4.3*): around a post, over a rail, through a branch... in your sleep. The second essential skill is to tie the slipknot up high (*figure 4.4*).

THE SLIPKNOT: STAYING SAFE BY LETTING GO   I use a rhyme to remind my students always to hitch horses with a slipknot in the lead rope:

> *Tie the horse fast and disaster will come to pass,*
> *But a knot that can slip will always do the trick.*

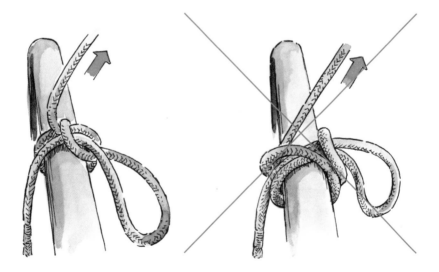

LEFT (4.2): A properly tied slipknot. This will release when given a yank.
RIGHT (4.3): An improperly tied slipknot. Notice that as the horse pulls harder against the knot, it will exert so much pressure downward that the knot will not release.

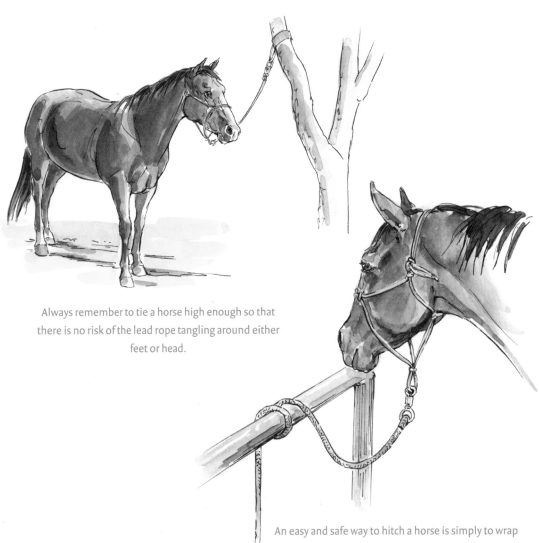

Always remember to tie a horse high enough so that there is no risk of the lead rope tangling around either feet or head.

An easy and safe way to hitch a horse is simply to wrap the lead rope two or three throws around the post.

Tying a horse fast, without being able to quickly release him, is dangerous — potentially deadly. In an adrenaline-stoked sprint for life, a horse simply cannot be stopped. Period. Individuals have been injured or killed because, in their instinctive rush to come to the aid of their horse, they forgot their own well-being.

There's a lot to be said for avoiding opposition rather than trying to overcome it. Do not become injured attempting to stop a 1,000-pound creature bent on saving himself through his prodigious might. If a horse is panicking dangerously, just let go. Let him fend for himself for a moment. Get yourself clear of danger. To do otherwise is foolhardy.

Often in life, it's not the crisis that hurts or kills us but the struggle we put up when we confront it. Working with prey animals drives home the lesson that not every situation calls for head-on confrontation. Keep the example of water in mind: more progress is made by flowing with events than by damming them. In the same way, letting go can be more effective than holding back. A slipknot that releases a horse with a quick snap will save humans and horses.

Practice the slipknot in different locations. Check the quick release (*see box on page 54*). Have a friend pull on the lead rope while you try to jerk the slipknot out. I cannot emphasize how much you need to practice tying slipknots until they can be tied effortlessly — and flawlessly. It takes a thousand perfect slipknots before you're ready to tie your horse.

TYING HIGH   Remember to tie horses high — at least four or five feet off the ground — so the horse cannot ensnare his legs in the lead rope. At that height, you can still easily reach the release.

THE VAQUERO AND THE KNIFE   Western riders owe a great debt to the unsung heroes steeped in the *Californeo* tradition of the *vaquero*, the earliest cowboys. A knife was one item every vaquero had on his person. It had a host of uses: trimming leather, cutting baling twine, or digging a pebble out from a hoof. But the number-one reason to keep that knife close at hand was to cut quickly through a lead rope or lariat if a horse got tangled up.

A knife is still the ultimate quick-release device. Get into the habit of heading out to the barn with a knife in your pocket or on your waist belt. A sharp, well-manufactured knife is a must.

Getting Grooming

■ ■ ■

AS YOU CAN SEE, there are many precautions to consider before you and your horse arrive at the hitching post. Make sure you select a spot where there is a clear and obvious escape route in case your horse panics. Is there enough room for your horse? Room for you too? Mental preparation and visualization set the stage for successful outcomes.

CULTIVATE EMPTY READINESS   One particular incident underscores the importance of anticipating escape routes before disaster presents the need. I was at a stable, getting ready to conduct a clinic. Four horses were tied to the hitching post, waiting to start the day. I was about to look the horses over just as one owner's child fired a potato gun. With a palpable thump, a large Idaho-raised spud the size of a small meteor came whizzing by at twenty miles an hour, to land among the four horses.

We were able to set two horses free by pulling the slipknots. The remaining two simply yanked the entire hitching post out of the ground. They ran off, awkwardly yoked together by a 150-pound welded steel post. It clanked against the asphalt as they sprinted to escape. Fortunately there was a long driveway available where the horses could run. They went far enough and then just stopped. A good escape route, fortunately, saved us all from any one thing.

Look around your own premises carefully. Allow your eyes to go slightly out of focus, as if you were trying to see through or beyond the horse. Take in the surroundings, the sounds. Is the wind blowing? Are there birds? What about the sky? Take in everything, without concentrating on any one thing.

Practice emptying your head of details. *If minutiae grab your attention, then your mind is trapped.* If you focus only on the horse, you'll miss the big picture. Suzuki Roshi, a prominent twentieth-century Zen Buddhist, wrote: "If your mind is empty, it is always ready for anything; it is open to everything."

Our observations should collect themselves unconsciously into a holistic feel for the grooming spot. The details — say, a loose plastic bag hanging from a nail, or a door groaning as it swings on its hinge in the breeze — should all coalesce into a sense of empty readiness, of attention without concentration. Awareness without anxiety. We learn to see the smallest detail without removing it from its context.

Once your mind is empty, go ahead and hitch up your horse.

GREETING: THREE-POINT FIXATION   In mountaineering, *three-point fixation* represents the combination of two footholds and one handhold, or two handholds and one foothold, to secure a climber on a vertical face of rock or ice. A climber never moves ahead with the ascent until he is certain of three points of solid fixation.

You greet your horse in the same way. With a horse, the three points (*see figure 4.5*) are voice, eye contact, and touch. You use all three to let the horse know where you are at all times. The more solidly you are anchored — the more modalities you use to engage the horse — the more freedom and safety you will have to explore.

The left is the horse's dominant side, squarely in his field of vision. The shoulder is a non-threatening area: predators don't attack at the shoulder because it is unlikely to deliver a lethal blow. Instead, they attack from above or beneath or behind. They do not approach from a position where the attack could be clearly seen and detected.

So we approach the horse from the shoulder. We draw near as a member of the herd rather than as a predator.

VOICE   Before beginning to groom, speak to the horse. Horses are not keen on verbal cues (they can learn a couple dozen spoken commands with practice), but they tune into the tone of the human voice. They can differentiate between a sharp, clipped speech pattern and a soft, comforting one. After speaking, look for acknowledgment from the horse. Did his ears perk up? Did he turn to focus on your voice?

VISUAL LOCK   Secondly, ensure the horse brings his eyes to bear on you. A visual "lock" is the only way to be sure he has localized his handler. This is a critical facet of personal safety: always make a solid, discernible visual

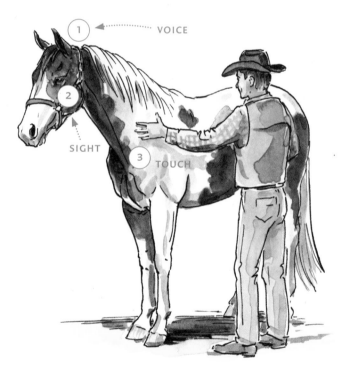

4.5 Three-point fixation using auditory, visual, and sensory contact with the horse

GROOMING AS A TEA CEREMONY

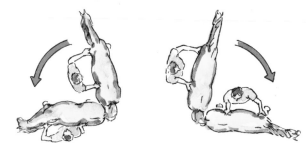

4.6 The handler is standing in a safe position at the neutral left shoulder. If the horse should suddenly jump or spook, the handler can easily step backward and stay in contact with the left shoulder. Similarly, if the horse should suddenly jump away from the handler, he can slide forward to remain in contact with the left shoulder.

connection with your horse. A recent statistic underlines the importance of eye contact. Motorcycle drivers are twenty times less likely to have an accident if they make eye contact with an oncoming driver who is turning the car into the same lane as the motorcyclist. The eyes have it!

I had an eerie experience approaching an acquaintance's mare just before setting off on a trail ride one morning. I needed to walk around this unknown horse to check the cinch on my own mount. As I went through my usual three-point fixation routine, I began talking to the mare. I noticed her ears swinging all around, trying to get a fix on me.

I made a deliberate effort to line myself up in her left eye. I could not detect any glint of recognition, but I made the mistake of just shrugging it off. As I placed my hands on her, she hauled off and kicked out viciously. Her hoof just missed me.

"Hey, sorry about that, man!" said my riding companion. "Don't sneak up on her left side. She's blind in that eye!"

It was my fault. I should have heeded my gut instinct that something was off when I detected no sign that she had locked on me visually.

TOUCH   The final point in the three-point system is touch. Be deliberate with your gestures. No tickling. Walk up and stroke the left shoulder. The left shoulder is the *neutral* or *safe* shoulder (*see figure 4.6*) where we always make initial contact with the horse.

The Safest Approach

■ ■ ■

THE LEFT SHOULDER is the safest place to stand next to a horse, even one you know well. After establishing visual and auditory contact, this is where you go to make your first physical contact with any horse.

The neutral shoulder is also where a trainer should start working with any client or student who is anxious or ill at ease around horses. This is where the instructor can best keep a client safe.

From the neutral shoulder, a stiff forearm against the shoulder will keep the handler in a safe position if a horse moves toward him or her. If the horse steps away, the handler has the choice to simply step with the horse or to disengage and put pressure on the hindquarters to make the horse face the trainer squarely and politely.

WITH YOUR HEART IN YOUR HAND Touch should be initiated by moving your hand softly but firmly with the grain of the horse's coat. Your reassuring, comforting touch should be filled with warmth. For the horse, being stroked around the face, neck, and withers is reminiscent of his earliest days as a foal, when his dam reassured him by licking and nuzzling his coat in a similar fashion.

Start at the neutral shoulder and gradually expand your strokes in larger circles, much as a painter increases the sweep of a brush stroke. And put your heart in your hand while you are stroking a horse.

ROUND THE WORLD AND ROUND THE BRAIN As your strokes expand, continue to talk to your horse and get ready to complete the Round the World maneuver. Move from the neutral shoulder and the left eye and go completely behind the horse. Finish on the right (or off) shoulder, viewed by the horse's right eye. This maneuver is carried out in discrete steps but should be practiced until it is one smooth, flowing motion, like a tai chi movement.

4.7 In Round the World, the handler uses her ribcage and armpit to maintain tactile contact with the horse. This light pressure on the hindquarters reassures the horse, reminds him where the person is as she passes through his rear blind spot, and reduces the risk of the person startling him.

Left Side, Right Side

...

HORSE BRAIN

HUMAN BRAIN

Comparison of sagittal sections of horse and human brains, showing the dramatic difference in the width of the corpus callosum that connects the right and left halves of the human brain.

4.8

ANOTHER IMPORTANT ADVANTAGE of the Round the World maneuver is that it compensates for the horse's unique brain. A horse's neuroanatomy (*see figure 4.8*) is different from a human's. In our brains, the left and right hemispheres are densely interconnected by millions of white-matter fiber tracks, through which humans gain a facility for *generalizing* cognitive tasks. It is easy for most people to teach themselves how to hold a fork with their right hand and then generalize that task so that they can pick up the fork to use it in the left one.

From an anatomical point of view, when we first acquire the ability to manipulate the fork in our right hand, the skill is processed in the motor cortex of the left hemisphere. The brain's wiring is crisscrossed: the right side of the body is actually controlled by signals originating in the left side of the brain, and vice versa.

Once the right hand has learned to use the fork, that information is encoded, packaged, and transmitted over a gigantic bundle of interconnecting white-matter bundles (the *corpus callosum*) to the right motor cortex. So what we learn on one side of the body can be easily swapped or generalized over to the other.

The horse, however, has a poorly developed corpus callosum. The equine brain has a limited capacity to generalize what is learned on one side of the body to the opposite side. Each side must be approached independently.

This is why it is so important to train a horse in a balanced fashion, first asking it to perform a task on the left and then repeating on the right. This explains why a horse will cross a jump from right to left but balk when first asked to jump from left to right. As far as the horse's brain is concerned, it is seeing two different jumps.

Australian horse trainer Clint Anderson points out that every horse owner actually gets two horses for each one they have purchased — one called "Righty" and a second called "Lefty" — and they need equal attention.

"SIDEDNESS" IN HORSES   Just as people generally are more dominant with one hand, which is more facile and dexterous than the other, horses also have dominant and weak sides. For most horses, the left side is dominant, so it will be easier for most horses to learn a task on the left side of the body before the right side.

A horse's preference for the left versus right side is easy to discover in the round pen. He will move better in either the clockwise (CW) or counterclockwise (CCW) direction. If the horse is right-side dominant, he will show slightly greater ease and fluidity when circling to the right (CW). If he is left-side (often referred to also as left-eye) dominant, then the horse will move better toward the left (CCW). About 95 percent of horses are left-side dominant. Every trainer should focus on building up the horse's weaker, less dominant side so he develops the same ease of movement on both sides. A good rule of thumb with a given task is to work a horse about 40 percent on his stronger, more dominant side and 60 percent on the weaker, nondominant side, to ensure that he learns and progresses with balance and symmetry.

TWO BRAINS IN ONE   The Round the World approach compensates for the horse's lack of ability to generalize by taking into account that the horse has two largely independent brains: one for observing the right side and another independent hemisphere for gazing to the left. By sweeping behind the horse through his blind spot (*see figure 4.9*) while providing ample tactile stimulation across the flanks and rump, we bombard both halves with reassuring signals as we cross over from one side of the horse's brain to the other.

With every task we undertake, we need to see the smallest detail from the horse's point of view. The intricacies of his perception and the sensitivities of his physiology should become the subjects of our lifelong study and devotion.

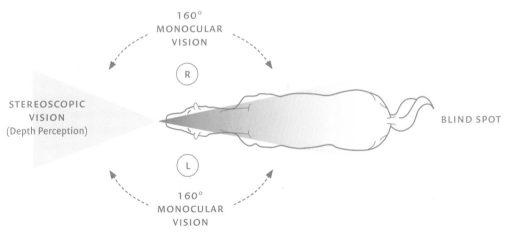

4.9 The visual fields of the horse. Most of the horse's world is seen through monocular vision, a single eye, with very little stereoscopic depth perception — just a small patch in front so he can see food and know where to step. There is a large blind spot behind a horse. Because there is little information crossover between the two halves of the equine brain for what's visually perceived, horses may spook at an object on one side after there was no reaction when they saw it on the other side.

Highlights

∎∎∎

Pick your grooming site with care.

∎

*Ritual transforms any task into an exercise
in awareness.*

∎

*Tack details matter: they convey your
grasp of design.*

∎

*The difference between being merely attached to your
horse and being connected to him is your
state of mind.*

∎

Envision dire consequences in order to avoid them.

∎

*Tie the horse fast and disaster will
always come to pass . . .
but a knot that can slip will surely do the trick.*

∎

Practice tying a thousand flawless slipknots.

∎

*A knife is the quick-release device of
last resort.*

∎

*Mental preparation paves the
way for success.*

CHAPTER FIVE

SEARCHING FOR CHI

From beasts we scorn as soulless,
In forest, field and den,
The cry goes up to witness
The soullessness of men.

■ ■ ■

M. FRIDA HARTLEY

From his headquarters in Pagosa Springs, Colorado, Pat Parelli has developed a systematic approach to training horses called Natural Horsemanship. There are wonderful concepts, acronyms, and aphorisms in Pat's writings. One of his most enduring concepts is compartmentalizing the horse's body into five separate, distinct zones of awareness (*see figure 5.1*), where pressure can be applied.

As depicted in the figure below, zone 1 is assigned to the area around the horse's mouth and muzzle. Pat insists students understand that this zone *begins* at the nose and extends for a mile and a half *in front of it*. Zone 5 is assigned to the tail and, likewise, stretches for a mile and a half behind the horse. These far-reaching zones of sensitivity in front and in back of the horse are linked directly to the survival of a prey animal. First, the animal is asking himself, "Is anything pursuing me?" Second, he wants to know, "Can I get out of here? Can I flee?"

It makes sense that the horse would develop an exquisite sensitivity to anything — movements, rustling, energetic auras — within zones 1 or 5. From a genetic point of view, any horse *not* tuned in to what was going on in front and behind was unlikely to survive to produce offspring. The less aware an individual animal was of what was transpiring, the sooner he'd end up as lunch for some saber-toothed tiger. In contrast, the sensitive horse, the one who could really spook, would survive to live a long, fruitful life and produce descendants. Being devoured is one of Nature's favorite ways of cleansing the gene pool, and horses arrived from prehistory with genetic proclivities to sensing and reacting explosively to whatever might be going on in zones 1 and 5.

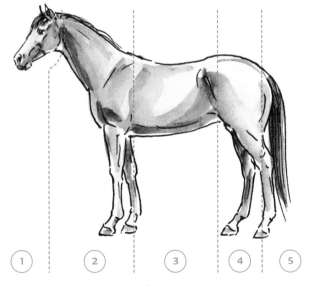

5.1 Zones of awareness on a horse

Bubbles of Awareness

■ ■ ■

THE AREA OF SENSITIVITY (or bubble of chi) around an individual horse can represent a volume greater than 15 million cubic meters. It is an enormous space that a vigilant horse must constantly probe, test, and sift through for threats. He must detect the kind of intensely focused energy that emanates from a stalking predator.

Undomesticated wild mustang herds living in federal Bureau of Land Management areas, such as those set aside in New Mexico and Nevada, are much more wary or vigilant than the average domesticated horse kept in the family barnyard. Wild horses have obviously maintained and honed their natural defensive instincts and would typically be sampling larger areas to detect predators. Unfortunately, in today's world, the wild horse's greatest predatory threat is from humans.

The dimensions of such a gigantic personal space are almost inconceivable to a human being. For comparison, consider an average person sitting down in his favorite lounge chair and watching TV (our equivalent of grazing, I suppose). That individual may have an envelope of awareness of a thousand cubic meters. In other words, a horse's awareness is nearly 15 thousand times larger than a human's in terms of volume. Why such a difference in orders of magnitude? Because we are predators. We don't usually worry about being attacked. We are the hunters. We do the attacking.

PROTECTIVE AWARENESS   Another component relates to the difference between a pack of predators and a herd of prey animals. Prey animals "pool" their awareness. When a herd of zebras is spread out across a stretch of African savanna, each individual animal is sampling the enormous volume of space around it. When a hundred animals are grouped, the volumes overlap and are additive (*see figure 5.2*), creating a huge "shield" around the herd. This is why prey animals are drawn into herds. The massive annual herd migrations, such as that of the wildebeest in Africa, can combine as many as two million individual animals, offering an enormous volume of protective awareness, sometimes covering hundreds of square miles.

Predators, on the other hand, move in the opposite direction; their attentive volumes are not additive but subtractive. As modern members of what used to be tightly knit hunting bands, often huddled in caves or fabricated shelters, we humans are adept at contracting down our sensitive personal space around us. For example, in crowded social situations, like subway cars, elevators, and packed cocktail receptions, most of us are socially

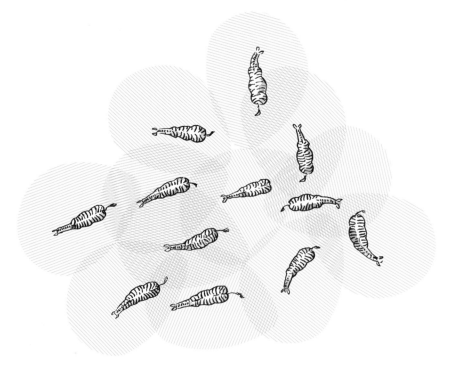

5.2 A herd of zebras with overlapping, additive components of volume

aware enough to pull in our antennae and pare down our reactive space to a handful of cubic meters. We prefer encroachment to confrontation.

Remember the airplane trip when you and your neighbor jousted over the armrest? Maybe you smiled and let your elbow slip down out of the way. In most routine social situations, boundary issues come down to a decision to contract or react. Horses do this too, in their own fashion.

For example, horses become uncomfortable and restless when first being loaded into a trailer because it constrains the volume available to them for detecting and evading a threat. Entering a trailer runs contrary to every instinct the species has acquired over millions of years. It takes practice to suspend his uneasiness and develop his trust enough that he willingly accepts the limited space in a trailer.

Intention

■■■

CHANGE IN ENERGY OCCURS because our brains package it to make anything happen. Every action, no matter how minute, occurs only with intention. Intention assembles and organizes energy so the action can be carried out. Then the energy dissipates. This change in energy state occurs because our brains must package energy to make anything happen.

The simple act of reaching out for your morning mug of coffee requires your brain to orchestrate the action before you can actually reach out. The brain "pre-thinks" what it has to do. Scores of muscles will need to be activated and balanced. Tendons need to stretch. Joints need to unfold. All of this has to be first organized as pure thought. This is a concrete, real way to think about intention.

Intention then proceeds to assembly and is finally translated into action. Only when a specialized area of the brain, the prefrontal area, has completely thought out the action and envisioned it from start to finish does our thought move over to the motor cortex. Here neurons fire up, sparking the muscles into action. They contract. Your hand goes out and your fingers extend. And the cup comes up. It all unfolds as if preordained, which it was — in your mind's circuitry.

The sequence within the brain includes these stages:

Thought, cognition (FRONTAL LOBES) $\longrightarrow$
Organization of action (PRE-MOTOR CORTEX) $\longrightarrow$
Firing of neurons (MOTOR CORTEX) $\longrightarrow$
Action potential $\longrightarrow$
Muscular contraction

This is how the sequence might be translated in terms of energy:

Chi collected (INTENTION) $\longrightarrow$
Chi focused (ASSEMBLY) $\longrightarrow$
Chi delivered (ACTION) $\longrightarrow$
Chi dissipation (RELEASE)

SENSING ENERGY   This notion of conceptualizing our thoughts, desires, and behaviors in terms of their energetic content might seem foreign at first. But this is how horses sense what we are feeling and how we are behaving. It is based on the foundation of how our central nervous system is organized.

At its most fundamental level, all nature is organized by energy. By exploring ground work with horses, we initiate direct physical interaction with chi. Through a skilled interpreter — our equine partner — we can translate the abstractions of energetic intention, assembly, action, and release into their physical equivalents. We can feel them, increase or decrease their amplitude, or move them faster or slower. We can practice these central spiritual concepts in a direct, physical way that allows us to understand them, to observe them, and to apply them.

Just as an archer translates the distance his arrow deviates from the center of the bull's eye as a *passive* measure of concentration and technique, the horse can serve us in a similar fashion. But the horse is far better because the success of our ground work becomes an *active* assessment of our proficiency. Working with a horse is equivalent to having a target that can speak to us, that can coach us while the arrow is in flight. To the extent that we allow our horses to teach us not just how to listen to chi but how to speak it, we open our hearts and minds to the living connections we can have to the whole Universe.

DEMONSTRATING CHI

Here's an exercise you can do to explore the volume of chi surrounding a horse. Take the rest of the day off. Grab a good book, a bottle of wine, and some cheese and fresh-baked bread. A bag of carrots won't hurt either. The latter is for the horses; the rest is for you. Head out to a nice green pasture with a few horses loose in it.

I know. Some of you will complain, "I don't have a green pasture." Is that all it takes to stop you? Get creative. We're talking about spiritual well-being. So go out and borrow one. Just get yourself out there.

Find yourself a spot of shade under a nice tree. Take out your book. Have a few sips of *vino*, a bite of cheese, and a nibble of bread. Let the horses get over the shock of seeing a human who just wants to hang out in their pasture. Remember: human beings usually come through that gate only when they want the horses to do something.

Once the horses have returned to grazing, randomly pick one out of the herd. Get up and start walking toward him. Envision yourself catching, collecting, and haltering that one particular horse. After you've

selected one, don't change your mind. Stay focused on that horse. Keep walking straight toward him.

Now watch what happens (*see below*). The horses you did *not* select will let you roam fairly close to them, but the one you intend to capture may start to pick up his head and maybe even move off. So what did the selected horse sense that the others did not? A noticeable change in the intensity of your energy state. Just making a selection in your mind produces a change in your chi that is easily perceived by the horse, even across an entire pasture.

INTENTION AND BREATHING One lesson horses teach us right away is that *intention begins with inspiration*. The foundation of training begins and ends with a breath. Deep breathing disciplines us to slow down. As predators, we like everything as fast as possible, preferably yesterday. Why? The faster the action, the quicker the reward. For prey animals it is just the opposite. The slower the action is, the more it gets absorbed.

Prey animals are patient. For them, rushing is inextricably linked to fear. Proper learning and reflection require tranquility and safety. As supercharged predators, humans need to purposefully slow themselves down. Breathing benefits the trainer by assembling and focusing her intention.

Horse as Awareness

■ ■ ■

TRULY ARCHETYPAL HORSE CULTURES appreciated the horse precisely for his enhanced awareness. Mongols, Bedouins, and Native Americans all treated horses like relatives and brought their most valued ones right inside their dwellings. A prized warhorse was zealously guarded. An enemy would have to display great courage and skill to sneak into the heart of his opponent's enclave and steal such a horse. Acquiring a man's warhorse was equivalent to stealing his power, his very soul.

To his human partner, a horse can appear to be a divine messenger, an ally with almost supernatural abilities. I've experienced this myself. On one particular trail ride, my friend and I rode deep into the foothills of the Santa Catalina Mountains, north of Tucson. We wound our way up the shoulder, shifting from one herd path to another. Pretty soon we were high up on the side of the mountain. As the horses scrambled up a scree slope of loose rock, their footing became more precarious. The horses grew skittish as we urged them up the slope. When we crested the ridge, we could see why: a huge storm was charging our way, right up the other side of the mountain.

One moment, the sky was clear and the sun was shining. A few minutes later, the air turned cold. Dark, threatening clouds engulfed us, and hail and snow began slashing at us. The horses jerked and twisted violently, looking around for a route to escape the pelting hail. Visibility was down to no more than a few feet ahead of us, and the snow and wind forced our eyes closed. It seemed any step, every step, was going to be our last.

Suddenly a voice inside instructed me to simply let go, to give it up to the horse and drop the reins. The horses were filled with panic. The idea seemed suicidal. But the voice kept insisting: drop the reins. *Drop them*. The voice was compelling, and eventually I listened. I just let go.

When I did, my Quarter Horse, Ace, calmed down immediately. A sense of determination seemed to infuse him. He began to patiently feel his way down the mountain. I could not see a trail. Every turn looked like a dead end, but somehow Ace managed to find another step. My companion's horse appeared to take heart from Ace's confidence and simply followed close behind.

Painstakingly, Ace guided us through the storm. There was no trail to follow; he felt his way down the entire mountainside. As he moved lower, the slope flattened out. Then I heard a dull, resounding thud: Ace had stepped out onto a small wooden bridge. The snow began to yield to a gentle rain. As I looked down, I saw the swollen stream rolling under the bridge. Ace had brought us back to the trailhead.

Napoleon Bonaparte (*see figure 5.3*) reported similarly about his own horse, Marengo: "When I lost my way, I was accustomed to throw the reins on his neck, and he always discovered places where I, with all my observation and boasted superior knowledge, could not."

I have no idea how Ace picked his way down the mountain. He did not follow the trails we had climbed up. I got the impression he seemed to be testing out the path, perhaps feeling it with his feet. But it doesn't explain how he was able to select a way down the mountain that did not dead-end in a cliff or walled-off canyon. Ace's negotiation of the terrain in those winter white-out conditions remains the single most amazing feat of navigation I have ever witnessed.

To me, such events are not exceptions. They are, instead, examples. They do not underscore what is impossible but illustrate what might be possible. They demonstrate the power of our horses' (and other animals') capabilities. Of course, the compass and the global positioning system are achievements of the human intellect. We want a map to show us the trail down the mountain, while animals just have faith one exists.

As humans, we draw comfort from the devices and machines we've derived from science, from cognition. However, animals place their ultimate faith in instinct and intuition. We may have questions about how or why such instincts engender behavior but we cannot doubt the power of their effect. To the contrary, humans find their faith sorely divided between intuitive versus cognitive behavior. While we hope to be the product of intellect, we remain creatures of instinct. To the extent we can engage ourselves with horses, we are returned to the home of our original, mammalian faith.

5.3 Painting of Napoleon Bonaparte depicted on one of his favorite mounts, an Arab stallion named Marengo (*Napoleon Crossing the Alps* by Jacques-Louis David, 1801)

CHAPTER SIX

GROOMING AS AN ACT OF LOVE

A lovely horse is always an experience....
It is an emotional experience of the kind that
is spoiled by words.

■ ■ ■

BERYL MARKHAM

T HE HORSE HAS A heroic and supernatural quality that inspires us to attend to his needs. In the details of grooming, we find opportunities to show our gratitude and respect for this magical species. Marilyn vos Savant remarked, "It is a lot easier to prove that you don't love someone than it is to prove that you do, but one of the best 'proofs' I know is the desire to devote time to the person with no expectation of any sort of compensation, including gratitude, in return." Grooming is an act of love.

The Grooming Toolkit

· · ·

HUMAN BEINGS DON'T SHARE TOOTHBRUSHES, and horses shouldn't share grooming equipment. Every horse deserves a personal tack box (*see figure 6.1*), with his own brushes, currycomb, and hoof picks. Assign each piece of grooming equipment to one horse — and only one. This also allows the handler to individualize the equipment choices for a particular horse. Some horses (such as mustangs) have thick, stiff coats, while others (such as Arabs and Thoroughbreds) have thin and silky coats. Different coats and environmental conditions require brushes with different bristle stiffnesses to meet individual grooming needs.

One size does not fit all. One set of brushes, one bit, one saddle — one approach — never works for all horses.

CURRYING FAVOR   The first instrument in our grooming ritual is the currycomb. Although most brushes are designed to work with the grain of the hair on the horse's hide, the currycomb breaks up wads of dirt that have become caked or stuck in the hair. It is used in broad circular motions and travels both with and against the hair's grain to dislodge dirt and grime.

Use it only with light pressure. A currycomb becomes uncomfortable on a horse's sensitive skin when it is pressed too hard. A horse can either look forward to or dread the currycomb: it's all in the pressure.

The currycomb is reserved primarily for the saddle blanket and girth areas (*see figure 6.2*). You can occasionally use it to dislodge dirt caked on the lower extremities of the horse, particularly the fetlocks, but you should scrupulously avoid the face.

BODY AND FACIAL BRUSHES   After the currycomb it's time for the body brush. Many brushes, especially the ubiquitous synthetic nylon

6.1

Each horse has a designated tack box to ensure there is no inadvertent contamination through brushes.

currycomb
body brush
soft facial brush

6.2 Specific areas of the horse for the currycomb, the body brush, and the soft facial brush

ones sold in tack stores today, are suitable only for scrubbing toilets. They should never be used on any horse. Find a brush with bristles of medium to light stiffness made from natural fibers (boar's hair is the best). Great Britain manufactures some of the best brushes in the world, and while they can be a bit pricey, they are worth the extra expense because of their durability. I figure a good brush should last the entire lifespan of the horse. If your horse was a good investment, so's a good brush.

The brush can be applied to the horse's entire body (except for the face). Brush *with* the grain. Dirt will migrate out in front of your brush strokes the way a wave washes sand up before it. If a horse is having a particularly bad hair day (i.e., his coat's filthy or he's shedding out excess winter coat), you'll need to clean out the bristles periodically.

The last (and my favorite) of the three grooming tools is the soft brush. The soft brush or facial brush (*see figure 6.3*) should be of the highest quality and have the softest bristles you can find. The best test for bristle softness is to brush your own eyebrows. If it feels good, purchase the brush. If not, your horse won't go for it either.

Start brushing the jowls first. Proceed to the forehead and, finally, the muzzle. Finish with the nostrils, mouth, and a gentle, light brushing near the eyes.

6.3

Use the soft brush lightly around the eyes and nostrils.

The Eyes Have It

■ ■ ■

IF THERE IS ANY DISCHARGE or crusted secretion around the eyes, remove it with a warm, clean, slightly moist washcloth. Avoid soaps or cleansers.

If the horse has signs of "pink eye," or conjunctivitis, clean around the eye with lukewarm water and then use my favorite recipe as an effective eyewash (*see box*). This makes a great solution for cleansing the eyelids and relieving redness or puffiness around the eyes. A thick discharge may be an early sign of conjunctivitis, indicating it is appropriate to start ophthalmic antibiotic ointment. Call the vet if things don't improve.

Use dye-free, natural, all-cotton washcloths (*see figure 6.4*). These can be vigorously washed in laundry detergent and bleached hundreds of times.

6.4 Pay gentle, careful attention around the eyes to clean away debris and help prevent conjunctivitis.

EQUINE EYEWASH

1. Place two quarts of filtered water in a saucepan.
2. Add 1 tablespoon of boric acid powder; stir until dissolved.
3. Drop two green tea bags into the water.
4. Add five grains of table salt.
5. Bring to a rolling boil; boil for at least five minutes.
6. Remove the saucepan from the heat.
7. Allow the solution to cool until it is barely lukewarm.
8. Test the temperature with your finger before using.

In my barn, we have a large bin brimming with fresh, clean washcloths to encourage the staff to be extravagant with them.

Never swap washcloths among horses. If one horse has conjunctivitis, sharing washcloths is an excellent way to spread it throughout the barn. If one eye looks infected, use a separate washcloth for each eye rather than risk contagion to the unaffected one. When in doubt, employ a fresh washcloth on each side of the face.

The Mane Event

■ ■ ■

I APPROACH BRUSHING my horse's mane and tail the same way I would want my barber to handle my own hair and scalp: respectfully. The majority of mane and tail brushes sold are poorly suited to tackling them. Most are glorified human hairbrushes, designed for a person's much finer hair but repackaged and marketed for equine use. The pervasive problem with these brushes is their long protruding bristles, anchored in a flimsy elastic backing, which inevitably pulls loose as you negotiate a horse's tougher, thicker hair fibers.

The horse's mane is shorter and easier to groom than the tail. It's important to get the entire mane on one side of the horse's neck. Most horses' manes have a preference for lying on one side of the neck or the other, like some folks' hair naturally parts on one side.

Initiate your brush strokes at the ends of the hairs, not at the roots. Thoroughly brush the ends and proceed up the mane until you get closer to the crest and poll of the neck.

6.5

A horse's forelock has a variety of uses and should be left long and thick.

SPARE THAT FORELOCK

I don't recommend fashion over purpose; keep the horse's forelock as long as possible.

Before you trim your horse's forelock and give him a set of short bangs, remember that this relatively modest patch of hair on the horse's poll has several protective functions:

- A thick forelock helps to protect a horse from banging his head.
- The profusion of hair around the top of the head helps warn him when his head is too close to an object, like the roof of your horse trailer.

- The forelock keeps flies out of his eyes.
- It serves as a UV screen, reducing the amount of sunlight reaching the horse's corneas, like a baseball cap.

A horse who is leery about having his forelock brushed out does not have a problem with his hair; he is telling you he is head-shy. So if he tosses his head, do not try to muscle him down by pulling on the halter. Go back to square one and teach him to overcome his head-shyness (*see chapter 19, From Sack to Saddle*).

The good mane and tail detangling products on the market are distinctly different from average conditioners. A conditioner is meant to remain in contact with wet hair for a period of one to five minutes and then be rinsed out. A detangler is rubbed into the hair and remains there. Most of them incorporate hydrating molecules that hold water well, so they add moisture to the surface of the hairs. They also include a lubricant, usually either glycerin or silicone, so the hairs can slide more easily over each other. Detangling solutions make manes and tails less susceptible to pulling out and breaking off.

The Tail End

■ ■ ■

IT'S TIME TO TURN your attention to the tail. First clean out any chunks of dirt, weeds, or burrs you see. Rub plenty of detangler into the tail hairs. Again, start by brushing the ends and work your way up.

Take your time. It's a delicious feeling when the brush begins to move smoothly through the hair. More and more, the fullness of the tail gradually registers in your hands as you brush. After a while, your brush will slip through the tail hairs as effortlessly as the slide on a trombone.

Working your way up toward the horse's rump, you'll begin to feel the caudal portion of the tail. This part of the tail is made of skin, flesh, and bone. It also has nerve endings, so use gentle brush strokes. As you move toward the dock of the tail, you will often notice some shorter frayed hairs around the base of the tail. These hairs have usually been damaged by the horse rubbing his rump back and forth. If there are signs of excessive

TAIL WRAPS

One effective way to prevent trauma from damaging or pulling hair out of the tail is to wrap it. Tail wrapping, however, should be undertaken with caution. Horses who are turned out should have their tails wrapped with a material light enough to tear easily if caught on a fence or tree. It needs to fray and rip easily to avoid damaging the tail. In a turn-out situation, a cheaper tail wrap is preferable.

6.6 A neglected tail, a mess of knots.

6.7 After applying detangler, start working hairs loose from the ends and then gradually work your way toward the tail dock.

6.8 The feeling is delicious when the tail, now smooth and free of tangles, has been completely groomed.

rubbing, there may be a problem with parasites or skin disease. Consult your veterinarian if you have any questions.

I think it is safe to say that many of us have a love affair with the horse's mane and tail. There is something sensual about their long, flowing, majestic qualities. I have found many students like to linger on this aspect of grooming, and I encourage them to do so. Remember the loving feeling that comes from brushing someone's hair or being the recipient of such devotion.

Hoofing It

■ ■ ■

The one who removes a mountain,
Begins by carrying away small stones.

CHINESE PROVERB

FEET EQUAL TRUST. Asking a horse to pick up his feet is like someone asking to hold your hand. It is not something you do until you know each other well. As a prey animal, a horse is symbolically putting his life into your hands when he allows you to hold his feet. While you are grasping his 100-pound leg is not the moment to discover that your horse feels ambivalent about the issue.

If a horse is starting to develop bad manners — or worse, a sullen state of mind — it will show first in how he picks up his feet. As soon as we see the slightest sign of hesitation, we must go back and practice. Raising his feet is something a horse needs to practice until it is second nature to hold them up at the slightest prompting.

In fact, a day should not pass that you do not lift and examine your horse's hooves. So it's something your horse *gets to rehearse every day.*

PICK IT UP   So how do we teach a horse to pick up his feet readily? Begin on the first day of his life. One of the first things I teach every foal is to get comfortable having his hooves handled. Handling the feet should be done with the utmost respect and gentleness; it will eventually be accepted as second nature by every domesticated horse.

If I'm dealing with a wild horse, on the other hand, the feet are the last thing I tackle. It will take dozens, sometimes hundreds, of hours to build up sufficient trust for that. The horse needs to become perfectly tame and completely at ease with being led, with having human beings around him, and with being handled and touched anywhere. And I mean anywhere: groin, teats, under the tail, inside the ears, mouth, or nostrils, and, finally, anywhere along his legs.

Once all of that is out of the way, we can teach a horse to pick up his feet easily. Because the ability to put his feet down and run is the horse's ultimate and final defense, we won't ask him to put that on the line until he has complete confidence in us.

The key to having a horse lift his leg is for you to shift his center of gravity (*see figures 6.9 and 6.10*). If I were gradually to push harder and harder on your shoulder, you would eventually pick up a foot because I would have moved you off balance. You would need to shift feet to regain your stability.

We use this same principle with the horse. Begin with the front feet, because it is easier for a horse to lift the forelegs than the hind. There is simply less weight to them; and because of the horse's front leg anatomy, only flexion is required to lift it, while the hind requires a combination of extension and flexion.

FRONT LEG PICKUP   When you're training a horse to lift his leg, begin by facing his hind end. Rest your hand quietly on his shoulder (*see figure 6.9*). Take a deep, cleansing breath. Every breath you take is shared with your horse. When you breathe mindfully, with the purpose of quieting your inner being, it is automatic that your calmer state will be transmitted to your horse. Breathe slowly, and you will physiologically entrain your horse to slow down.

The motivating pressure for the horse to raise his foot comes from your leaning against his shoulder, *not* from your lifting the lower leg and hoof. Lean in until he shifts his weight onto his opposite leg. As soon as you see the horse's weight come off the near foot, slide your hand into position and lightly press the flexor tendon. When the hoof lifts, slide your hand under the hoof to support the pastern and hoof (*see illustration sequence*).

Here's the sequence of cues:

- Balance the horse's weight to the rear
- Bend down next to the horse
- Lean against his shoulder
- Run your hand down the back of the horse's leg and pinch the flexor tendon
- Once the foot lifts, slide your supporting hand under the hoof

Breathe as you work on the hoof. When you're ready, exhale while you softly place the foot back on the ground. As you release his foot, offer praise and a reassuring stroke; he has complied with your request.

It may take dozens of trials before the horse responds to our cues. Meanwhile, we want to get him into the habit of anticipating our requests.

When the horse understands a request is coming, it is time to give up a cue. Let's say the horse shifts his weight as soon as he feels you lean against his shoulder. Great! That means we can eliminate that cue from the sequence in the future. Soon you'll reach the stage where your horse will shift his weight whenever you bend over and start to reach for his hoof. The last refinement is to ask the horse to hold his leg up for progressively longer periods of time and then put it down on cue.

HIND LEG PICKUP   Now it is time for the hind legs (*see figure 6.10*). Here is the slightly different sequence of cues:

- Face rearward and stand parallel to the hind leg
- Slide your hand down along the back of the inner hind leg
- Lean against the horse's hip
- Rest your hand on the flexor tendon, a hand's width above the fetlock, and give it a slight squeeze
- When the hind leg flexes upward and the hoof lifts off the ground, slide your hand along the underside of the leg to support the pastern and the hoof

FRONT LEG PICKUP

HIND LEG PICKUP

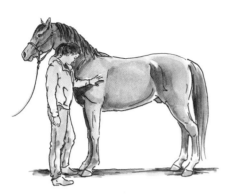

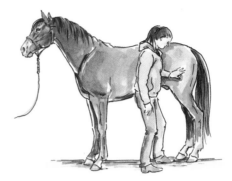

As you exhale, glide your hand down the back of his leg.

As you slide your hand downward, lean in against your horse's shoulder. This pushes him onto his far leg and unweights the foot you wish to lift.

As your hand arrives at the large flexor tendon along the back of the lower leg, exert light pressure in the groove between the cannon bone and the tendon. Then lift the leg and cradle it on your thigh or between your legs.

BREATH SEQUENCE: FRONT LEG

Practice carrying out this sequence of cues slowly and smoothly. Make each step correspond to a phase of your breathing. Our goal is to make our cues and movements flow along the leg, like our breathing.

- • INHALE: Stand at the shoulder, facing rearward, hand on the horse's shoulder
- ○ EXHALE: Slide hand down the shoulder
- • INHALE: Lean against the shoulder to shift the horse's weight
- ○ EXHALE: Lightly pinch the flexor tendon
- • INHALE: Lift and support the hoof on your thigh or between your legs
- ○ EXHALE: Work on the hoof or gently place it back on the ground

BREATH SEQUENCE: HIND LEG

Practice the hind leg sequence of cues slowly and smoothly, with each step synchronized with your breathing.

- • INHALE: Stand at the hip, facing rearward, hand on the horse's hip
- ○ EXHALE: Slide hand down the back of the thigh and leg
- • INHALE: Lean into the hip to shift the horse's weight
- ○ EXHALE: Lightly pinch the flexor tendon
- • INHALE: Lift and support the hoof
- ○ EXHALE: Extend the horse's leg behind him
- • INHALE: Support the leg on your inside thigh or pass it between your legs and clamp it between your knees
- ○ EXHALE: Work on the hoof or gently place it back on the ground

6.11

Rasping the hoof on a hoof stand

One important difference between the front and hind legs is the additional step of asking the horse to relax and extend the hind leg. Gently stretch the hind leg into extension while you walk the extended leg out behind the horse. Be sure to walk the leg straight out, directly behind the horse. Pulling the leg slightly off to the side can be uncomfortable for the horse and make him skittish about yielding his leg. In case he jerks his leg free, so he can place it back on the ground, stand parallel to the horse's hips, with your feet safely off to the side, out of range.

As the horse becomes confident about holding his hind leg up, ask him to do so for ten to fifteen seconds each time. After that is mastered, you can be confident that it's safe to brace the hind leg on your inside thigh or pass it between your legs — the so-called farrier stance — so the hoof is clamped between both knees, leaving both hands free to work on the hoof. Alternatively, instead of steadying the front or rear hooves with your hands, you can safely put the hoof on a hoof stand (*see figure 6.11*).

Establish this hoof-handling sequence not only to accustom the horse to picking up the requested hoof but also to get him used to the painless but sometimes time-consuming process of cleaning his feet out with a hoof pick. You'll use this hook-like instrument with its strong handle to pull out pebbles and debris wedged into the nooks and crannies around the sole of the hoof.

Breathe while you work on the hoof. Once the hoof is clean, exhale and respectfully lower it to the ground. Many folks simply let the hoof drop like a brick. Instead, lower it gently and stroke the leg when the hoof is back on the ground. This serves as a sensory cue to the horse that his foot is being returned to his control. It also encourages the horse to place his weight on that particular limb so you can prepare to lift another hoof.

In addition to occasional but necessary cleaning to ensure healthy hooves, introduce the experience of the vibration used when filing or rasping the hoof. You will lightly rasp an unshod hoof until you have taught the horse to stand still.

All of your care, attention, and training with respect to hoof handling will eventually be put to the test, because, sooner or later, the farrier will arrive.

THE FARRIER IS HERE   For more than a thousand years, metal shoes or rims have been nailed to horses' hooves to improve their durability. Today, shoeing horses is the province of the farrier.

There are differing notions of how the term *farrier* arose. Some believe it is derived from the Latin *faber ferrarius* (*faber,* meaning craftsman or manufacturer, and *ferrarius,* from iron): in essence, a blacksmith (*see figure 6.12*). Another theory holds that the designation came from a Norman lord named Henri de Ferrariis. He apparently had a knack for doctoring horses and accompanied William the Conqueror during the conquest of England in 1066. The nobleman took his name from the town of Ferrières, near Paris, an area rich with iron (*fer* in French) ore mines.

When it's time for the farrier to come and shoe horses, his or her visit is associated in a horse's mind with many different stimuli. For example, most farriers like to pull their vehicles up close by the barn, because they may be loaded with more than 1,000 pounds of metal: horseshoes of all sizes, anvils, nails, sledgehammers, and perhaps forges. My farrier drives a huge diesel truck and pulls his gear right up to the barn door. So I must ask myself: is my horse accustomed to loud diesel trucks coming up that close and maneuvering nearby? If not, I must get to work on it.

Many farriers wear thick leather aprons to protect themselves from hot sparks when they hammer the heated metal horseshoes coming out of the forge. The apron slaps loudly with each step they take. I recommend that

6.12 *De Schmidt (The Smith)* by Jost Amman, 1568

trainers simulate this novel sound by putting on leather chaps or chinks so they can slap the surface and edges back and forth on their legs and get the horse accustomed to the noise.

Horse handlers also have to contend with the banging of the steel tools. Farriers use sledgehammers to hammer the shoes to a customized fit. That's a lot of racket. We can reproduce that by placing hoof nippers, trimmers, files, and hammers in a heavy coffee can; then shaking it around to produce the sound of "heavy metal."

Your horse must become accustomed to having his hooves tapped and rasped. As the horse's confidence grows, increase the amplitude of these movements until you can tap the bottom of the hoof wall without the horse flinching. Ask the horse to hold his hind leg in the farrier's stance, or place the hoof on an actual hoof stand (*see page 84*). Again, you need to simulate as closely as possible anything the farrier might do. Borrow a hoof stand to train your horse to be at ease with resting his feet on it. By the time your horse needs his first trim, it will be no big deal.

A plea on behalf of all farriers: don't make your farrier responsible for teaching your horse how to properly and politely pick up his feet. That is not the farrier's responsibility; it's the owner's duty to ensure that each horse has learned proper hoof etiquette.

LEARNING TO STAND QUIETLY   Every horse needs to learn to stand quietly without moving his feet as a prerequisite to lifting his feet safely for cleaning or trimming. Two techniques can help the horse be ready for this task.

The first is simple: never ask a horse to stand still unless he is ready to do so. If a horse is frisky and rambunctious, that is not the time to address how to stand still. Seek the conditions that allow the horse to succeed. Try to set up the training scenario so the solution you are looking for is easy for the horse to find.

Earlier, I mentioned that prey animals prefer to learn lessons in a slow, unhurried fashion. They digest both food and information slowly! So, as counterintuitive as it may seem, the best time to introduce a horse to a novel experience may be after a demanding physical workout, when he's tired. It's a bit like teenagers who figure that the best opportunity for asking to borrow the car is when their parents are relaxed and in a good mood.

The second technique is to ask the horse to stand on a surface that discourages him from moving. This training tip falls under what I call the *uphill–downhill* principle: namely, it's easier to go downhill than uphill. If I establish an objective, my intention is to discourage anything that is non-productive by making the horse feel as though he's moving uphill, which takes work. If it's a step toward the objective, I want the horse to feel as though he's moving downhill, because it's easier to go down the slope.

That's why I use footing made up of 3- or 4-inch-diameter river rocks to teach my horses to stand quietly. It provides a rough, heavily textured surface, more uneven than traditional pea-sized gravel, and exerts pressure on the bottom of their hooves, so the horses feel more uncomfortable when they keep moving their feet than if they find one spot and stand still. It's a great tool for the horse that's fidgety or inclined to shift constantly from one side of the hitching post to the other.

Using river rocks is a time-honored technique dating all the way back to the great horseman Xenophon of Greece, who taught horsemanship to Alexander the Great. His text *The Art of Horsemanship* is a classic that became the keystone of natural horsemanship, as well as dressage.

KEEPING IT SAFE   Always position yourself safely when attending to your horse's feet. I make this admonition from experience; my toes have been broken no fewer than three times after I've been stepped on by horses. I wish I weren't so inclined to learn the hard way! Consider protecting your precious feet with steel-toed construction boots that meet the Occupational Safety and Health Administration standards.

Also visualize the area around and under the horse where he is most likely to place his feet if he jerks a leg free. I call it the landing zone (the LZ), a term borrowed from the military. It refers to the footprint on the ground where a helicopter sets down, like a helipad. Anticipate where your horse's hooves will land, and keep your feet out of the LZ.

When handling your horse's lifted foot, apply slight upward pressure by placing the wide-open palm of your inside hand firmly under the pastern. Supporting your horse's foreleg from this location makes the hoof accessible for inspection and cleaning. It provides the horse with sensory feedback so he is aware when you're letting go of his leg. This also helps you position your feet away from the horse's LZ.

Evaluate and patiently clean each hoof when you groom your horse. Do not rush this step.

The Tea Ceremony

■■■

OUR APPROACH TO GROOMING can help set the stage for each training session. By immersing ourselves in the details of the ritual, we develop a method to cultivate mindful awareness. Grooming is the equine equivalent of a tea ceremony. Paulo Coelho, the author of *The Alchemist*, had the opportunity to experience a tea ceremony in Japan; he wrote:

> You go into a small room, tea is served, and that's it really, except that everything is done with so much ritual and ceremony that a banal daily event is transformed into a moment of communion with the Universe.

The tea master, Okakura Kakuzo, explains what happens:

> Tea ceremony is a way of worshipping the beautiful and the simple. All one's efforts are concentrated on trying to achieve perfection through the imperfect gestures of daily life. Its beauty consists in the respect with which it is performed. If a mere cup of tea can bring us closer to God, we should watch out for all the other dozens of opportunities that each ordinary day offers us.

Strive to use grooming as an interval in which you can shift your attitude from an *everyday* state of mind to an *every instant* state of mind.

CHAPTER SIX

Highlights

Grooming is an act of love.

Choose your grooming brushes with discrimination.

Shifting the center of gravity lifts the leg.

When your horse begins to anticipate a request, drop that particular cue.

Make it hard to do the wrong thing and easy to do the right one.

Turn your everyday *state of mind into an* every instant *state of mind.*

CHAPTER SEVEN

THE MAGIC DOG

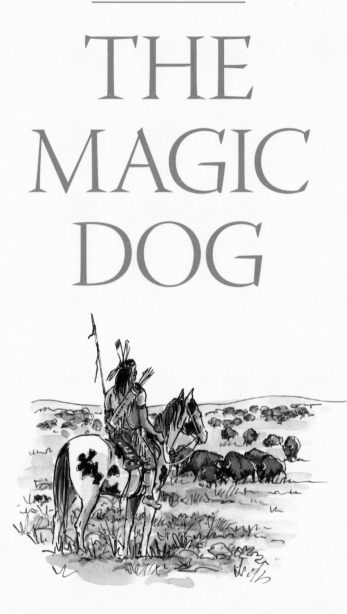

When I bestride him, I soar, I am a hawk:
He trots the air; the earth sings when he touches it;
The basest horn of his hoof is more musical than
the pipe of Hermes.

■ ■ ■

WILLIAM SHAKESPEARE, *Henry V*

A LIFE WITH HORSES OFFERS opportunities to look inward, to find new points of access for further self-improvement and self-awareness. The path of horsemanship honors both horse and human: the longer we pursue it, the more profound the revelations become.

There is an old Celtic proverb: "A friend's eye is a good mirror." Because horses so easily reflect back our inner state of mind, as I noted earlier, they serve as "divine mirrors." They return to us our emotional truth; what we feel is what they see.

Coyote's Mischief

■ ■ ■

NATIVE AMERICANS CALLED the horse "the magic dog," conveying a deep, abiding appreciation for the unique qualities of this animal, which they believed was given to the People by the Creator as a special gift. The Plains Indians believed that maintaining and appreciating all life forms around us, both visible and invisible, was a sacred duty. They also believed the Creator gave the People two special companions to take along on their journeys. The first was the dog. Later came a second, more significant

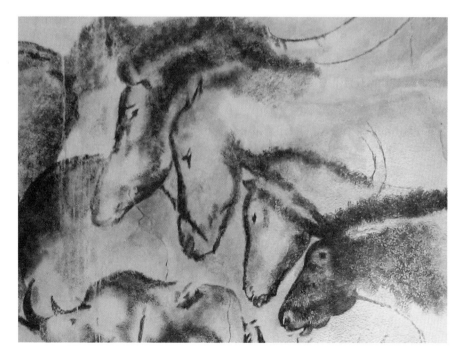

7.1 Humans have an ancient and unique bond with horses. These drawings from the Chauvet Cave in France are believed to be 15,000 to 30,000 years old.

contribution to the well-being of the tribes. This ally they called "the magic dog" — what we call *Equus caballus*, the domesticated horse.

A Native American folk tale explains the special connection among horses, dogs, and humans. In an earlier time, the "two-leggeds" (humans), the "four-leggeds," and the "winged ones" all lived as one people in one great hoop: a single, great tribe of all creatures. Everyone spoke the same language, and all lived in harmony, as the Creator had intended. Each was able to see the needs of the greater common good. No one creature was seen as better or lesser.

One day, a cold wind began to blow out of the North, and with it came Coyote to visit his two-legged brothers. Coyote was always full of mischief and gossip. As he sat next to the humans, he talked of the need for the two-leggeds to invent a new, separate tongue — one that only they could understand among themselves, so no other animal would be able to speak their words. Many humans nodded their heads with approval, and soon a new language was created, filled with words, something only men and women could decipher.

The Creator looked down from the sky and saw all the mischief Coyote was instigating around the campfires. Angered, the Creator ordered Coyote to leave the camp. Coyote skulked away, but he sneaked back to the campfires after nightfall to spread more gossip. This is why, to this day, Coyote comes around the campfires only when the shadows are long and dark and the Creator cannot see him lurking about.

Soon all the two-leggeds were fluent in their secret tongue. Slowly human beings forgot the other sounds they had originally shared with their fellow creatures. As time went on, the two-leggeds listened less to the other animals and began to think of themselves as separate and better.

The human beings began hunting the four-legged and winged ones. The animals became frightened and ran deep into the forest. They learned to hide their voices from the human beings, lest their sounds help the humans hunt them down and kill them.

So it came to pass that the animals felt they could no longer trust the human beings. They went to the Creator and told Him how the human beings had become terrible enemies. The Creator listened, and it became clear that human beings would always try to maintain dominion over the animals. As punishment, the Creator decided to send a giant earthquake down and split the world asunder so that the animals and humans would be forever kept apart.

The Earth trembled and shook, and the ground cracked open. The chasm left the two-leggeds on one side and all the other animals and birds safely separate on the other rim. Seeing the Earth suddenly gape open, the human beings cried out in fear. They realized how much they had angered the Creator with their hidden secrets and selfish ways. They understood they would be forever kept apart from the other creatures.

They called out across the chasm, begging the animals to forgive their past transgressions, pleading with the other creatures to jump across the ever-deepening canyon between them. Because most of the animals had learned to distrust the two-leggeds, they shrank back into the forest. The earthquake continued, and the crack in the earth's crust grew deeper. The human beings saw they would be exiled forever without any animals.

At the last moment, the Horse and the Dog came out of hiding and jumped across the chasm to stand on the opposite rim with the human beings. The two-leggeds rejoiced and promised the Dog and the Horse they would be permitted to live forever among the humans as honored guests. And so it came to pass that the Creator was pleased and asked the two-leggeds always to remember that the Horse and the Dog had voluntarily joined the human beings. They were admonished never to forget to honor these most special and unique friends among all the creatures of the World.

So according to Native American folklore, the horse is handed down as the most special of gifts — given to us as both our friend and our teacher.

PRIDE OF THE PEOPLE   In a handful of cultures, the horse has come to embody the heart, the soul, and the pride of its people. The Arab (*see figure 7.2*) and Mongol cultures (*see figure 7.3*) are two of the most ancient. Another culture that seizes the imagination is the Native American Plains tribes (*see figure 7.4*). Many American horse trainers have drawn inspiration from the exceptional bond between Native Americans and their

7.2 Bedouin horsemen

7.3 Mongol horsemen playing the traditional game of *Buzkashi*, where competitors must swoop down at full gallop to steal a goat carcass off the ground

7.4 The natural ease and elegance of the Native American Plains horsemen are evident in many of the archival photographs taken by Edward Curtis at the beginning of the twentieth century.

horses. GaWaNi Pony Boy, a mixed-blood Cherokee, developed a method for training horses that not only introduced Native American nomenclature but also paid homage to the natural and graceful harmony that exists between the Native American horses and their riders.

Redeemed through a Horse

· · ·

FROM 2003 TO 2006, I worked with several residential facilities that offered rehabilitative services for juvenile delinquents. These young men and women came from the inner city, an environment dominated by gangs, drugs, and violence. Most of them had learned to put their faith in their fists, their ammunition, and little else. Many had gotten caught in the revolving door of the juvenile court system.

To begin their reorientation, when they arrived at the facilities, they were immersed in a new culture imbued with notions of individual honor and commitment, borrowed heavily from Native American folklore. These facilities had hundreds of youngsters and scores of horses in their adventure programs, and I approached the governing boards about developing rehabilitative programs based on equine-assisted learning (EAL) and equine-assisted therapy (EAT) — as a pivotal component of the daily schedule for the youth. Many of these young people, I argued, had never been able to count on anyone or anything. But with the horse, I could guarantee them a different outcome and a new paradigm: whatever you give, you will get back. To start the process, I would make the horse the center of the program.

MUSTANG IN THE ROUND PEN   The round pen was a good place to start, because when we step into the round pen we are all equal in the eyes of the horse. Once inside its walls, there is no starting point or finish line. The round pen is the center of all horsemanship.

TAKING IN A MUSTANG

Adopting a mustang is a wonderful, inexpensive alternative for an experienced horse lover looking to raise and train a young horse. Without the Bureau of Land Management (BLM) adoption program, many of these mustangs would either die from starvation or be slaughtered. However, they are some of the wildest of horses, and training them can be quite dangerous. It should be considered only by trainers with experience, skill, and patience.

7.5 Wild mustangs are beautiful, but training a wild horse from the BLM is not for amateurs.

I began developing round pen techniques for the program based on Native American concepts and symbols, adding some of my own ideas about chi in the introductory groundwork. Many of the Sioux and Crow concepts were familiar to some company staff members, who were of Native American descent. However, the equine professionals were leery about working on the ground at all. They rode horses. They taught kids to ride horses. That's what they did. What else could we expect horses to do?

My strategy was to win the staff over first with a demonstration in the round pen. I asked the wranglers to bring me their troublesome horses for this purpose. It was my hope they would select horses that resembled the youths in their program: unruly, stubborn, and prone to violent outbursts. And they did; they brought a cantankerous, explosive four-year-old horse recently adopted from the Bureau of Land Management (BLM) wild mustang program (*see figure 7.5*).

These mustangs run wild over thousands of acres of BLM land before they are caught. Then they are rounded up by helicopter and driven into holding pens. Many have never seen a human being before the moment of their capture. Their transition to confinement and the imposition of rules by human handlers is often associated with tremendous stress and violent confrontations.

The wranglers brought the horse trailer right up to the gate of my round pen and opened the rear door. A dun-colored mustang exploded out the back and leapt into the middle of the pen, nostrils flaring, every hair on his body erect. I could see there was genuine interest (maybe morbid curiosity) among my wrangler spectators about how I would handle this wild horse. The first step, I thought, would be to defuse the situation for the horse by just letting him stand peacefully in the center. I walked away from him and went over to the rail.

I leaned over and asked the wranglers to tell me a few of the behaviors they had observed with this horse.

"He kicks!" someone yelled.

"He'll try to bite you," warned another.

"He won't lead at all."

"You can't even touch him."

I let the litany go on for awhile.

The cowboys shared their theories about the sources of some of the mustang's behaviors. "He's used to having his own way."

"He's never had to live with real discipline."

"He's not used to consequences for his behavior."

I said, "Man, he sounds like a lot of trouble, like a lot of the kids you're being asked to work with every day." Heads nodded. Meanwhile, left alone and completely forgotten, the mustang had been snorting, drinking in our collective smells through his nostrils, and he had taken one curious, tentative step toward our little discussion group. *Yeah,* I thought to myself, *just let him take his time.*

I kept the conversation about the youths going and asked the staff how they handled unruly juvenile delinquents when they arrived. They explained how behavioral boundaries were carefully established for the kids. They reviewed the importance of being clear, fair, and honest with each youth. The wranglers told me how they went out of their way to demonstrate to the kids that staff members were dependable and trustworthy. For too many of these unfortunate juvenile delinquents, it was the first time they had ever met an adult, especially a man, exhibiting those qualities.

The horse was two steps closer, not more than ten feet away now.

"If this horse were a new youth coming into your program, what's the first thing you would want to make clear to him?" I asked.

"Trust."

"So how do I tell this horse he can trust me? What can I do to prove it to him?" I asked.

Some proposed bribing him with a bucket of feed. Others suggested roping him first and then teaching him to lead. I pointed out the horse was already standing quite near me.

I suggested we start with something simple: just have the mustang look at me. I began to circle toward the horse's hindquarters, moving closer until he looked straight at me. The nearer I stepped toward him, the more he felt on edge. He'd look at me to see what I was up to, but as soon as he turned to look at me, I'd take a step backward and breathe.

My message was simple: just look at me and we'd both get to relax. Look away from there, there's going to be more tension, more palpable energy increasing in the round pen. The horse began to follow me consistently with his eyes. As long as he kept his eyes on me, there was no pressure. If he looked away, I'd send him out around the round pen.

With a few simple interactions, the horse was stepping around and facing me. I never challenged him, never asked him to do anything but move out. I let him feel the release every time he followed my direction. Within ten minutes the mustang was standing right behind me. The horse was now moving in sync with me, following me where I stepped, much as we wanted the youths to follow the lead set by the staff.

I asked the wranglers why the kids couldn't do the same ground work with the program's horses. It was as if a light bulb came on. It was clear the youths would have to exhibit self-control in order to succeed with training a horse. They would have to be patient and build trust slowly — just the traits the staff wanted to instill in the kids. In a few days, we were given the green light to go ahead with an EAT program.

More than a thousand youths and a hundred horses have gone through the programs since then. Best of all, I think, is that more than a dozen kids earned the right to adopt the horses and take them home when they successfully completed the program. Horses change the way we see ourselves.

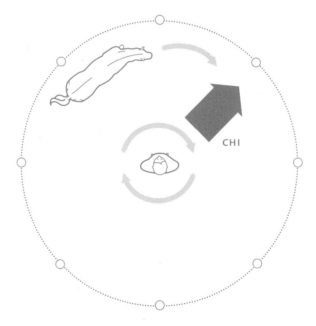

7.6 Working and training horses within a round pen

WHY IT WORKS   The symbolic concepts we employed were easy to grasp. From above, the round pen is a circle, without beginning or end, a reminder of the sacred hoop of all creation. The round shape converts a horse's typical straight-ahead flight distance of a quarter mile into a few laps around the circumference of the pen. This has advantages. Without the round pen, we couldn't keep up with the horse; he would cover too much ground. Circling the horse around the trainer creates an interactive space where pressure can be amplified.

In the early stages of round pen work, the closer the trainer is to a horse, the greater the energy on the horse. The effect of release can thus be easily amplified by stepping back away from the horse toward the center of the round pen (*see figure 7.6*).

The round pen is a physical representation of a circle of hallowed, sacred ground. When we cross the threshold of the round pen, we need to clear our minds and eliminate whatever woes and worries the day has brought. No boss. No spouse. No stock market. No agenda. We're going to work on a task — without attaching ourselves to the outcome. Within this sacred space we will also vow to maintain our integrity toward our horse.

PLAY, NOT PRACTICE   Part of the respect we demonstrate in the round pen is to avoid excessive repetition. Focus on play, not on practice. The old notion of using longeing or circling to tire a horse out (to get rid of the "fresh" when they're full of piss and vinegar) is misguided. You don't want to work with your horse only when he's tired. Think back to when you sat in a classroom near the end of the afternoon, with your eyelids sagging, your head resting on your hand. Was that a great state of mind in which to learn? Hardly.

On the contrary, you want your horse full of energy, jazzed up, ready to play. Then you're ready to start working together in the round pen. Pat Parelli wisely points out: "A round corral or a longe line is the easiest way to develop a relationship with a horse, if used naturally." I would add that if it's abused, it's the fastest way to sour one.

There's a fine line between dedication to mastery and the slavery of compulsion. For me, it lies in how we approach the minutiae. If we obsess about every little detail, that mindset chokes off the flow of creativity. Rules and guidelines are not the objectives of the exercises; they're the context for them. They are useful to help germinate meaningful linkages and metaphors. With time and patience, maybe they'll help distill universal principles.

The Four Aspects
of the Round Pen

■■■

SOME NUMBERS JUST FIT SNUGLY. Four is one of them. It's the first composite number, meaning it's the first number that can be created by multiplying numbers other than itself. The simplest geometric solid, a tetrahedron, must have four sides. There are four seasons, four races of human beings, four primary elements. Time is the fourth dimension. And there are four directions.

To me, looking at the round pen encircling my horse and me, it seemed only natural to amplify my groundwork by attaching specific concepts relating to each of the four cardinal directions on its circumference (*see figure 7.7*).

These four directions are assigned colors in the Native American tradition. Traditionally these four colors, all pigments found in the natural environment, also representing the four races of humanity, were assigned as follows: black for the North, white for the East, yellow for the South, and red for the West.

THE NORTH   North, associated with the color black, embodies the concept of empathy. Derived from the Greek *empathēs* (from *em-* + *pathos*, feelings, emotion), empathy is defined as "the action of understanding, being aware of, being sensitive to, and vicariously experiencing the feelings, thoughts, and experiences of another of either the past or present without having the feelings, thoughts, and experiences fully communicated in an objectively explicit manner." It is epitomized by the expression "seeing the world from someone else's perspective."

North represents the direction of the leader, the alpha mare — the one who takes responsibility for the group. It is also the embodiment of the Golden Rule: namely, "Do unto others as you would have them do unto you." North is the faithful, invariant direction upon which we depend for our moral compass, to show us the way when we are lost, to help guide our next steps when we wonder where to go: to make sure we do the right thing.

Why black? Yes, it is the color of darkness and shadows, but it is also the color painted under the hunter's eyes so he's not inadvertently blinded by the sun or the snow. It is the color of charcoal — what's left after everything is burned, consumed by fire. It is the color of death. Grief also implies empathy, the ability to see loss and comprehend the world through the suffering of others. Empathy is a fundamental ingredient for

COLORS OF THE ROUND PEN

NORTH

COLOR: Black
CONCEPT: Empathy
ROLE: Leader
ADDITIONAL: The Golden Rule

SOUTH

COLOR: Yellow
CONCEPT: Intention
ROLE: Visionary, entrepreneur
ADDITIONAL: The archer is one with the target, seeing the end before beginning.

EAST

COLOR: White
CONCEPT: Learning, illumination
ROLE: Teacher
ADDITIONAL: Imprinting, ritual

WEST

COLOR: Red
CONCEPT: Wisdom
ROLE: Shaman, elder
ADDITIONAL: Walking the red road

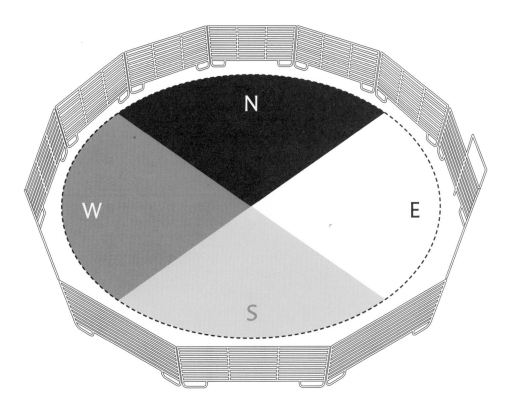

The NORTH is the leader, responsible for the herd or group. The EAST is the educator, the teacher, and stands for illumination and knowledge. The SOUTH is the visionary, the one who sees the goal, the objective. The WEST is the shaman, the individual responsible for bridging what is physical to what is not, for lending meaning to the existential struggle.

compassionate leadership, embodied in legendary horseman Tom Dorrance's concept: "Feel what the horse is feeling, and operate from where the horse is." Every effective trainer needs to see the world through the eyes of his or her horse.

THE EAST   East is the direction of learning and is represented by the color white, the hue of illumination. A cardinal direction, it embodies the rising of the sun, the light that comes after the night (the North) but it also encompasses the illumination of education, the clarity brought by knowledge. This concept of recurrent, repetitive learning reminds trainers that they must help a horse acquire a skill on both sides of the body first. Because of the nature of his corpus callosum, the horse must relearn each task separately on the right and left side. The East embodies the duality of learning and relearning, as well as teacher and student.

THE SOUTH   South is the direction where the sun reaches its apogee at noon. It represents the ascendency of growth and life and is symbolized by the color yellow. In this direction, we place the concept of intention: visualizing the end before we begin. We discussed earlier how intention brings about the assemblage and the concentration of chi. Intention is what a horse tunes into when we ask it to do a task. The clearer our intention, the more likely the horse will succeed. Clarity of intention becomes the heart and soul of our training and the pivotal concept of the Southern direction.

I am reminded of the Zen archer whose concentration is so intense that the individual and the target become unified. Eugen Herrigel, a German philosopher who studied the art of *kyudo* (archery), thus described it in his book *Zen in the Art of Archery:*

> *The archer ceases to be conscious of himself as the one who is engaged in hitting the bull's-eye which confronts him. This state of unconscious is realized only when, completely empty and rid of the self, he becomes one with the perfecting of his technical skill, though there is in it something of a quite different order which cannot be attained by any progressive study of the art.*

In the south lies the role of the visionary, the entrepreneur, and the innovator, because intention describes not just how the goal validates our actions but also how it is the seed from which actions blossom.

THE WEST   Lastly, we come to the West, the direction of the setting sun. It represents the phase of life when wisdom becomes preeminent. The

West is associated with the color red. This is where we put the concept of pressure and release — the fuel for the learning engine of our horse. It is the direction of the shaman and the tribal elder. The setting of the sun is symbolic of the end of life, of our mortal legacy.

"Walking the red road" (toward the West) is another spiritual concept. It relates to a sacred journey in the good, correct, and balanced way. To choose the red way implies to be in harmony with nature, to travel down a road devoted to worship and spiritual inquiry.

FINDING THE CENTER   The balance of these four directions, with their explicit values, keeps us centered in our approach to the horse. As trainers and handlers, we need to return to the round pen for reminders and for inspiration and resolution from the four cardinal directions.

Balanced Leadership

...

THE FEELING OF CONNECTION arises from a sense of inclusion, being part of a team. We are *being* included when we *feel* included. Our left hemisphere has a natural tendency to make us see ourselves as alone and apart, while the right side of our brain pleads for a sense of companionship and community.

THE FOUR Cs   The horse thus introduces us to another Native American concept: balanced leadership. A crowd with a leader is a herd; without one, it's a mob. Horses can't survive long in a mob. They're looking to see who's in charge. Horses seek four qualities in their leader: the four Cs.

COMMAND

CONTROL

COMPASSION

COMMUNICATION

First, a leader has to look like a leader. A leader, horse or human, transmits an aura of authority in his or her bearing. Body language can tell you if an individual is accustomed to a position of command.

A leader has to not only be *in* control but also *under* control. Good leaders don't lose their cool. They make good decisions, even in pressured situations. They exert control over those under their command. When conditions are demanding and dangerous, leaders are able to mobilize their charges so they respond even when panicked.

Compassion is also an essential ingredient of good leadership. No leader will stay in charge for long unless he or she can demonstrate that the good of the herd is the highest priority. Even though we think of bravery as a human quality, horses value it too. They look to see if the alpha horse makes certain there is no threat before leading the band to water. Does the leader keep the herd together, so the weakest benefit from the presence of the strongest? Finally, leaders need to show they can empathize, sense the needs of those they lead. Leaders can be ambitious but the best leaders are ambitious for all to succeed, prosper, and be at peace.

The fourth vital quality of good leadership is effective communication. A successful leader uses clear cues and unequivocal signals to communicate. It is vital that a leader make his or her wishes known and that every member of the group knows what is expected in response to these requests.

OTANCAN: THE LEADER   No herd leader, however, can take his or her position for granted. Every horse, every member of a herd, asks one question of the leader: *are you in charge or am I?* Each horse is looking for someone to lead the herd — even just a herd of two. The horse needs an answer. If you exhibit the four Cs, then the horse will accept you as *otancan* — the leader. If not, the horse must assume leadership over you.

7.8

The leader must constantly prove his or her worthiness.

Otancan is the Lakota word for "leader, the greatest." Once the horse recognizes you as otancan, he has two obligations to fulfill. The first is to follow you. In return for this, the horse expects you to look after him by exhibiting the four Cs. The horse's second duty — one many humans find difficult to accept — is to repeatedly challenge you as *otancan*. As the trainer, you are not permitted to remain otancan unless you consistently prove you deserve to be.

That's the *otancan*'s burden. If you accept becoming otancan, being worthy in the eyes of your horse, you must rise to the challenge by bringing impeccability into your relationship. You develop a partnership with the horse that is free from your personal agenda, your private needs. Instead, you listen and look for the needs of your horse.

Finally, to be truly in charge, you can't really *need* to be. Leadership is something your horse bestows upon you, never something you get because you demand it. Being a leader is a reward, not a right, and it should come to you because your horse recognizes the leader in you. You must shift perspective from the left-hemisphere position, where you believe you deserve something, to the more right-brain perspective, of seeking to earn the recognition. With respect to the results of natural horsemanship, I am inspired by the quote from the Taoist philosopher Lao Tzu: "When the effective leader is finished with his work, the people say it happened naturally." So it should be with your leadership of your horse.

The Mind of a Warrior

■ ■ ■

ALTHOUGH HORSES ARE SOME of the most peace-loving animals in all creation, undertaking to learn horsemanship calls for a warrior's mindfulness. The concept of warrior, the *samurai*, is best expressed in the code of *bushido* that comes from feudal Japan (*see figure 7.9*). The word samurai means "one who serves." But it does not imply servility. Hardly. Rather, it reflects the honor of meeting, even anticipating, the needs of one's lord before one's own, even at the risk of losing everything, including one's life. In the complete subjugation of his ego, the samurai acts with total clarity and integrity.

It's no wonder the samurai meditated on death as an expression of strength. To will yourself to die is the ultimate act of fierce dedication. Translating old texts about the codified behaviors of bushido, Justin Jones writes:

> *The realization of certain death ought to be renewed every morning. Every morning you must prepare yourself for every kind of death. With composure of mind, think of yourself as shattered by bows, guns, spears, swords, as carried away by great billows of water; as running into a great fire; as struck by thunder and lightning; as shaken by severe earthquake; as diving from a cliff; as a disease-filled corpse; as an accidental death corpse.... This is not mere precaution but the experiencing of death in advance.*

To be of service, one needs to be free of an agenda, unfettered by the self, and uncluttered by one's own thoughts. In other words, you must effectively *die*, ridding your behavior of any trace of your own concerns. The notions of impeccability and service are intertwined.

As in Japanese samurai culture, Castañeda described the similar notion of the warrior as central to Yaqui shamanism:

> *Impeccability begins with a single act that has to be deliberate, precise and sustained. If that act is repeated long enough, one acquires a sense of unbending intent which can be applied to anything else. If that is accomplished the road is clear. One thing will lead to another until the warrior realizes his full potential.*

Horsemanship develops and strengthens our intent, helping us along the path to become warriors. We gradually recognize that the horse's ability to attain success in his training is a measure of the clarity with which we see our own purpose joined to his needs. The clearer we see, the quicker the horse learns. Our intent becomes action.

7.9 The samurai was always aware that his greatest opponent was himself.

Highlights

■ ■ ■

Horses are "divine mirrors,"
reflecting back our inner emotional truth.

■

In the round pen, we are all equal in the eyes
of the horse.

■

The round pen represents the hoop of life.

■

Before you cross the threshold of the round pen,
clear your mind.

■

Separate devotion to mastery from
slavery to compulsion.

■

To become otancan *you must exhibit command,*
control, compassion, and communication.

■

Leadership is a reward, not a right.

■

Horsemanship develops the
mindfulness of a warrior.

PREY, PREDATOR & THE RULES OF LEARNING

*If your horse says no, you either asked
the wrong question,
or asked the question wrong.*

■ ■ ■

PAT PARELLI

The history of horsemanship has at times been a hit or miss affair. Sometimes equitation was marked by inspiration and insight; other times, training methods were mercilessly, and even mindlessly, imposed. In the twenty-first century, however, we are the beneficiaries of a wealth of knowledge about animal behavior. If learning is what the student does to acquire a particular skill, then training is what a teacher (or a trainer) does to facilitate that process. We really don't teach anything so much as assist a student or the apprentice to learn the material or task at hand. In this chapter we will review the principles that govern how learning shapes our methodology and predicts what cues and techniques will work best.

The Paradox of the Horse-Human Pair

It seems inconceivable that two species as different in attitude and demeanor as the human predator and the equine prey animal could be ruled by the same learning principles. For example, consider the table on the next page summing up the characteristics that distinguish predator versus prey.

In the introductory chapters, I emphasized that one of the horse's gifts is to draw out and reinforce emotion, intuition, and transcendence, all trademarks of output from right-hemispheric brains. As with the contrasts we see when comparing predator-prey characteristics, significant differences are underscored when we enumerate the attributes of the left and right sides of the human brain, outlined in Table I on page 110.

8.1

Human and horse in harmony

Many of the tensions and anxieties we experience in our professional lives, as well as our inability to find true satisfaction, stem from this left-versus right-brain dichotomy (*see illustration on page 112*). That's the predator's curse. We crave rewards. We want to know: where's the cookie? Where's the money or the next promotion? This endless thirsting after the next prize guarantees a restless nature. It creates an itch that can't be scratched.

The horse brings a different perspective. His motivation is to be left in peace and to be free from demands. A horse looks for a right-brain sensibility in his handler. So, as predators, we must learn we have as much (or more) to gain from dedicating ourselves to letting go as we do from grabbing for more. We need to learn how horses learn, and, in the process, we can adopt a new approach to life.

TABLE I
TRAITS OF PREDATOR AND PREY

CHARACTERISTIC	PREDATOR	PREY
Eyes	front of face	sides of the head
	stereoscopic	monocular
	reduced visual field	vast visual field
	high acuity	low acuity
	color vision	black and white
	poor night vision	superb night vision
	intense focus	wide, diffuse view
	large fovea (focus area)	small fovea
	small retinal surface	large retinal surface
Direction of travel	straight ahead	oblique
Learning (positive)	reinforcement	release
Learning (negative)	punishment	pressure
Motivation	inquiry/curiosity	avoidance
Learning profile	repetition	one time
	large number of trials	minimal number of trials
Predominant posture	offense	defense
Weapons	tooth and claw	hooves
Emergency response	fight or flight	flight
Living space	den/cave	open/pastures
	(cozy)	(unrestricted)
Community	packs	herds
	family groups	
Pursuit of foodstuffs	intermittent	constant
	explosive pursuit	browsing, grazing
	ballistic	roaming

The Psychology of Learning

...

WHILE EACH OF US may possess different abilities to draw upon our right-hemispheric functions, the principles of training are universal. For example, I can "bribe" my dog to lie down. He will do it willingly and look up expectantly for his just reward — say, a piece of hotdog. But I can't get my horse to vault over a jump standard for a carrot.

Why? Predators thrive on rewards — the foundation of stimulus-response (SR) training. The principle of SR is that the occurrence of a desired response will increase if we pair the behavior with a reward.

PLEASURE CENTERS IN THE BRAIN   Ultimately the nature of our ability to acquire experiences and link them as stimuli to a particular set of responses (be they positive or negative) directly relates the basic wiring of our brains. Deep within our cerebral hemispheres there are structures that qualify and quantify our experiences by connecting them to positive or aversive sensations. These loci include the *hypothalamus* (deep behind our eyes at the bottom of our brains), the *septum pellucidum* (a structure in the midline of the brain several inches above the plane of the eyes), and most importantly the *nucleus accumbens,* a pair of structures that are located both in the right and left sides, approximately in the middle of the skull and lying a few inches off the midline.

The nucleus accumbens and septum pellucidum are important not only in the immediate sensations of pleasure, like sex or eating, but also in behaviors like altruism or learning or education. For example, when we feel happy about helping someone in need or learning a favorite subject matter in school, these activities are linked in our memories with pleasant sensations generated in the nucleus accumbens and septum pellucidum. We tend to try to repeat or reproduce those behaviors that are associated with more activity in these centers rather than less. In fact, addictive behavior, be it gambling or heroin, is directly linked to excessive and repetitive stimulation of brain activity in these regions.

The hypothalamus, on the other hand, seems to function more in matters of generalized mood, such as fear or happiness.

All of these structures have been well-preserved throughout evolution, and they function in humans much as they do in other animals. In the end, these mysterious collections of neurons and axonal fibers determine how well we learn; what experiences and relationships give us joy; and to a larger extent, what gives our lives purpose, be it love, wealth, or spiritual insight. Their electrical activity and circuitry lies at the heart of the matter, of the reasons we want to live and the purposes we wish to fulfill.

TABLE II

ATTRIBUTES OF RIGHT VS. LEFT HEMISPHERE IN THE HUMAN BRAIN

LEFT BRAIN	RIGHT BRAIN
direct	oblique
verbal	visual
logical	emotional, intuitive
words	pictures
past, future	present, now
singular perspective	common bond
I	we
them	us
individuality	community, tribe
hoard	share
dominate	cooperate
debate	compromise
reason, thinking	feeling, emotion
engineering, sciences	creative arts
god is on our side	oneness with god
religious	sacred
wealth	abundance
reward	release
accomplishment	fulfilment
rationality	spirituality
insight	empathy
relationship	connection
population	humanity
ecosystem	nature
coincidence	synchonicity
study, analysis	prayer, meditation
conclusions	awareness
danger, risk	fear, anxiety
athletics	dance
accomplishment	legacy
warrior	shaman
experiment	experience
heroism	self-sacrifice

HOW HORSES FIT IN   Given this behavioral paradigm, horses are, at first glance, something of an odd fit for SR training. Horses have a dramatically different notion of reward. The predator's brain might assertively say something equivalent to, "Hey, I want something to eat." A prey animal's brain, on the other hand, may politely inquire, "What do I need to do to avoid unpleasantness?"

In the context of training, although we can easily pair a stimulus ("Lie down!") with food (hotdog), release is far more vague and elusive. How do we define avoidance? And what priority for avoidance readily comes to a horse's mind? Is a small amount of avoidance sufficient, or must it be substantial?

With training our hypothetical dog, the size of the hotdog is immaterial. While avoidance may be a more difficult reward to quantify and incorporate into training, we can use it effectively to reinforce specific behaviors during training. For this reason, we employ the notion of *release* as our reward system for SR training. In this context, release is simply defined as a dramatic reduction in pressure: that is, a significant decrease in the amount of chi applied to the horse.

We must be familiar with two important, overarching principles of learning theory in order to understand the structure of training. The first is *behaviorism*. The second concept is a specific aspect of behaviorism called *flooding*.

Behaviorism

...

8.2

BEHAVIORISM IS THE SCHOOL of psychology that posits that the principle of SR is what shapes learning. It asserts that any organism, from the lowliest bacterium to the highest order primate, learns by *conditioning*. Behaviors are learned because they are coupled with a particular reward. The conditioning, the pairing of behavior and response, can be subdivided into classical or operant types.

Ivan Petrovich
Pavlov

CLASSICAL CONDITIONING   An early pioneer in behaviorism was the great Russian scientist Ivan Petrovich Pavlov, often heralded as the father of classical conditioning in psychology, though the moniker seems improbable because his research had nothing to do with psychology.

Pavlov was not initially interested in psychology or learning. In the late nineteenth century, he was performing physiological experiments to understand the reflexes that triggered digestion. His masterful unraveling

8.3 Classical conditioning. The sensation (stimulus) of being burned will produce a reflexive reaction (response) of withdrawing the foot. (Engraving from Rene Descartes, *Traité de l'Homme*, 1664)

of the autonomic regulation of the gastrointestinal tract would ultimately lead to the Nobel Prize in 1904.

By the 1890s, Pavlov discovered that digestive processes in the stomach would not begin until salivation had been initiated in the mouth (*see figure 8.4*). He studied the chemical nature of secretions from canine salivary glands. While Pavlov was measuring the salivary output of dogs in his laboratory in St. Petersburg, he found canines (and humans too, by the way) begin salivating as soon as they are presented with something to eat, long before the food is actually tasted in the mouth.

Pavlov was in the habit of having a metronome tick away while the dogs ate. One day, he noticed that just hearing the sound of the ticking was enough to initiate salivary output in the dogs, even if no food was put in front of them. In other words, the sound of the metronome had become paired in the dogs' minds with dinner time and was eventually sufficient on its own to initiate saliva secretion. He called this phenomenon a *conditioned reflex*, as opposed to a naturally occurring one. He reasoned:

Stimulus (SEEING AND SMELLING FOOD) $\longrightarrow$ **Salivation** (NATURAL REFLEX)
Pairing Stimulus (HEARING METRONOME) + **Stimulus** (FOOD) $\longrightarrow$ **Salivation**
Stimulus (HEARING METRONOME) $\longrightarrow$ **Salivation** (CONDITIONED REFLEX)

Ironically, he is far better known for his incidental discovery of the effect of the metronome and conditioning than for his Nobel Prize–winning work in digestion.

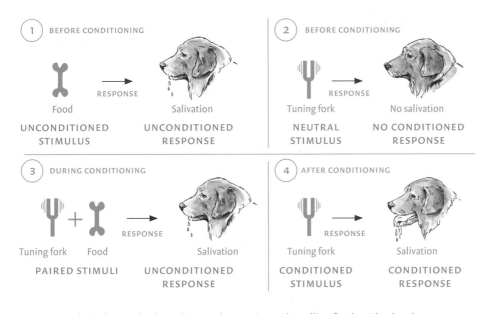

① BEFORE CONDITIONING

Food
RESPONSE
Salivation

UNCONDITIONED
STIMULUS

UNCONDITIONED
RESPONSE

② BEFORE CONDITIONING

Tuning fork
RESPONSE
No salivation

NEUTRAL
STIMULUS

NO CONDITIONED
RESPONSE

③ DURING CONDITIONING

Tuning fork + Food
RESPONSE
Salivation

PAIRED STIMULI

UNCONDITIONED
RESPONSE

④ AFTER CONDITIONING

Tuning fork
RESPONSE
Salivation

CONDITIONED
STIMULUS

CONDITIONED
RESPONSE

8.4 Pavlov's dog. 1. The dog salivates when seeing and smelling food. 2. The dog does not salivate when hearing a tuning fork. 3. The dog salivates when seeing and smelling food and hearing the tuning fork. 4. The dog salivates when hearing the tuning fork alone.

This particular kind of coupling between an initially neutral stimulus (such as the sound of the metronome) with a natural reflex (such as salivation at the sight of food) is called *classical conditioning*. Classical conditioning thus pairs a normal physiological response with what is originally perceived as a neutral stimulus. Rene Descartes maintained that all human consciousness emerges from SR experience itself (*see figure 8.3*).

Classical conditioning occurs in all organisms, including horses. For example, most horse owners have experienced what happens every evening when they go out to put the horses up in the barn at suppertime. The horses learn to queue up next to the gate to be taken into their stalls for food. Our appearance at the entryway is similar to Pavlov's ticking metronome. In the horses' minds, we've paired the natural desire to eat with what was initially a neutral stimulus: namely, our showing up at the gate to collect them.

8.5

OPERANT CONDITIONING   B. F. Skinner was a Harvard psychologist who coined the term *behaviorism* to describe the causal and temporal relationship between an event (the stimulus) and the stereotypic behavior that follows the stimulus (the response). Behaviorism reflects learning framed in the context of the SR model.

Skinner developed a system of training pigeons in a so-called Plexiglas "Skinner Box." A bird placed in the box was trained by trial and error to

B. F. Skinner

peck at black or white levers to receive a kernel of corn or a food pellet as a reward.

Operant conditioning is a method of training that occurs when we move away from natural reflexes and into neutral stimuli. For example, let's say I use the Skinner box to teach a pigeon to peck at a black lever in order to receive a food pellet. Black levers are not a part of most pigeons' natural environment; there is no natural response to a black lever among pigeons. In this example, however, I couple a neutral stimulus (black lever) with a reward, or a positive *reinforcer* (the pellet). A reinforcer (also called a reward or reinforcement) is anything intended to increase the likelihood of a response taking place. In our example, we will soon have reinforced the pigeon in such a way that it will start pecking at any reasonably similar black lever. So when I pair a physiologically neutral stimulus (black lever) with a reinforcer (pellet), I am carrying out operant conditioning.

HOW IT WORKS WITH HORSES

Let's look at an example in the horse's world. I can train my horse to step to the side by applying pressure on his flanks, as in figure 8.6.

Eventually my horse learns to carry out this side-step because I pair the release of pressure on the flank with his taking a step. I have used operant conditioning to teach my horse to side-step.

Pressure on flank (STIMULUS) ⟶ **step to the side** (RESPONSE) ⟶
release of pressure (REINFORCEMENT)

8.6 Light pressure being applied with a training wand to the horse's flank

Positive and Negative Reinforcement

...

AN ENDLESS VARIETY of reinforcements can be used to shape behavior. As trainers, we often think of reinforcers as being *positive*: a piece of food, verbal praise, or a stroke on the neck. But there is also *negative* reinforcement, and this concept is often misunderstood. A negative reinforcer, like a positive one, increases the probability of a behavior.

For example, the ringing tone that reminds you to secure your seat belt is negative reinforcement. The tone is slightly annoying (some might even say nagging) to increase the odds that we will buckle up to stop the sound.

Many folks think of a negative reinforcer as punishment. This is incorrect. For example, if I whip my horse with a crop (not recommended) as he approaches the jump, the whip is a negative reinforcer because it *increases* the likelihood my horse will get over the jump. If, on the other hand, I whip my horse with the riding crop right after he balks, my horse may attempt to balk less at the jump in order to *avoid* being struck. That is a punishment.

A second, unfortunate aspect links negative reinforcement and punishment: both are widely used in the everyday world of horse training even though both are *notoriously ineffective* at eliciting behavior when compared to positive reinforcement.

PUNISHMENT IS A PREDATOR'S TOOL As predators, punishment comes to us quickly and easily. Watch a pride of lions, and look at the speed and violence they employ to reprimand a member who violates the social hierarchy when it comes to sharing a carcass. It is noteworthy how many of the manifestations of our societal ills are addressed with punishment rather than by reward. Meanwhile, the best teachers and most efficient trainers are adept at looking for opportunities to apply positive reinforcement.

YOUR THREE-SECOND REACTION WINDOW Paradoxical as it may sound at this juncture, there are situations where real punishment is appropriate with a particular horse. For example, we never want a horse to get the idea it is alright to bite a person. Biting is an aggressive behavior. We need to react to it quickly and decisively.

In this regard, I am a firm supporter of the "three seconds of pure homicide" rule. This means we have three seconds from the instant the bite is delivered to symbolically "kill" our horse. *More than three seconds,* and our reaction will no longer be associated in the horse's mind with having delivered the bite.

We have a very brief window in which to create an association in the horse's mind between the attempt to bite and the punishment, the consequence. We use whatever is at hand in that instant: the lead rope, fists, a dressage whip, anything.

If more than three seconds pass (counting, one thousand-one, one thousand-two, one thousand-three), we absolutely must *not* react. At all. The horse simply cannot make the connection in his mind between his actions and a punishment delivered with an interval greater than three seconds. That very brief window must be respected, no matter how angry or physically hurt we are.

To be quite clear, I do not routinely condone violent reaction by a human being against a horse. But there are exceptions. Serious, vicious biting is one of those exceptions. I want my horse to remember for the rest of his life that biting me, his leader, was a bad decision on his part. It's a mistake that should never be attempted again! A swift punishment, judiciously applied with correct timing, is an effective way to deliver that message. If you think about it, there is no other response, other than a full-blown, self-defensive reaction, you can provide. So punishment may be appropriate if reserved for exceptional situations in which a horse directly and imminently threatens the physical well-being of his handler.

The reason punishment and violence are so often applied in training sessions relates to our predatory nature. Our genetic heritage as hunters predisposes us to attack automatically, to inflict damage with tooth, claw, or tool. As a species, we have a heritage of violence and physical abuse toward horses that stretches back thousands of years. Until very recently, it was considered acceptable to routinely whip horses. As Monty Roberts points out in his book *From My Hands to Yours:* "Violence is only for the benefit of the violator."

Abuse and punishment destroy a horse's trust. Period.

PUNISHMENT VS. REBUKE   We often use rebuke to train our horses. If our horse balks at a jump, we might gently scold it: "Oh, come on, you goof!" Then we'll move on to a more positive regimen. If our horse pulls out in front of us while we're leading it, we're going to say, "Quit it!" We'll reproach him with both the tone of our voice and a quick tug on the lead rope.

Some trainers labor under the misconception there should never, ever be any scolding of a horse. That is incorrect. A trainer should never rebuke a horse when he is in the process of *learning* a task. But if a horse knows better and has already mastered the task, then we can reprimand that horse when he misbehaves. It is no different than a lead mare scolding a horse for surging ahead of the herd. So the rule of thumb is: don't be afraid to scold if circumstances warrant it — but check any impulse to punish.

THE TIMING OF REWARDS   If we return to our version of B. F. Skinner's famous pigeon-pecking experiments, we can decide that every single time our pigeon correctly pecks at the black lever, it should receive a pellet of food. This timing, where every response is associated with a positive reinforcer — one push, one pellet — is called a *fixed ratio*.

WHEN TO REWARD   A *fixed interval reinforcement* occurs when the food pellet arrives only after a certain interval has passed, say 10 seconds, after the pigeon has pecked the black lever. Fixed interval responses can be inefficient. For example, getting a paycheck every Friday is a fixed interval response. The paycheck arrives a week after the work is actually performed and the time card has gone in, so it has no direct correlation to how well we performed that work in that particular week. Maybe we're learning to make widgets in the factory, and we don't do it very well in the beginning. On the other hand, fixed interval responses like a paycheck may be a great method to keep a person incentivized once they have learned to do the job well.

A *fixed ratio reinforcement* occurs when the pellet arrives only after a certain number of responses (e.g. peck ten consecutive times) has been reached.

HOW FREQUENTLY TO REWARD   *Variable intervals and ratios* are difficult to understand but vital in learning theory if one wants to become a good trainer. Returning to our pigeon, in a variable interval modality, the pigeon pecks at the black lever, but a pellet appears at some random time after the pigeon pecks the lever: maybe a fraction of a second or several minutes afterward. A *variable ratio reinforcement schedule* is when the number of responses required changes randomly before a pellet is delivered. Because the reward comes randomly, the pigeon pecks like mad to get the reward.

To teach a task initially, fixed ratios or intervals are most effective. Once the response is well established, use variable ratio and interval reinforcement schedules to maintain and strengthen it. Variable ratio and interval reinforcement create a learned response that becomes resistant to extinction (*see page 120*).

To return to an equine example, you want to reward your horse after every successful jump while he is in the process of learning how to jump.

But once he is successfully completing jumps, you can begin gradually reinforcing your horse intermittently, after a succession of jumps or after completing a full course of jumps. That helps solidify his learning.

The Mystery of Extinction

■■■

EXTINCTION IS THE ERADICATION of a behavior. If we stop producing response when the pigeon pecks on the lever, eventually it will learn to quit. Pecking behavior will be extinguished. If we train our pigeon with a fixed interval or ratio schedule of reinforcement, then the behavior will quickly stop when the reinforcement stops. By contrast, if we use variable ratio or interval schedules of reinforcement, then we produce a learned response that is much more difficult to extinguish.

EXTINCTION BURST   Right before a behavior is about to disappear (i.e., become extinguished), there is often a burst of *increased* frequency in the behavior. Our pigeon pecks faster right before it gives up pecking for good.

It's critical for every trainer to recognize an *extinction burst*, because it so often occurs right before we're about to achieve our goal of eliminating a behavior. The behavior will dramatically increase for a few moments before it disappears.

Extinction bursts explain how a horse can seem to be learning a new behavior — let's say standing still while we mount — and then experience a setback. The horse begins to understand the idea and gradually holds himself more still. Just when we think we've got the problem licked, the horse will suddenly seem to forget everything. The horse now squirms around. We become frustrated, believing all of our teaching has been for naught.

What we're actually seeing, however, is an extinction burst just before the horse solidifies the training in his mind. The good trainer recognizes this response, as frustrating as it may be, as an indication that success is close at hand. This is when it's time to very gently rebuke the horse and coax him on through.

The Great Secret:
Baby Steps

■ ■ ■

THE CORNERSTONE OF HORSE-TRAINING techniques is *successive approximation*. At first we reward the slightest attempt or tendency toward the final behavioral goal. Let's say I want my horse to come over to me in the center of the round pen from the rail where he's standing. At first, I encourage him to turn toward me, then to turn and take a step toward me. Then two steps. I encourage the horse to get closer and closer to the final behavior I am looking for and reinforce him along the way for every step he takes.

8.7

Secret of success

This is exactly what we mean when we talk about breaking down our training tasks into baby steps. Baby steps are the individual stages we proceed through to arrive at the final, desired goal. The more steps we can build into the process, the easier it will be for our horse to succeed, because we have built in adequate successive approximation.

SYSTEMATIC DESENSITIZATION   *Systematic desensitization* is a process that combines the principles of successive approximation and classical conditioning. A noxious, frightening experience (such as handling a live spider) is broken down into baby steps until you reach some level (such as looking at a photo of a spider rather than holding it) that is not frightening. That neutral, acceptable level is then paired with something pleasurable that induces a calming, relaxing effect (such as deep breathing). Then we slowly increase the stimulus (such as looking at the spider in a jar) until we bring ourselves along to the desired endpoint.

Because, at first, almost everything we ask of a horse, from taking a bit into his mouth to standing at a hitching post, is either noxious or frightening or both, we will frequently use systematic desensitization.

The sacking-out process (*see chapter 19, From Sack to Saddle*) is an example of systematic desensitization. The horse is frightened of a fully unfurled burlap sack, flapping in the breeze. So we start by reducing the sack's size until it's balled up in our fist like a brush. Now it is a neutral, acceptable stimulus. We start stroking the horse with the balled-up burlap bag. Gradually we increase the size of the bag by unfolding it as we continue stroking and encouraging the horse. Eventually, the horse can be made so comfortable with the presence of the bag that we can snap it out to its full size and simply throw it over the horse's back. Think about how frightened a horse may be the first time he sees a saddle blanket. But eventually he becomes completely relaxed and nonchalant when a saddle blanket is thrown over his withers while being tacked up.

Dangers of Flooding

* * *

FLOODING IS AN EFFECTIVE but inherently dangerous training technique. Unfortunately, it was the stock and trade of breaking horses before the popularity of natural horsemanship displaced it. *Flooding* simply means to totally overwhelm the trainee with excessive stimulus (say, dropping the subject into a room filled with snakes, as in the scene in the 1981 film *Raiders of the Lost Ark*).

The subject might go crazy with fright, but, with no way out and no release, he eventually has to accept the frightening stimulus (or outright die from it). An example of flooding in horse training is the old technique of snubbing a wild horse tight to a post and cinching a full Western rig. The horse is let loose. Wild with fear, the horse runs hither and yon, bucking and kicking, trying everything to get the saddle off his back. The horse puts up a good fight but in the end, exhausted, trembling, covered in a sweaty lather, he stands and accepts the saddle.

Flooding is generally a poor system to use with horses, because of their genetic proclivity to become frightened. It can still be found in many of the old-fashioned training techniques. In his book *The Man Who Listens to Horses*, Monty Roberts describes the shock he felt as he witnessed his father use brutal, old-style flooding techniques to subdue wild mustangs rounded up for the rodeo. Those seminal experiences in his youth led Monty toward a whole new understanding of a nonviolent, respectful approach to training horses. The evolution of equine training toward natural horsemanship is evident in the fact that systematic desensitization as the guiding principle has gradually displaced flooding techniques.

Learning and Teaching

* * *

WE HAVE NOW REVIEWED the rules of learning, which explain the mechanics of training: how a stimulus and a response become paired together in an animal's mind. What they do not elucidate, however, are the principles of experience, the overarching laws that transcend species or intellect. These speak of a universal applicability that refers to common mammalian brain structures and neurochemistry that bind us as learners and teachers.

Highlights

▪ ▪ ▪

*Learning is the acquisition of a new skill,
teaching is the facilitation of the process,
and mastery is the expression
of intention.*

▪

*Behaviors are learned because they are
coupled with a response.*

▪

*Predators yearn for rewards and
prey animals for release.*

▪

*In behaviorism, learning comes from linking
a stimulus to a response.*

▪

*Conditioning is subdivided into classical and operant types.
Classical conditioning links a stimulus to a
physiological response. Operant conditioning links a
nonphysiological stimulus with a response.*

▪

*Fixed-ratio reinforcement produces reliable
responses but is easy to extinguish.*

▪

*Variable-ratio reinforcement produces enduring
responses that are resistant to extinction.*

▪

*Before behaviors suppress completely,
we see an extinction burst.*

▪

*Positive reinforcement works
better than negative.*

CHAPTER NINE

PATIENCE

*A handful of patience is worth more
than a bushel of brains.*

∎∎∎

<small>DUTCH PROVERB</small>

A SINGLE CHARACTERISTIC separates great trainers from the rest: patience. Whenever an impasse is reached with a horse, stop. Ask yourself: *How I would approach this problem if I were given a hundred years to solve it?* More patience guarantees success.

I was not originally a patient man by nature, but I've learned a lot from horses over the years. Training horses has made me more aware of my own impatience, because they falter when they feel they are being rushed. The speed and efficacy of their learning decrease as soon as they detect the distracting change in the energy I transmit whenever I am in a hurry. The focus of my chi shifts from sustained, focused energy into a sharper, darting version that is palpable to the horse.

I would liken such energy shifts to the difference between the breathing of a long distance runner versus someone in a panic. Both individuals are breathing rapidly, but one has a purposeful focus and the other is chaotic, almost destructive.

One of my great regrets is that I did not learn the lessons of patience sooner in life. I eventually began to understand how horses could teach me to slow down and suspend the pressures I inadvertently imposed: deadlines, schedules, and expectations. To this day, whenever I feel impatience or frustration welling up — when I am stuck in a line or at a meeting or waiting for someone to finish what they have to say — I remind myself that a horse would not feel the internal turmoil that's chewing away at me. A horse would simply remind me: either we give this all the time in the world, or we stop this second.

TRAILER WORK AS A MODEL Trailering horses is one of those problem training areas where human impatience plays a significant role in our horse's inability to carry out the task successfully. First, schedule practice time going in and out of the trailer on a weekly basis to keep a horse well-versed in trailer work. Most owners simply do not move their horses in and out of the trailer at regularly scheduled intervals. Often, the only time their animals see the inside of a horse trailer is when it counts — namely, whenever a horse has to be taken to a show or the vet.

When we are in a hurry to get things done is hardly the time to find out our horse needs practice. But that is precisely what happens, almost every time. As I grow older I've learned that the scarcest resource of all is time. The paradox is that the more I hurry, the more time I waste, and the only way to hold on to it is to slow myself down.

When I remember all the harsh utterances I wish I could take back, the anger I wish I had swallowed, the days lost to frustration and rage, I can imagine nothing more practical than to gain greater equanimity in the face of adversity. Shakespeare wrote: "How poor are they who have not patience!" Horses teach me every day to enrich my life by cultivating patience.

The Gelding:
Rephrasing the Problem

■ ■ ■

I ONCE WORKED with a gelding who was notoriously reluctant to trailer. He was owned by a nice couple in their early fifties who had inherited the horse when their daughter went off to college. They could not recall an instance when the daughter had put the horse in a trailer. He had lived in the pasture next to their house since the day their daughter had acquired him when she was a young teenager.

Every time the owners tried to load the gelding in to the trailer, it would turn into an ordeal. Eventually they learned to stop making any trail-riding plans. With each attempt to force him into the trailer, the gelding and the couple grew embittered and entrenched; fuses burned shorter. The couple actually tried to use a block and tackle to drag the horse into the trailer, against his ever-growing rage. This all came to an abrupt halt when the horse kicked out and shattered the husband's leg.

I was called by the wife because she was afraid that, as soon as he could, her husband would stagger out into the pasture on crutches and shoot the horse. They told me I could have the horse if I would just haul him away. I told them I didn't want their horse, but I would be happy to help them train the gelding to load into the trailer peacefully and willingly. Yeah, right.

It was clear we needed to change the nature of the problem before we could hope to find an answer. I also noticed the trailer looked like it hadn't been out on the road since the days of the Roman Empire.

I made a decision. I announced, "This gelding can't trailer for an entire year!"

"What? Are you crazy?" yelled the husband. He turned to his wife. "I told you he wouldn't be able to do anything. Didn't I say that horse won't trailer? We should just go ahead and put him down."

"I didn't say he won't; I said *can't*."

"What do you mean he can't? He's got four perfectly good legs!" he said, looking down at his own right leg in a cast. "There's no reason on earth this horse can't trailer!"

"Sure there is. He's not ready," I said. "You cannot make this horse trailer any more than you could make an infant run a marathon. He is not developmentally ready."

"Bull! If he can walk, he can trailer."

"Not quite. I can promise you he will trailer ... eventually. It will take a year, though." I watched the husband mull that over. He looked as though

I had stuck a pin in him. All the pent-up frustration seemed to be hissing out of him; the frame of his large body deflated.

We had turned the problem of this gelding upside down by rephrasing it as something that would happen, but way off, in the distant future. The goal of getting this horse into the trailer had lost its immediacy. It was no longer a need that demanded to be satisfied *now*. It was something to schedule on the calendar.

Suddenly there was no friction being generated by some imagined, artificial deadline. The owners were instantly less frustrated by what they had perceived as the horse's lack of willingness to cooperate. I asked them to promise me that no matter what transpired with the horse, they would under no circumstances attempt to get him back into the trailer.

"Give me your word," I said. "You'll treat the trailer like kryptonite. You won't try to get him near it."

They were reluctant to promise. But I also knew if they could not let go of their previous agenda, they'd never regain the horse's trust. Eventually, however, with a little coaxing, both husband and wife agreed to honor the request.

SETTING A NEW COURSE   Now we were going to set sail on a different course with the horse. I had learned about trailering the hard way — the fast way. Since then, I had watched and worked with hundreds of horses and trailers, and I knew that rushing the process was always its undoing. We needed to symbolically move ourselves away from a position where we were trying to literally drag the animal into the trailer to a new place, where we would let the horse flow into it naturally, of his own accord. And that meant we were going to slow this trailering experience way, way down.

The first thing I did the next day was tow the trailer right into the middle of the fine pasture next to the owners' house. The gelding was there and watched warily. I unhitched the trailer, opened the back doors, and tied them wide open so they would not accidentally be slammed shut by a gust of wind. I wanted to start with a statement: the last thing I cared about right now was closing the trailer doors.

I left the gelding at liberty in the pasture. This gave me a chance to gauge his reactions to the trailer. I sat 400 yards away, where I would not disturb him. A book gave me something unobtrusive to do under the shade of a cottonwood. No wine or cheese this time; instead, I had a pair of old Swarovski binoculars. Periodically, I would sneak a glance, like I was stalking game. I could see him eyeing me through the tall grass.

By the end of the first week, I would enter the pasture and deliberately make my way over to the trailer. The gelding would pick up his head, give a rebellious snort in my direction, and then trot off to the corner of the field that was farthest away from me and the trailer. He'd give me one final perfunctory perusal and then lower his head and settle back to grazing. Through the binoculars, I could see he never took his eyes off me, though he seemed to be feeding so casually and absentmindedly.

FROM CURIOSITY TO COMMITMENT My routine, not his, soon changed. I walked up to the open doors of the trailer and placed two small, fresh carrots on the floor, barely 12 inches inside the threshold. I placed them tantalizingly close to the outer edge so the gelding could get a strong nostril-full. If the smell was to motivate him to go after those carrots, he would have to make up his mind to lean inside to grab them. My goal was simple: make the gelding commit to being interested in something inside the trailer, on his own terms.

I returned the next morning. Carrots? Gone. That day I left him a new present: four pieces of apple, strategically placed 12 inches deeper inside the trailer. Through the Swarovskis I made a quick mental calculation based on his size and build. I estimated the horse would still be able to stretch his

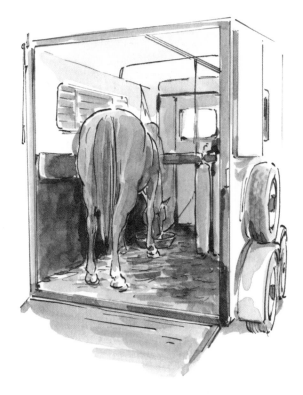

9.1 A horse who is reluctant to trailer can often change his attitude by learning to eat his meals quietly in the trailer. Soon he will be eager to see the inside of the trailer.

neck far enough inside the trailer to reach the sweet apple slices without having to venture in with a single hoof. Again, I just wanted him to commit to reaching inside the trailer for what he wanted.

I was in no rush. I had given us a year to do this. It was up to the horse.

The next day I left slices of honeydew melon. A few horses don't have much of a sweet tooth, but most certainly do, and they go nuts over sweet melon. I was hoping he would be drooling at the edge of the trailer.

Patience is key. The issue is not the apple or the melon but the horse making a commitment and having freedom of choice. If that gelding had a hankering for melon, it would help him decide.

BREAKTHROUGH   The next morning, he had. There was no need for the Swarovskis; the gelding was standing meters from the trailer, waiting. We could easily overlook the significance of this new position, but remember: horses speak in a language of subtle changes in gestures, posture, and stance.

The gelding had made a momentous decision. Now I had to acknowledge his commitment. We had opened up a kind of diplomatic negotiation. This was no time for ruses or trickery. I walked up to the trailer and began slicing a fresh and crispy (and excessively noisy) Granny Smith apple. I slid the slices halfway inside. Yesterday the horse would have put at least one hoof inside the trailer to get that melon. Today was going to require three additional hooves to get the apples (*see figure 9.1*).

Over the next two weeks, I moved his grain bucket, pellets, and hay to the farthest end at the back of the trailer. Every time the horse wanted to eat, he had to enter. There was a big difference in his attitude. Now he was standing patiently alongside the open doors when I approached. No longer did he feign grazing as I approached. Now he scrutinized the operation first-hand, up close and personal.

ONWARD TO ACCEPTANCE   By the end of the first month, the horse had accepted the trailer as a part of his environment. It was a stall to him, a place to feed. He had made every decision on his own, including always waiting for me to leave before he entered to eat.

Now, however, it was time to up the ante and ask more from him. I wanted him to accept my presence while he ate in the trailer. But how to convince him? I knew he would be very leery of my being that close while he was in a vulnerable position.

I reminded myself not to think in a direct line. Linear logic is useful to predators. I needed to think obliquely, like a prey animal. Patience is valued among prey animals as a display of peaceful intent. When we humans seek efficiency or productivity we emanate an aggressive, predatory purpose.

REVERSING THE PROBLEM AGAIN

I applied the principle of reversing the problem 180 degrees: if I wanted the horse to be in the trailer with me, I would have to prevent him from doing so. I'd convince the gelding to accept me in his trailer by closing the doors and making it off limits to him. Without constant access to food, the gelding's appetite would make him take note of when he could get inside the trailer. He'd have to either accept my presence or go hungry. His choice.

I gave the gelding one hour a day when the doors of the trailer were open so he could eat his groceries. If he failed to take advantage of that hour, he waited another 23 hours for the latch to reopen. I stacked the deck even more — and not just a little bit. I drained the water out of his pasture stock tank! Now I arrived each day with a feed bucket in one hand and a water bucket in the other. As the gelding got thirsty and hungry, motivation sparkled in his eyes.

I walked into the trailer and placed the buckets all the way at the far end of the trailer. He put his nose deep inside the trailer. He sniffed and then licked his lips. I stood patiently in the back of the trailer. He was going to have to decide which he wanted more: sustenance, or me out of his trailer. I gave him exactly one hour. The first day he made the wrong choice. I stepped out and closed the doors behind me. As I walked away, the gelding pawed the ground near the rear of the trailer. Good. He was thinking.

The next day, the gelding was standing next to the trailer. I opened the doors and climbed into the trailer. I went to the back of the trailer and stood next to the bucket of water. The gelding was resolute. Today, he would not lose his opportunity to drink. He stepped aggressively with his front hooves into the trailer, snorting in protest. I stood my ground and, with the edge of my boot, edged the water bucket six inches closer to him. The gelding's ears perked up, and then he stepped all the way in. Gathering up all of his resolve, he sank his muzzle greedily into the water bucket.

Some readers might think withholding water from a horse is cruel. I would never recommend denying water to a creature to the point that the animal would be in physical danger. But remember that in some situations a herd of horses in the wild can go for days without water. And every horse in that herd becomes completely focused on reaching water. So the level of motivation I produced in him was only a fraction of what he might have experienced countless times had he been a member of a wild herd.

When I was sure the gelding had almost had his fill, I asked him to back out of the trailer — to deliberately leave his bucket of water. I had reversed the situation again. He was now the one who wanted to climb back in the trailer, and I was the one stopping him. Consider what a long way we had come!

I backed the gelding out, held him outside, let him stand for a minute, and then let him step back in. I stroked his neck and petted him as he put his muzzle back into the bucket. My presence, the water, and the food were now inextricably linked as stimulus and response. When his thirst slacked again, I backed him out. Next he stepped back into the trailer, and I let him eat in peace until the hour was up. The entire time I stood inside the trailer with him.

FREE CHOICE   The next day, the gelding climbed freely in and out of the trailer more than a dozen times for me. It had taken us a month and a half to accomplish this, but now he was going in and out of the trailer of his own free will. No one had laid a hand on him. The horse had been given the opportunity to make choices and, in the process, had displayed great courage and respect.

The story does not end here. There was still plenty of work to be done to ensure the horse would eventually go in and out of the trailer on command and certainly without the promise of food or water. All that could now be easily accomplished.

I should add that, as a rule, I do not favor the use of food bribes for teaching horses to trailer. Most horses can be easily taught to accept the trailer with simple pressure and release techniques, but horses constantly call on us to employ novel strategies to resolve their training needs. If food can do it, then use it. Confident horsemanship requires the development of an open, fearless attitude about discovering new questions. There's no arrogance — no "I've already used the technique with a thousand horses a thousand times before" mindset — but rather an honesty (humbling as much as bumbling) that allows answers to unveil themselves with natural grace.

Patience with Ourselves

■ ■ ■

IMPECCABILITY AND INTEGRITY are founded upon patience. If we are hurried, then our chi reflects that edginess, emerging from us with a frenzied, chaotic quality. When we are tense, we see our horses "squirt" into action. There is no smoothness in our chi. It simply is applied too forcefully. It demands a response and our horse bolts into action because he is overly anxious to escape.

Clumsy chi is no feathered caress; it's like a slap. When we focus on properly modulating our chi, it flows from us with elegance and softness. When we are patient about seeking change within ourselves, then it will come quickly.

Rushing causes delays. If you want to get a horse to do something quickly, *then quickly slow down.*

9.2 When you slow down, time becomes your partner in training.

Highlights

■ ■ ■

Patience separates great trainers from the rest.

■

*When your horse is ready to enter the trailer,
back him out.*

■

Food and water can open a horse's mind.

■

*To get your horse to do something quickly,
slow him down.*

■

*To keep your horse inside the trailer,
keep the doors open.*

LEADING THE WAY

*People in their handlings of affairs often fail
when they are about to succeed. If one remains as careful
at the end as he was at the beginning,
there will be no failure.*

■ ■ ■

LAO TZU

WHILE LEADING may seem mundane, there's nothing casual about the it. The act should be undertaken with impeccable intent to establish your energetic connections to your horse. The instant you lead your horse away, you are making a conscious choice: teach or be taught.

Leading is not about being out in front. It's about being in tune.

The Line and the Lead

∎ ∎ ∎

WHEN YOU PICK UP your horse's lead line, yes, you're holding your horse at the end of a 14-foot (or longer) piece of rope, but your horse is also holding you. So prepare yourself. When you take up the lead, do it with awareness of creating connection. You're defining an energetic relationship through a simple piece of rope.

POSITION AND BODY LANGUAGE   You can lead your horse from any one of a dozen different positions. Some are more difficult to master than others. Always start your training with the easiest position: namely, with your right shoulder aligned with the horse's left eye.

As soon as we lead off, we must depend exclusively on our body language to give directional cues. Do *not* look at the horse. Instead, focus your chi on the horizon. That is where you intend to go.

How often do our goals take shape after we are able to visualize them? In a similar fashion, you want to establish the direction of travel for your horse by focusing on where you want to go. We gain insight from looking at the most common mistakes novices make when leading: they take one step forward, stop, and then turn to look back at their horse (*see figure 10.1*). Alternatively, their energy is focused on the ground (*see figure 10.2*).

It may be human nature to want to maintain visual contact, but that's not true for equines. The lead stallion or alpha mare does not look back to see if the herd is following. He or she focuses on the horizon, where the herd needs to go. And the herd follows, searching ahead for where the lead mare is gazing.

10.1 This handler has stopped leading and has turned to coax the horse by pulling on the lead. This is a sure sign to the horse that the handler is not exhibiting confidence in a leadership role.

10.2 Another common mistake: looking down at the ground while leading the horse.

10.3 A tug of war with a lead rope is a losing proposition. By keeping our chi aimed ahead of us, we avoid this pitfall.

The Chi of Focus

■ ■ ■

WITH YOUR CHI FOCUSED on a distant point, step off confidently, with the first three or four feet of your lead rope in your right hand, hanging slack between you and your horse. Now the horse must decide: follow or stand still?

Let's first consider the possibility that he decides not to follow. Alas, freedom is about making choices. There may a hundred different reasons why he doesn't follow, but you will discover his decision in the first two strides. If your horse elects not to follow, the slack in the lead will grow taut. Restrain yourself from instinctively yanking forward.

We cannot engage in a tug of war with a horse. Any time we try to muscle a horse into doing something, we'll always fail (*see figure 10.3*). When we physically challenge him, we create an opportunity for him to exert his prodigious strength. As trainers, we can only exert power based on the bond we've created with the horse's mind. This is the power we want to exercise and develop. We need an algorithm to teach our horse to follow us when we lead.

ARDP: Ask, Request, Demand, and Promise

10.4

The ladder of ascending, escalating chi

■ ■ ■

WHILE TRAINING HORSES, we will use a deliberate, four-step approach that I call ARDP. This stands for:

ASK   REQUEST   DEMAND   PROMISE

We will apply the same four-step method to every task we teach our horse. Implicit in this algorithm is accepting that our goals cannot be grasped in one fell swoop, one quick, desperate grab. Instead, approach your aims deliberately, patiently, and with a careful, measured, timely application of energy.

The first step is to ASK. It is a peaceful process, tranquil. The voice tone associated with this level is that of a quiet sage: "Would you mind doing this?" The pupil's response is framed in the same equally graceful, elegant fashion. The image of the chi being applied is the caress of a feather.

The second step is to REQUEST. It is similar to how a supervisor might make his or her intention known: "Have this on my desk by Tuesday, will you?" There is insistence and assuredness in the request. The image of the

CARDINAL POINTS

The four steps are reminiscent of the four cardinal directions of the round pen outlined earlier. Each step is an incremental ascent upward in pressure.

To **ASK** is to be aligned with the **North**, the direction of empathy. We see the world through the horse's eyes and ask accordingly.

Next we turn to the **East**, the direction of affirmation and reaffirmation. We **REQUEST**. We educate to get the response we seek.

As we step up the process, we move to the **South**. The **DEMAND** makes our intention crystal clear. We create a deliberate, firm picture of what we want to see.

And our last resort is when we face the **West**, the direction of our final steps. Conclusive pressure lies this way. There is unwavering commitment to get the response we seek and see the process through. We have made a **PROMISE** to ourselves and our horse to get results. And we only make promises that we can keep.

pressure applied here is that of a finger pushing against your shoulder, prodding you to action.

The DEMAND is the third step. We are now at the level equivalent to an officer's order or command. Your entire shoulder is being gripped by a firm, insistent hand. The amount of chi exerted is substantial.

And last comes the PROMISE. It carries the weight of a royal decree, the force of law. A penalty is in store: "I promise you shall do as I command or face dire consequences." This level of pressure should be visualized as a hand laying a scepter (or a whip) on your shoulder. The chi imposed is overwhelming and irresistible.

PACING — AND PAUSING   This incremental escalation allows our horse to create a firm picture of how our training requests will be framed. When we first work on a new lesson, we simply ask our horse to try to carry out the assignment. Obviously, if our horse is making an earnest attempt to learn, to respond, we never do more than ask; especially with younger horses, give them plenty of time before you take the next step in the ARDP process.

Once a horse understands the pattern in which all requests will be posed, a trainer can feel more confident about accelerating through this hierarchy. Except under the direst circumstances — an emergency, when either human or horse may be injured — there should always be a pause between each level of request. The pause must be at least a few heartbeats; a long, deep breath is better. The most common error committed by trainers is not letting the request sink in, not waiting long enough for the horse to respond of his own free will. What a waste.

TREACHEROUS TERRAIN: FROM ASK TO PROMISE When we first ask a horse to respond, we are also inviting him to make a mistake. The horse must have the opportunity not only to react but also to *commit an error*. As Mark Twain said, "Freedom is not worth having if it does not include the freedom to make mistakes."

Remember, our goal is to teach our horse the joy of cooperating, of playing with us as his human partners. When training is experienced as fun, it engenders a positive feeling in the horse and a desire to cooperate. When training focuses on correction (or worse, nagging coercion), it fosters resentment — and occasionally rebellion. Forceful training asserts we do not trust the horse to choose. If we find ourselves on the fourth level, the promise, more than once or twice while attempting to teach a horse a task, that is firm evidence that something is amiss with our instructions — with us.

Lead On

■■■

LET'S APPLY THE ARDP HIERARCHY to leading our horse — impeccably. Prepare by silencing your own thoughts. Become as still as a fencepost.

THE ASK Stand next to your horse's left shoulder and inhale deeply from your core, from around your belly button. The first three or four feet of the horse's lead will hang slack from the halter. Take up the surplus lead in figure-8 loops in your left hand, which is farthest away from the horse when you lead from the horse's left shoulder.

Your first step away should be a deliberate, strong step forward with your right foot. It is an effective body signal, similar to the body language an alpha mare sends to the herd when she is leading. Knowing the language makes all the difference. Step away and observe the focal point on the horizon you've selected. Take in every detail. The smaller the detail, the better, because it draws your chi into focus. Exhale. Focus.

Lead off with determination. Expect your horse to follow. If he does, the first three or four feet of the lead will remain slack (*see figure 10.5*).

If the lead becomes tight in your hand, you'll know he has not stepped out. Let a few more feet run out through your hands and then brace yourself to move to the second level in the hierarchy.

10.5 The ASK. This handler is leading the horse in a relaxed starting position, eyes aimed at the horizon. Note the slack in the lead and the relaxed loop of surplus lead in the left hand.

THE REQUEST To request the horse to follow, your right hand closes, and you'll produce a pulse, a snap of energy, in the lead that travels to the halter (*see figure 10.6*). Note, I didn't say a *pull*. You are not tugging on your horse. You're delivering a quick, decisive "pop" by bringing your right elbow tight against your ribcage, which helps brace your right arm.

Continue to maintain forward pressure on the lead and keep your eyes on the horizon. When horses are being taught to lead for the first time, most make up their minds to follow when they reach this second level, the REQUEST.

The timing of your release needs to be impeccable. Back the pressure off as soon as you notice any sign that the horse is even *thinking* about carrying out your request. This is one of the holy tenets of horse training. You'll know your horse is thinking about following you when you feel the lead first begin to lose its tautness. Try then to let the lead soften a little more. You want to encourage your horse by rewarding the least effort, *not* the completed task.

HONING YOUR SENSE OF TIMING When you first try these techniques, it's only natural to be a little clumsy with the timing of your cues, requests, and releases. Don't worry about that; just keep practicing. Rest assured your horse is patient and will forgive you for anything — except for being

10.6 The REQUEST. This handler is at the second stage. Notice that her arms are locked against her ribcage and the lead is momentarily taut. Her chi is solidly focused ahead.

unfair. As your sophistication as a trainer increases, the timing of your release improves. You will *sense* when your horse is ready to respond correctly before you can actually *see* it with your own eyes.

Watch for the first twitch in your horse's muscles as he prepares to answer your request. With an impeccable release, you will notice something magical: your horse seems to be rewarded from within. Look for that moment. Find it. Learn to recognize it. The very first time may require numerous tries before you reach it, but once you do, it becomes easier to consistently find that impeccable release.

THE DEMAND   Most horses will lead off at the level of the request, but some may require the next step up the hierarchy. For the DEMAND, you will turn sideways, with your chest parallel to the flank of the horse, and take a step toward the hindquarters (*see figure 10.7*).

Shift the surplus lead rope from your left to your right hand. The left hand still urges the horse forward, but now you lift the end of the lead in the right hand until it is level with the horse's croup.

In the ASK and REQUEST phases, chi was concentrated in zones 1 and 2 (from the poll to the girth line). Now most of your chi will shift toward the horse's rear, just behind the hips. This stance shift and raising the lead are the cues for the DEMAND stage. You are exerting substantial pressure on the horse's hindquarters to move forward.

At this point, most horses are inherently sensitive enough to take a step or two forward. If the horse thinks about stepping forward, release the

10.7 The DEMAND. The handler is standing to the side of the horse, parallel to the flank and slipping toward the rear. Notice the upheld lead rope focusing chi on zone 5.

pressure from the upheld lead in the right hand and return back to your leading position (see below). The surplus coils of the lead rope will be back in your left hand. Walk ahead, putting your gaze back on the horizon. Quietly lower the coils to your side, below your waistline, as the horse moves out; and we are back in the leading position next to the horse's head (*see figure 10.8*).

THE PROMISE   Now let's assume your horse has stubbornly refused to move forward. Next comes the PROMISE. As Shakespeare wrote in *Macbeth*: "If it were done when it is done, then t'were well it were done quickly." Now your horse absolutely *must* move forward. Use the end of the lead in your right hand to slap the horse on the back of the left hip with the end of the lead rope.

You may be surprised that I've even suggested slapping a horse with a lead. It is not intended to be punitive nor painful. The slap is an instantaneous, abrupt delivery of chi. Remind yourself that horses rebuke their fellow herd members with deep, forceful bites and with steel-capped hooves, propelled by hundreds of pounds of muscle. A single snap with the end of a lead rope is not very noteworthy in terms of the horse's discomfort but it does tell him to move out — now.

It reminds me of some of the Zen meditation exercises where the teacher delivers a blow, the *kyosaku* — a quick, forceful slap between the shoulders with a stick — to help the pupil clear the mind and become more mindfully aware during *zazen* practice. That is as much as the slap with the lead needs to accomplish. And we usually should only need it once.

Having been slapped hard enough on the hindquarters, any horse will eventually propel himself forward — a fraction of a step or 20 steps, it does not matter. Look for any indication, no matter how great or small, that your horse is trying. As soon as your horse moves out, drop your chi level instantly, and peacefully resume leading from alongside. You want him to move into "the praise phase" for having stepped forward. It is not the slap across the rump we want the horse to remember but the support and encouragement you give him for stepping out.

At this stage, don't give any thought to stopping or slowing your horse. Don't be concerned if he moves out one step, one lead length, or one trip around the racetrack. You want him to make the connection between feeling chi applied to zone 5 and stepping forward.

Now every horse is moving out, even the stubborn ones.

For now, be content with letting the horse walk out and stop on its own. Repeat the maneuver again, starting with the ASK level. Pause between each escalation. Let the horse resolve in his own mind that you're asking him to move forward.

10.8 The handler is now back in position to lead the horse after getting him to step out. Eyes are focused back on the horizon and the rope coils are at the handler's side.

LIP LICKING

Take note whenever your horse licks his lips. Some animal behaviorists believe lip licking is a gesture indicating a subordinate, submissive status. The licking is thought to symbolically evoke chewing on grass, indicating he is a fellow herbivore, a nonpredatory creature who represents no threat. We see foals and young horses exhibit an exaggerated version of this gesture when they try to appease older, more dominant horses.

Monty Roberts, who has consulted for hundreds of high-strung Thoroughbreds on racetracks all over the world, believes that when horses begin to lick their lips, it is a sign they are now willing for the trainer to become "Chairman of the Board." Monty believes the horse is asking if he can make a deal to become the follower and let the trainer lead. Either way, lip licking is definitely significant, and a good trainer will pause to allow the horses to complete this gesture.

You'll soon be able to figure out when your horse's light bulb switches on. Look for a softening quality in his eyes, especially if he exhibits a slightly downward or submissive head tilt and licks his lips (*see box, above*).

Between the Rungs

■ ■ ■

SUBTLETY AND ELEGANCE are attributes of any great horse trainer. Consider the adage: "If it doesn't look easy, you're doing it wrong." If the application of a technique feels difficult or strained, it will look inelegant and ineffective.

All of us have moments when our training can seem off, ungainly. Such moments are related to one of two problems. Either we have not practiced sufficiently to get the mechanics smoothly worked out, or we are not framing our question properly. Nine times out of ten, it's the latter.

Mechanics become more significant as we seek to enter that eloquent area between zero chi and the first rung of the ladder, representing everything that lies *below* the first level of asking.

Below asking is where mastery lies.

ACHIEVING QUIET MASTERY   Leading a horse seems like a simple task, but an entire palette of subtlety lies within it. For example, we can train our horse to lead off just from an exhalation. Mastery is related to an appreciation of seemingly invisible cues we communicate to our horse.

We have defined the four rungs of chi in ARDP, but we want to learn to display the quiet expertise that comes from training our horse in the space between the ground and the first rung of the ladder (*see figure 10.9*). In that space is another, smaller ladder with four more subtle steps: the first step is to breathe and the final one is to ask. And under *that* ladder is another: the first rung is to think and the last rung is to breathe. And below that is another, and so on.

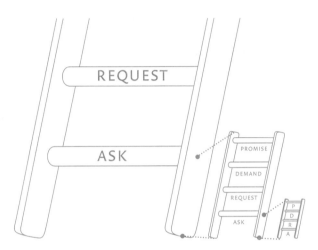

10.9 The mastery of horsemanship lies beneath the first rung in the ARDP paradigm. Under each rung lies a whole new ladder of more elegant, finer adjustments.

There are always infinitely smaller increments of chi to be mastered, because the horse's capacity to respond to the imperceptible units of psychic energy is limitless. Without the horse to help us interpret it, we would not be able to grasp the subtlety of our own chi.

The more the horse teaches us about energy, the more we can accentuate the quiet between our gestures, just as the silence between notes creates the music. We also learn to delight in assembling the least chi possible. I estimate that horses are anywhere from one hundred to one thousand times more sensitive to chi than we are. This is how we tune our thought processes into the horse's response. Training in harmony with our horse is how we become transformed. Horsemanship provides access to higher levels of self-awareness.

PLAYFUL PRACTICE

As predators, humans love repetition. When we see a dog assimilate a lesson, we tend to repeat the trick over and over. Prey animals, on the other hand, take a dim view of reiteration. Horse trainers should seek to create brief lessons and revisit tasks in multiple sessions rather than in a single exposure. Incorporate tasks into the horse's training at discrete intervals, keeping his mind engaged and entertained.

I try never to ask a horse to repeat a task more than four times in a row. It does not matter if he is passing over the same jump, following the same figure-8 patterns, or leading away. After four repetitions of any task, it's time to move on.

A good trainer places a premium on play because horses never tire of it. As herd animals, horses give themselves whole-heartedly to play when they feel secure and out of harm's way. Playfulness is thus one of the highest expressions of joy and freedom — a rare state for a prey animal.

10,000 HOURS The paradox is that no matter how subtle you think your body language is, it's never subtle enough. How long does it take for us to figure this out? The more subtle our training techniques become, the more refinement we perceive can still be added to our technique. It is a never-ending spiral.

I once asked the master horse trainer Ray Hunt how long it took before a person could no longer be labeled a novice rider.

He pulled on his chin for a moment and then smiled. "Well, at least ten thousand hours. How's that sound?"

"Wow," I said, "that sounds like a lot!"

"Really? I thought it might be too little."

To grasp what Ray was getting at, consider this. If you spent two hours a day with your horse 365 days a year, you would need to ride for nearly fifteen years before you could say you were no longer a novice. I dread to think how many lifetimes it would take to become an intermediate!

Enlightenment smacks of a lightning strike accompanied by Hollywood-like special effects. But it never is. It's the product of a long journey, usually years, filled with disciplined practice. It seems like an instantaneous transformation only to the outside spectator.

Infinite Patience and Tiny Steps

. . .

WE CAN TRAIN OUR horses to do anything if we can satisfy two stringent conditions. First, place no time limits on when a goal will be achieved. Second, every task must be broken down into small, achievable components — baby steps.

In the previous story about the gelding freely choosing to walk into the trailer, I was able to help that horse succeed because I removed time limits on the task. It didn't change the horse's attitude; it changed mine. I converted the trailering task into smaller, incremental steps, sometimes moving a treat no more than a foot or two a day. Remember: we cannot fail at training a horse if we break the task down into small enough baby steps (*see figure 10.10*).

In the 1920s and 1930s, many traveling carnivals and circuses trained horses to ascend a ramp to a platform 20 or 30 feet off the ground and then to dive into the swimming pool below. It was a great crowd-pleaser, but it took months to teach each horse to scale even a small ramp, and then more time to have it step off into a pool and eventually to dive in (*see figure 10.11*). Then the ramp had to become longer and slowly be raised higher. The pool got deeper and the drop longer.

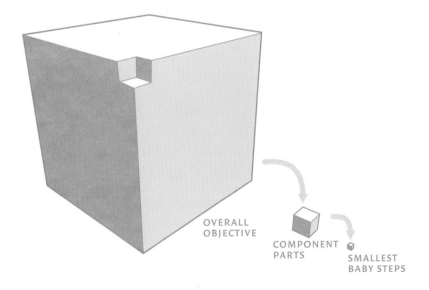

OVERALL
OBJECTIVE

COMPONENT
PARTS

SMALLEST
BABY STEPS

10.10 The concept of baby steps: every global objective needs to be broken up into smaller component parts, which can always be broken into even smaller steps.

10.11 A horse diving into Lake Ontario in 1908, featured in a Toronto Island equine show

The impossible will remain insurmountable until each of us learns to develop our own personal system of disassembling a training goal into the smallest achievable components. Then success, imperceptibly attained, is assured.

For the making of the movie *Hidalgo*, Hollywood trainer Rex Peterson had to teach his horse to be buried alive for a scene (it took nine separate takes). Think of what it must require to train a horse to willingly undertake such acts. That's why I state categorically you can teach horses to do anything, with enough patience — and baby steps.

LETTING GO OF THE OUTCOME   Caring too much about outcomes can cause trouble. How important is it that you get your horse to lead off properly a second time today? The question seems silly; it's only natural you'd want your horse to lead off more than once. But on a deeper, symbolic level, do you really need your horse to lead off today? The more you care about the outcome, the wiser you'd be to postpone working on it.

This is one of the paradoxes in horse training: when you don't care if your horse leads off is a good time to teach it. If you do care, it's not. Wait until you no longer have an emotional investment. Horsemanship can be maddening in this regard.

Clinics are amongst the most frustrating situations I encounter as a trainer. When I'm teaching techniques to attendees, I want to demonstrate a successful outcome. But I can also become too intent on demonstrating the result and overlook what's going on with the horse. Things break down because, as a trainer, I risk losing my integrity in the eyes of the horse when I am too concerned about how I might appear in the eyes of my audience.

Because of these very issues, one of the worst accidents I ever suffered on horseback occurred at the conclusion of a clinic. We had wrapped up for the day. The students were filing out, and the horses were tied quietly to the round pen rail, waiting to be led back for the evening feed. At the last minute, a couple of reporters showed up with a photographer. They wanted to do a magazine article and needed just one picture of me on horseback. Couldn't I do them this favor?

Sure. I went over to the round pen, intent on getting them the darn photo they needed. I jumped over the top of the railing and leapt onto the back of one of the horses in the round pen. He had been asleep. I offered no three-point fixation, no thought about how surprised he might become.

The horse exploded. I was suddenly in the rodeo event of my life. He dumped me with a thump on the ground; no photo op. I landed hard! I heard an ominous crunch in my back. With everyone looking on, I dusted myself off and stoically limped out of the round pen. Later I learned I had actually broken my back; it would take ten hours of surgery and several pounds of titanium to put Humpty Dumpty back together again.

What was the root cause of this mishap? I was no longer a leader or a partner in my horse's eyes. I was a predator, bent on extracting what I needed from my horse: a photo.

DIVINE MIRRORS   When we face problems in training our horse, we can resolve them only once we face the relevant issues within ourselves. This is why I referred to horses earlier as "divine mirrors," because they show us a true reflection of ourselves. To find the solution to the problem we see in our horse, we have to look for its origin within ourselves.

Nuño Oliveira, legendary dressage master, wrote in his book *Reflections on Equestrian Art*:

> The good [trainer]... is not he who, seeing resistances and serious difficulties appear in a new exercise, tries to conquer them at any price, sometimes raising violence and brutality, but rather he who, on seeing the resistance rise up, knows how to return to the beginning, to the preparatory exercises, until he has obtained the flexibility and relaxation necessary to start the exercise he is trying to teach.

Finally, never hesitate to reward too quickly or frequently. No matter how rapidly your central nervous system attempts to react, it will never be premature with respect to praising your horse. I have these words written by French cavalry officer Etienne Beudant inscribed over the doorway to my barn: "Ask for much, be content with little, and reward often."

Walking in Harmony

...

WHEN YOUR HORSE LEADS OFF, release all pressure, and give him complete freedom to follow. Walk together in harmony. For how long? How far? The answer — I suspect you have already guessed — is to walk together just as long as it feels right to you.

When the moment has passed, let it go. To paraphrase a famous Buddhist aphorism, to remain attached is to bring forth sorrow. So contentedly walk your horse a mile down the lane, or three paces. It makes no difference. Maybe one day your horse will respond instantly to your request to walk off. But if today is not that day, it does not matter.

Enjoy those carefree moments when your horse walks with you. Give no mind as to whether he leads slightly ahead or behind. Problems will always present themselves. Unclutter your trainer's mind. Silence your anxieties over what *might* happen, what *might* go wrong, what bad habits *might* arise. If, if, if... the mind befouls itself with concerns about if.

If stands for *In the Future*, which is unknown, unknowable. Love your horse enough to stay focused in the moment. That is the only place where true bliss dwells.

Highlights

■ ■ ■

When you lead your horse, you make a choice:
teach or be taught.

■

Where we look is where we focus our chi.

■

Always use the ARDP four-step incremental approach:
(1) Ask, (2) Request, (3) Demand, and (4) Promise.

■

If you find yourself at the level of Promise more than
once or twice, you are doing it wrong.

■

When teaching your horse,
always let him reflect long enough to make his
own choice.

■

Release your pressure as soon as
your horse begins to think about doing
the right thing.

■

There are always smaller increments of
chi to be learned.

■

You can achieve a goal quickly when it has no time limit.

■

The smaller the baby steps, the quicker you'll finish.

■

Outstanding achievements are obtained with
inexhaustible patience.

■

Walk with your horse as long
as it feels perfect.

NOW & THE OCEAN LINER

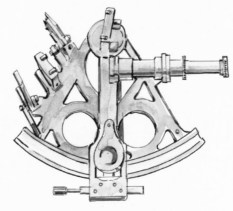

Having spent the better part of my life trying either to relive the past or experience the future before it arrives, I have come to believe that in between these two extremes is peace.

■ ■ ■

AUTHOR UNKNOWN

H OW DO WE VISUALIZE the now, this moment? One image from my childhood always does it for me: an ocean liner.

As a kid in New York, I loved going down to the piers to watch the big steamships coming and going. The Hudson River was thick with ocean liners, like the *Queen Mary*, the *Cristoforo Columbo*, and the *SS United States*. When I was old enough to head down to the wharfs by myself, I'd visit whichever ships were in town.

But something better was in store for me. My grandfather sent for our family to come to Europe, and my father was nervous about us traveling by plane. "I don't trust 'em to stay up," he said. That meant we would cross the Atlantic by ship. So began a series of great adventures in my life. Those ships always stirred me to my core, and they still do.

The Deck Beneath Your Feet

■ ■ ■

F OR A MOMENT, imagine yourself a passenger, standing on the deck of one of those great ships. From the stern, you watch the ship's wake, already slipping behind into the past. If you walk all the way forward and stand at the bow, you can stare out at what lies ahead: the future, where you will be in the next instant, the next heartbeat. But no matter how much you might study the vast sea before the bow of the ship, there is no way to know precisely where your ship will go among the endless, rolling waves. This is the nature of the future; it lies ahead but is unknowable.

So where is the present? The ocean liner reminds us that we are standing on it. The present is right beneath our feet (*see figure 11.1*), in the planks of the deck, from where we constantly gaze longingly at the past or anxiously guess about the future. The roll and pitch of the ship, the shudder of

PAST

11.1

FUTURE

the engines, the slapping of the waves against the sides of the hull — these constitute the present, which is so immediate, so real, and so attainable.

Peter Matthiessen wrote in his book *The Snow Leopard*: "In this very breath that we take now lies the secret that all great teachers try to tell us, what one lama refers to as 'the precision and openness and intelligence of the present.' The purpose... is to pay attention even at un-extraordinary times, to be of the present, nothing but the present, to bear this mindfulness of *now* [italics added] into each event of ordinary life."

Nothing but the Present

■ ■ ■

FOR WARRIORS, there is one overarching goal: to discover self-awareness, to stalk it and take ownership of it. That can be accomplished only in the present, "the very breath." The horse is the incomparable teacher of that keenness, because he dwells in the present, the only tense in which a horse can live. He grazes on today's grass, growing in today's pasture. There's no *Guide Michelin* to identify where four-star grass might be served in future pastures, no history of yesteryear's ten best forages. And the horse can't fret about whether there will be enough grass next year.

But we're not horses, so it takes great determination and self-control to stay in the moment. The horse needs us to focus on now. We cannot connect with him if we worry about how he misbehaved yesterday, or glance at our watch and wonder if there's enough time to prep for the afternoon's meeting with the boss. Guess what? Through all of that distraction, not for a second were we in that round pen connecting with our horse. We could just as fruitfully have turned the horse out to pasture.

This is the horse's great gift. He's always asking, "Are you here with me?" If we want to work with him, practice some lesson, do anything, we have got to be there with him. Every conversation in our head about what we should have done or what we're going to do is a marker. We should acknowledge each one as proof — irrefutable evidence — that we are not in the moment.

We all have regrets, dreams, worries. That's our nature. But they also plunge us into paroxysms of distraction. They throw us off the scent, and we lose the trail to the one place in our heads where we need to be: the present. Only there can we become proficient in mindful awareness. And more importantly, only by finding that place can we learn how to get back there, repeatedly and at will. So we must practice leaving our agenda and anxieties at the gate. And when we stay in the moment, our horse is there, waiting for us to step into the ever-present circle.

Highlights

■ ■ ■

The past is written and the future unknown;
both waste the mind.

■

The present lies where you are, beneath your feet.

■

Transformation happens only in the present.

■

Horses are always present,
so they point the way to self-awareness.

■

"Should have done" or "will have to do"
tell you that you're not
in the present.

TINY BUBBLES OF CHI

A horse is a projection of people's dreams about themselves — strong, powerful, beautiful — and it has the capability of giving escape from our mundane existence.

∎∎∎

PAM BROWN

L EADING A HORSE IS the best way to assess the amount of chi we generate as handlers. There's a bubble, a force field of energy, around us, as there is around all life forms. Some days, when we are feeling strong and positive, that bubble is large and energized. Other days, perhaps when we may be sad or anxious, the bubble around us is contracted, giving off a confused, weakened aura. Horses are very responsive to the quality of the aura given off by our internal emotional state.

Colliding Chi

■ ■ ■

IN A HERD OF HORSES, each member emanates a unique bubble of chi, almost like a fingerprint. Each individual is acutely aware of not just his own bubble but also when his bubble may encroach on or encounter others. Horses are keen managers of chi. The extent to which one horse's bubble probes, imposes, or intrudes on another's is no accident but a measure of that horse's power and position in the herd's hierarchy, a collection of closely knit, energetic beings.

Every horse also sees his human handler in the same energetic context. When we are leading a horse, he will try to detect how much chi we generate in the first few steps we take (*see figure 12.1*). If it's a first-time encounter, then leading is a critical first assessment on the part of the horse that serves to size up our energy status.

Within a few strides, the horse will start nosing closer to us, crowding us from behind, and probing our space from alongside our inside elbow. If our chi has a dominant, energetic pattern, the horse will back off and

12.1 A horse uses the first steps of leading to probe the bubble of chi around the handler. Notice how the horse is probing behind the handler and then close to the inside elbow to detect how much chi she is generating.

Even if you see and work with your horse every day of his life, he will still conduct a daily reassessment of your chi. It's like trying to read what mood your spouse is in when he or she first gets that first cup of coffee. You put out feelers. You look for a sign.

Your horse does the same thing: he may crowd you at the gate, or stand too close inside your personal space, or just toss his head in your direction. None of the gestures are accidental; they're all designed to test out your energy state, the status of your chi bubble.

quickly fall in behind us. Alternatively, if the horse senses our chi is vague, weak, or indecisive, he will assert himself by genuinely encroaching into our space and pulling ahead, effectively seeing if he can establish himself as the leader.

Bumping or jostling is how horses affirm their status in the herd. Such behavior is readily apparent, for example, when individual horses crowd around a flake of hay (*see figure 12.2*) to gain control of it. A dominant horse will assert himself by projecting significant amounts of chi against the more submissive adjacent horse.

As the dominant horse moves closer to the subordinate, he cranks up the amount of chi he is exerting. If the subordinate is already close to the flake, or actually eating it, then the dominant horse will drive him away by applying concentrated chi against his head, neck, and shoulder areas. This drives the submissive horse into a tight circle away from the flake of hay. We're going to apply chi in a similar fashion to get our horse to circle away from us by pivoting on the hindquarters.

12.2 A dominant horse drives a subordinate horse away from a flake of hay.

Turning on the Hindquarters

■ ■ ■

IF YOU ARE LEADING your horse in a straight line (let's say you're on the horse's left) and decide that you want your horse to circle away from you, to the right, you can hold up your right hand and forearm to block the left side of the horse's face, as in figure 12.3.

This gesture applies focused chi to drive the horse's head, neck, and shoulders away from the handler. It sends a message to the horse to step away, just as the dominant horse did in the example of the flake of hay.

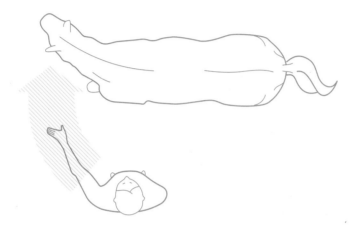

12.3 The trainer uses his hand to block and then drive the horse's face, neck, and shoulders over to the right, causing the horse to step away from him.

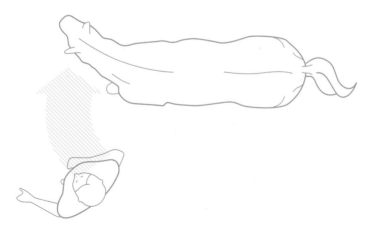

12.4 As the trainer's use of chi becomes more adept, he can simply use his right or inside shoulder and elbow as the source of chi to shift his horse to the inside or to the right.

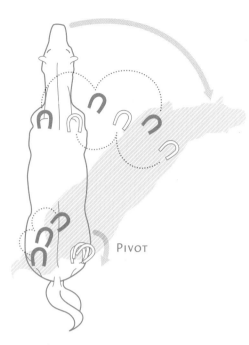

12.5 Turning on the hindquarters. The horse steps over, his left leg crossing in front, with a pivot on the right rear hoof.

Driving the horse over in a tight circle forces the horse's forequarters to swing to the right (away from the trainer). This large shift in his center of gravity also makes the horse step over with his left leg, which usually passes in front of the right foreleg as the horse pivots on his right hind foot (*see figure 12.5*). The more sharply our chi drives the horse's forequarters over to the right, the more the horse will have to rotate on the hindquarters to depart.

This may sound like a lot of little movements for a trainer to control. But if our goal is to expand our awareness of how our own energy can interact with our horse's to cause such maneuvers, then we must study our horse's movements. We need to carefully analyze how our horse moves. If stepping across with the outside leg is part of the movement we're asking our horse to perform, then we need to appreciate how we can pre-position our horse's feet so the movement is easy to carry out.

Then if we're asking our horse to initiate the outside turn by pivoting on his inside hind leg, we must precisely plan how, when, and where we will apply our chi to the horse's face, neck, and shoulders to create the necessary shift in his center of gravity to make that turn happen. We'll also amplify our chi as soon as we see our horse's left shoulder begin to rise. It will feel as if we are assisting the horse to lift up his whole left foot, leg, and shoulder while pushing the entire forequarter over to the right (*see box, next page*).

Each horse knows instinctually how to pivot on the hindquarters; this movement is part of his natural repertoire. *Our* difficulty as human trainers and handlers arises in getting the horse to carry out that maneuver smoothly and sequentially on *our* command, when we want it and how we want it. By studying the turn and breaking it down into its discrete components, we get a better grasp of how and where our chi needs to be applied to elicit the pivot from our horse. We learn to understand the balanced simplicity of the horse's natural, four-legged, athletic choreography.

Turning on the Forehand

■■■

MOVING THE HIPS, or turning on the forehand (or forequarters), is an essential element of our horse's repertoire not only for the purpose of moving the hind end over but also as an integral part of stopping. By turning on the forehand the horse is basically disengaging his hind legs, the main engine of propulsion. We will use this later to train the horse for both the casual stop and for the emergency stop.

For now, we will focus on positioning the horse's legs in such a way that the horse can easily step over with the hindquarters, by passing the near leg in front of the far leg and pivoting on the inside front foot. In order to begin getting the horse to move its hindquarters over, we need to be able to apply chi to zone 4.

EMPLOYING ARDP   In this maneuver the ASK will simply be to lean and look at the hips. There is substantial chi being exerted by our eyes, and this will usually be enough to cause the horse to take a step over, first passing the near hindleg in front of the far one, and then bringing the far hindleg back into position next to the near hindleg.

For the REQUEST phase, we will crouch and assume a slightly more predatory, focused body position (or pose) as we look toward the hip. For the DEMAND phase we will begin shaking the end of our lead rope with the popper at zone 4 to move the hips over. Finally, the PROMISE phase is simple: we'll give the horse a slap on the side of the near hip so he steps over.

START WITH ONE STEP   The trick to moving the hindquarters over is to get just one step. This has a number of advantages. First, the horse is getting frequent rewards for side-passing with the hindquarters. Second,

As our application of chi becomes perfected, so does the horse's execution. The real training does not occur in the horse. The horse is actually teaching us how he carries out the movement in nature and then providing us with feedback as to how effectively we are applying chi to replicate the movement. As we get better, so does the movement. It becomes less awkward and jerky.

This is one of the essential values of working with horses, even for novices who have no real interest in how horses are formally trained. Each horse is a miniature laboratory where we get to experiment with different individual energetic combinations to see when and where we effect the largest improvement in his response. In doing so, our personal energetic awareness grows in countless ways.

The position of the horse's front legs in turning on the hindquarters: note the distinct pivot on the right rear hoof.

the trainer is learning to turn down his or her chi in order to get just one step instead of three or four. Finally, as we become more elegant in applying the chi to zone 4, we are able to gradually pulse it so that we can get one, two, or three steps or have the horse turn around on the forequarters in a full circle.

The point is to be able to pulse the chi against the hip for each step. If a horse gives you particular problems turning on the hindquarters, it can help to substitute a training wand for the lead rope. This will amplify the chi that you're applying to the horse's hips.

Moving off the Forequarters

...

PART OF THE MYSTERY and artistry of working with horses involves learning to appreciate how movement in one part of the horse engenders a reactive movement somewhere else. Sometimes I have to stop in the middle of training to remind myself of the exhilarating quality of this equine poetry in motion. Other times, I just hang my elbows over the fence and watch my horses in utter amazement as they chase each other in the pastures, running full out, exuberantly expressing the joy they must feel at being so alive, beautiful, and powerful. Don't worry about the balanced poetry. The horse will take care of that.

Start with your horse standing still. Check the position of your horse's hind feet to make sure you have positioned your horse to be able to step diagonally forward and across with the near hind leg. Now apply chi against the side of the hindquarters (zone 4). At first, you want a single step, even if it is a bit clumsy. The application of chi makes your horse sidestep with his rear end; the near hind leg crosses in front of the far one (*see figure 12.7*). Once your horse is accustomed to this maneuver, you can pulse your chi against his hip, asking for a second and a third step over with the hind end.

Eventually you'll be able to get your horse to do complete circuits, pivoting on the forehand and walking his hips around in either direction. Look carefully for him to pivot around his planted inside foreleg. Eventually he should practically "drill" a hole in the ground with his near front hoof. You can help your horse at the earliest stages of this exercise by slightly flexing his neck to the inside, toward you. However, don't rely on this pressure for long. Reserve using lead pressure on the nose for small corrections when asking him to tip his nose, head, or shoulder toward you.

PIVOT

12.6 Turning on the forequarter. The left hind leg steps over as the hindquarters shift to the left. The pivot point is the right front hoof.

Moving off the Hindquarters

∎ ∎ ∎

WE HAVE ALREADY PUSHED our horse's neck and forequarters over by applying chi *alongside* the horse's face, not *at* the horse's face. We want to aim our chi at the cheek, behind the muzzle and below the eye; otherwise our horse may get in the habit of jerking his head up. That's just the opposite of how we want our horse to initiate the step-over with his front legs. We want our horse to drop his head, gently and smoothly flexed away from us, and then step across to bring his near foreleg across and in front of the far front leg and shift the forequarters away from us.

To carry out this maneuver, it helps to put your horse into the proper position. Prompt him by swinging his face and neck away from you. You accomplish this by applying pressure to the side of the cheek (away) with downward pressure on the lead rope. Pulling the lead downward puts pressure on the horse's poll through the halter and helps your horse to flex down at both the poll and the neck (this gives you the downward component). Then gently push the near shoulder over with your hand. This helps him to understand you are asking him to cross over with the front legs. Insist the foreleg closest to you passes in front of the foreleg on the far side. Be generous with stroking and petting when your horse succeeds.

As your horse grasps the maneuver, gradually ask for more than just a single step. Keep mixing it up so your horse doesn't fall into a rut. Sometimes ask for three or four consecutive steps and then just a single one. Throw in plenty of single-step exercises; they keep the horse light on his feet and teach us to be parsimonious with the amount of chi applied during each pulse. Too little, and your horse won't move his feet. Too much, and you'll get more than one step. Once your horse is working well to move off the hind- and the forequarters, consider laying down a little obstacle course to help improve your horse's footwork.

From Leading to Circling

∎ ∎ ∎

AT FIRST GLANCE, the interactions of chi might seem more complicated as we move from leading to circling. They're not. They're simply more dynamic. To see how easily leading can turn into circling, go down to the stable. Bring a cup of coffee (freshly brewed, of course). Pull up a bale of hay. Sip. Watch. You will witness the invisible bubbles of horse and human bumping into each other like billiard balls.

Usually the horses are doing most of the driving. It's only natural, I suppose. It would be much the same for Jedi knights from the *Star Wars* films. They would probably be very aware of the Force around them, while the rest of us, the non-Jedis, would walk around oblivious to its presence and power.

That's how it is with horses. They're zinging and zapping with chi all day long. It's crackling and rippling all around them. I often become aware of all the energy flying around only when I tune into the horses and watch them at work and play.

Look for the pivotal moment when leading a horse evolves into circling. A good time to observe this is when people lead their horses out of a stall. The gate, wherever it leads — a stall, a pasture, or the round pen — offers a singular instant where we can see intention at work.

When a person is leading a horse up to gate (*see figure 12.7*), there are only two possible outcomes: the handler goes first or the horse does. About 75 percent of the time, the handler will go through the gate first. When the trainer is not paying attention, the horse gets through first. One thousand pounds customarily wins that one. If the horse pulls ahead through the gate, the handler will usually pull back on the lead. The horse will turn back around in a circle once he is through the gate.

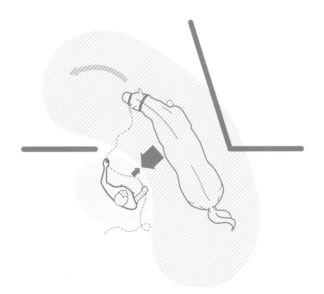

12.7 This diagram shows what happens to a handler's chi as the horse advances through a gate ahead of his trainer. Automatically, the trainer's chi diminishes; the horse slips ahead and begins to circle in front of the trainer.

THE INTRASCAPULAR LINE AND SHIFTS IN CHI

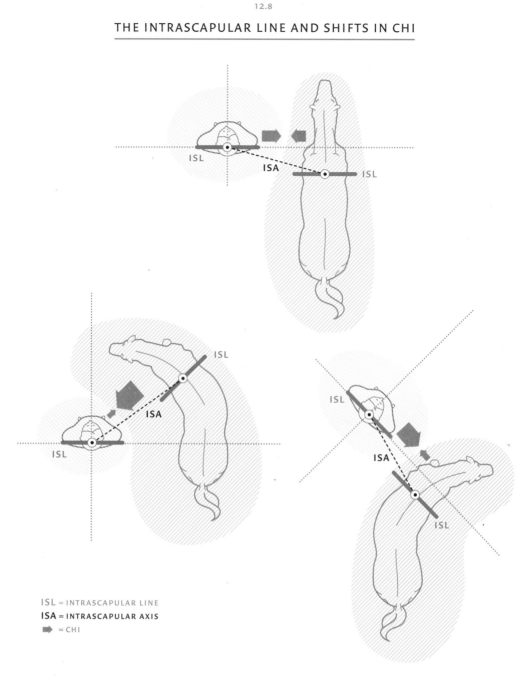

ISL = INTRASCAPULAR LINE
ISA = INTRASCAPULAR AXIS
➡ = CHI

Shifts in chi produce changes in the relationships of the ISLs. As the ISLs change relative to each other, we can predict how the horse will circle. In the top figure, the handler and horse are relatively balanced and moving straight ahead. In the middle figure, the human's chi is diminished, and the horse slides ahead. He will circle in front of the handler. In the bottom figure, the handler moves in front of the horse, driving the horse to circle behind the handler.

Lining Up the Shoulders

■ ■ ■

THE QUESTION ARISES: why does the horse automatically circle back so quickly? If we observe trainers closely, we'll see that they walk slightly ahead of their horse's left shoulder while leading him in a straight line. The trainer's shoulder blades are lined up ahead of the horse's shoulder blades. We can draw an imaginary line through the shoulders of the trainer and another through the shoulders of the horse. Each of these lines is called an *intra*scapular line (a line drawn between the shoulder blades of a single individual), or ISL (*see figure 12.9*).

We can draw another imaginary line starting from the center of the human's ISL and connect it to the center of the horse's ISL. We'll call this the *inter*scapular axis: ISA. *Inter-* signifies something shared or commonly held between creatures. So this ISA links the human ISL to the horse's ISL.

When the handler is walking alongside the shoulder or head of the horse, roughly even with each other, the ISA is more or less perpendicular to the forward direction (*see figure 12.8*). The chi between the pair is balanced, and thus they move off, straight ahead.

If, however, the handler allows his or her chi to diminish, then the horse's ISL will ease ahead of the trainer's. Now the ISA slopes forward, and the horse moves off in a circle ahead of the trainer. In figure 12.11, the trainer is leading the horse from the left side. As the trainer falls behind

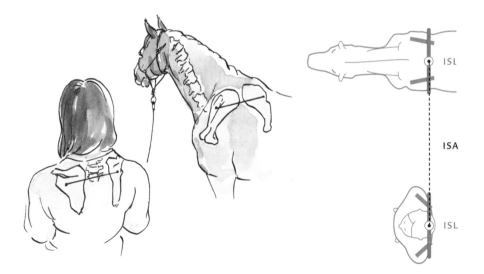

12.9 The line drawn from one shoulder blade (scapula) to the other is called the intrascapular line (ISL). The ISL is shown for both the handler and the horse.

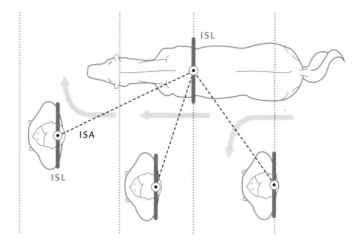

12.10 The alteration in the ISA (i.e., the relationships between the handler and the horse) can change the direction of travel.

the horse's left shoulder, the horse will circle ahead and to the left. This is precisely what happens when the horse passes through the gate first.

As we pull up to a gate, our chi automatically decreases. Most of us just say, "Oh, well. The horse got there first. I'll let him go through first." That simple acquiescence automatically reduces our chi's intensity. We shrink back a little to let the horse through, and the horse circles ahead of us.

Instead, if the handler increases his or her chi's intensity while pulling ahead of the horse, the ISA slopes far behind the trainer. This will make the horse circle behind the trainer. Again, the horse will move to wherever the energy is lower; in this example, that is behind the handler. Now the pair will curve off to the right (*see figure 12.10*). The trainer goes first, and the horse slips behind into the procession.

This is how it's possible to make our horse circle toward or away from us simply by increasing or diminishing our chi relative to the horse. Allow the chi's intensity to drop, and the horse slips forward and circles ahead of us. Boost the chi, and the horse falls behind and circles behind and away from us.

Directional Reversal

∎ ∎ ∎

DIRECTIONAL REVERSAL is a wonderful little trick to learn at this stage. If your horse is pushy and seems to be always trying to lead (or reach every gate first), allow him to slip slightly ahead of you. Let him start to circle around your shoulder toward you. Now simply turn sharply inside, rotate 180 degrees around to your left, and then head straight off — dead ahead (*see figure 12.11*).

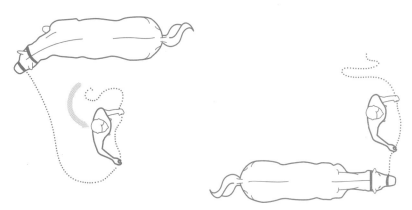

12.11 The handler uses directional reversal to turn inside the horse and get back into leading position.

CHI AND YOUR FOOT POSITION

A critical facet of learning more about energetic connection through chi is to pay attention to your feet. The key to your manipulation of chi lies in mastering your feet: less feet, more hooves. The more proficient you become at manipulating chi, the less your feet have to move and the more the horse's feet move in response to your intention. This resembles a mathematical formula:

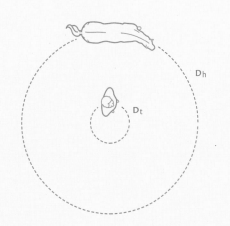

$$\text{Chi} \cong \frac{D_h}{D_t}$$

Less feet, more hooves. The larger the D_h (distance traveled by the horse) and the smaller the D_t (distance traveled by the trainer), the more control the trainer is exerting through chi.

In effect, because the circle you are making is so much smaller than the one your horse is making at the end of the lead, you effectively turn more tightly and get "ahead" of your horse. You return to an assertive, balanced position where you can lead off again in a straight-ahead fashion. This simple, fluid movement allows the handler to turn inside the horse. It is a perfect demonstration of how chi, applied at the right moment, in the right place, helps us effortlessly maneuver our horse.

We can also transfer chi from next to the horse's shoulder, while we are walking straight ahead, and shift it to zone 4 (*see figure 12.12*). When we do this in combination with simply turning around in place, we effectively make the horse move around us.

12.12 When the trainer turns while placing chi on zone 4, the horse's hips are driven over, so the horse effectively circles around the trainer.

Four Ways to Direct a Horse

■ ■ ■

We have now employed four methods to produce directional changes or circles while leading our horse:

- We used our right forearm to drive our horse to step over and away from us.
- We shifted our position and chi relative to that of horse to make him circle in front of or behind us, sliding the ISA forward or rearward, respectively.
- We used directional reversal when necessary to regain the leading position.
- Finally, we used spinning in place while shifting chi onto zone 4, the hips, to circle our horse around us.

It is important to practice these maneuvers. It conveys to our horse that we are developing control of the leading process. We decide how the team will move, when we go from moving ahead in a straight line to a circle, be it large or small. Also, we assert ourselves; no matter how hard our horse may try to pull ahead of us, we can always put ourselves effortlessly back into the leading position.

ADVANTAGES OF DIRECTIONAL REVERSAL   Harnessing directional reversal, in particular, has a dramatic impact on the horse, because in doing it we transmit patient, focused chi. As in *aikido* martial arts maneuvers, you've used the horse's unopposed forward movement to put yourself back in position to lead.

Directional reversal has much to recommend it. It is a tranquil, gentle, and patient method of asserting directional primacy over our horse. There's no physical struggle or coercion. Your authority is established by skillful, effortless changes in position. Often, spiritual leadership establishes itself through gentle, nonviolent action rather than an obvious demonstration of power.

Conservation as Motivation

∙∙∙

SOME TRAINERS MAINTAIN that horses are inherently lazy. This is false. What they label laziness is actually a potent survival mechanism: conservation of energy. True, given the choice, a horse would rather move from one end of the arena to the other at a walk rather than a gallop. But there's no laziness in such behavior. By analogy, if I brought a cup of tea down to one end of my house and realized I'd forgotten my newspaper in the kitchen, would I sprint to retrieve it? If I just walked, would you label me as lazy? No. I walk for the paper and run if the house is on fire.

Over thousands of years of history, horses have, in fact, shown themselves to possess a mythic work ethic. The self-sacrifice of horses on behalf of their human masters is legendary. Human civilization has been carried on the backs of horses. Our temples, our palaces, our fortresses all stand on foundations laid over the bones of millions of horses.

HORSES IN HARM'S WAY   My grandfather helped me understand the utter horror that engulfs horses caught in the grasp of murderous modern warfare. He was a cavalry officer in World War I, a conflagration in which more than four million horses perished. My Opa had the misfortune of having both of his horses shot out from under him in the midst of battle. It was also his great luck that those two horses gave their lives to save his.

Decades after the war, when I was about twelve, my grandfather took out a leather box from his writing desk. Inside, there was a spectacular medal. He handed it to me: a beautiful red and white enamel cross, wreathed with gold, hanging from a wide red and white-striped ribbon. To my eyes it shone greater than any jewel.

"This is the highest decoration my country, Austria, gives for valor," he said. "This medal was placed around my neck by the emperor himself, in the *Reduntensalle* of the Habsburg Palace in Vienna. I received it after I was wounded and my second horse, Otto, was killed. Many people thought I was a brave man, I suppose. But let me show you something."

He lifted the velvet backing of the box. From under the liner, he took out a small black-and-white photograph, not much larger than a postage stamp. It was a picture of my Opa as a young man. He was dressed in uniform, sitting proud and tall astride a beautiful dark horse. He placed the photo on top of the medal in my hand. (*See figures 12.13 and 12.14.*)

"This was my Otto," he said. "Look at him! His strength and carriage. His absolute loyalty...." My grandfather's eyes welled with tears, and his notoriously resolute voice became tremulous. "The absolute loyalty Otto

12.13 My grandfather as a cavalry officer in World War I

displayed...was remarkable. I told your Oma, before I went off to the front, that she need never worry about my well-being. I would come back alive because Otto would be there to look after me." Tears rolled down his cheeks.

I handed back the photo. He collected himself. "Otto deserved this medal. He saved my life. He shielded me from the shell. He laid down his life for me. He died because...because he loved me."

When I was older, my grandfather shared more details with me. He told me that although he himself had been injured by the artillery blast, he was able to rise to his feet. He recovered his bearings in the midst of the smoke and confusion of the battle and rushed over to where his horse lay. Sadly, two of Otto's legs had been completely amputated by the blast, and his abdominal cavity had been torn open by shrapnel.

It must have been a sickening scene. My grandfather threw his arms around Otto's neck and kissed him. Sobbing, he pressed his revolver against the side of Otto's head and ended his suffering. I can only imagine how Opa felt having to kill his beloved companion.

A few years later Opa took out the medal again and gave it to me to keep. Forever. It was the last time we saw each other. Reading through some of his journals from that period, I think he had an inkling the end of his own life might be near.

12.14

A priceless legacy
of my grandfather

"When I saw the Emperor standing there smiling," he said, "and my family there, the generals, officers, friends, all filling the hall in the Habsburg Palace — I could think of nothing else but Otto. None of it," he stated emphatically, "was worth losing Otto. Much too high a price, my boy," he added wistfully. "I never would have agreed to pay it, had I known."

"You mean Otto?"

"Had I known what was going to happen to Otto...to horses. To friends. Enemies. I'd never have gone. I'd have found myself a clever desk job in Vienna. Then I could have been riding Otto in the park every Sunday. He'd never have been...sacrificed."

You can imagine how my grandfather would have reacted if someone suggested to him that horses were lazy. No, horses have a great sense of duty and hard work. But they need to conserve energy; they evolved into large foraging prey animals that must be ready, in an instant, to exert themselves explosively to avoid a predator's attack. They save their energy for when it counts.

WORKING WITH A HORSE'S ENERGY   You employ this conservative trait when you train with directional reversal (*see figure 12.11*). A horse uses less energy moving in a straight line than when he has to stop, turn, and start up again. Every time a horse pulls ahead of you, slipping out in front of your ISL, you apply directional reversal. Eventually, the horse figures out he'll expend less energy if he stays behind and just lets himself be led in a straight line.

To make this concept easier to grasp, test it out. Find a reasonable stretch of lawn or open space somewhere. Pick out roughly a 100-foot long stretch and walk it back and forth once, for a total distance of 100 feet. Now mark out a spot that is only 20 feet away and go back and forth five times, to and fro, until you have again walked a total length of 100 feet. You'll discover that moving forward in a straight line uses far less energy than multiple round trips.

With some horses, directional reversal takes time to sink in. But there is no physical struggle or tug of war between trainer and animal. You should employ directional reversal every time your horse tries to muscle himself into the leadership role (and he will). Especially early on, directional reversal causes the horse to use up energy. The horse begins to see it is futile to try to pull ahead because you, as the handler, simply spin around and lead off. The horse soon realizes it makes more sense to simply follow. What's more, you have let your horse learn this lesson for himself. Your horse will see that you demonstrate control, command, communication, and compassion as leader.

Pushing and Pulling Chi
from the Shoulder

■ ■ ■

THE NOTION OF "PUSHING" OR "PULLING" with chi has nothing to do with mechanical energy transmitted through the lead or halter. It relates, instead, to the chi — the psychic vitality — emanating through the trainer's arm and shoulder nearest the horse (*see figure 12.4*).

It takes about ten times more chi to push than it does to pull a horse in the same direction. Because it is more difficult to master pushing than pulling, I recommend learning first how to pull with chi before learning to push with it.

Leading your horse forward is the most straightforward "pulling" task you can tackle. Imagine a string running from your right shoulder to the tip of the horse's muzzle. As you step forward, this invisible string pulls your horse forward. Keep your chi moving in a rhythmic, bouncy fashion. It helps to exaggerate your gait in a kind of sailor's swagger while you lead your horse. The horse is sensitized by the small pulsing movements of your right upper torso.

Bring up the swing of your gait slowly and gradually. Accompany it with soothing verbal encouragement so your horse has some lighthearted fun with it. Be patient while playing this game and teaching your horse to move into the vacuum of chi you leave behind. There will be occasions, especially early in the process, when leading off by pulling with energy can break down a bit. Horses get bored. Their attention drifts. Like humans, the younger the horse, the shorter his attention span. If a horse loses the rhythm of leading, shrug it off. Start over or move on to something else. Never be afraid to return to the beginning.

Pushing is harder; it takes more practice. The focus of the practice is to first learn to predictably drive the horse's face and shoulder over. Over time, you can reduce the need to hold up your hand to help project chi powerfully. Gradually you'll bring the chi down into your elbow and shoulder and learn to drive the horse over with just the chi focused in your elbow.

Watch horses interacting with each other in the wild. This is one of Monty Roberts' enduring contributions to the field of horsemanship: trainers should rely on direct observation of untamed horses (like wild mustangs) in their natural state to understand the methods horses use to communicate with each other and to teach each other. Pure *Equus* is spoken out in untamed, open spaces. Roberts insisted that natural training methods must use the same basic vocabulary, based on the horse's body language and behaviors in the wild.

Not all of us can spend days in the field watching wild mustangs through binoculars the way Monty did. But you can watch chi at work between a mare and her foal in a stable. Within a matter of hours after the foal's birth, the dam is able to direct her foal forward, backward, sideways (laterally), and even upward and downward, if necessary.

As she teaches her offspring vital survival skills, there's only the lightest physical contact between mare and foal. A mare does not nudge hard or shove her foal outright, except in a dire emergency. Almost all physical contact between the mare and her foal consists of stroking or nuzzling for reassurance. As you watch the mare teach her foal to lead off, she will cue the foal with — what else? — her leading shoulder. In fact, most foals position themselves right behind their dam's ISL (*see figure 12.15*).

12.15 The natural alignment between dam and foal is the same as that between handler and horse.

Highlights

■ ■ ■

*If a handler's and horse's output
of chi is constant and balanced along the ISA,
the pair will travel in a straight direction.*

■

The shoulder is the key to leading with chi.

■

$$Chi \cong D_h / D_t$$

■

*The greater one's command of chi,
the more the horse's feet move and the less the trainer's do.*

■

Horses are not lazy; they conserve energy.

■

*Directional reversal is a peaceful,
gentle way to bring yourself back into
the leading position.*

■

*Horses move instinctively
from areas of higher chi to areas with lower chi.*

■

*It is ten times easier to pull than to
push with chi.*

PICKING UP THE PACE

Where in this wide world can man find nobility without pride, / Friendship without envy, / Or beauty without vanity? / Here, where grace is served with muscle / And strength by gentleness confined / He serves without servility; / he has fought without enmity. / There is nothing so powerful, nothing less violent. / There is nothing so quick, nothing more patient.

■ ■ ■

RONALD DUNCAN, *The Horse*

WE WILL INCORPORATE two other important properties of chi into leading. First, chi has a volatile component: it is easier to add it to our interactions than to drain it out. It's a little like starter fluid on the charcoal grill — less is better. Novices often err by adding too much chi too quickly into an exercise, and this makes the horse overreact and "squirt" into action.

The second characteristic is chi's inherent elasticity. Chi stretches and thins out as you move away from your horse, like a piece of salt water taffy drawn out between your fingers (*see figure 13.1*).

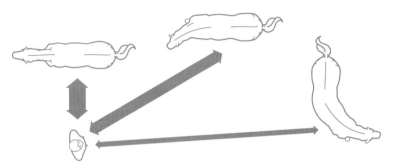

13.1 Chi stretching between trainer and horse as distance increases

Artful Persuasion

∎∎∎

WHEN YOU FIRST add variable speeds into your leading exercises, do not put too much distance between you and your horse. This way your chi will stretch but still exert a strong pull on your horse. If you walk away too fast, the chi will snap (as if you stretched the taffy till it broke), leaving your horse behind, in the dirt.

Begin by gradually increasing the length of your stride for a few paces. See if your horse will keep up and bring his muzzle back in line with your ISL. If your horse responds appropriately, turn, breathe, and stroke him. Reinforce the baby step that he's taken in the right direction.

After a short pause, lead off, again at a slow, steady pace. Then, in three or four places, increase the speed of your stride so your horse has to hurry to stay with you (*see figure 13.2*). If the horse keeps up, release him, reward him, and rejoice. If your horse cannot hang on, you might have been overzealous, so start again — slower, more gradually. Breathe. Begin again. Behold.

Sometimes a horse won't follow. Worse, he just stops dead in his tracks. The rookie mistake is to walk back to the horse, stroke him a few times, and then try to cajole him into moving. Wrong. Doing this rewards the horse for standing still. He is learning he can stop — and be released — when he lets his handler walk away and does not keep up. It is important to keep the horse moving and the energy flowing. Chi must be applied like measured, artful persuasion.

Leading Off at the Jog

∎∎∎

AS YOU LEAD OFF, keep it simple. Like a treadmill, you may change speed but not direction. Having your horse keep up with you at faster speeds is accomplished in two ways:

* Working solo, using the lead rope behind you to exert chi on the hips
* Enlisting an assistant to drive the horse forward from behind while you lead from the front

If you're working alone, first ensure that your horse has solidly learned the idea of stepping forward every time you ask. Then pick up a slow jog. Check if your horse sticks with you. If he does, praise him profusely. Return to the walk and stop. Praise. Start again at the walk, then speed up to the jog, and so on. Speed up and slow down with your horse until he becomes comfortable sticking with you regardless of speed.

Don't be concerned if your horse needs verbal encouragement to keep up with you. You may need to throw in a kiss or a cluck to your horse at first. Any horse (but especially a young one) can become confused. If your

13.2 This handler is jogging and using excess coils of lead to put pressure on zone 4 to keep the horse trotting even with her ISL.

horse begins jogging along with you easily, hearty congratulations to you (and your horse). When a horse readily jogs alongside, that is an indication the chi between you and your horse is strong. It's stretching but not breaking.

Many horses need encouragement to keep up at first when you start to jog out. If there is no response from your horse, then take the excess lead rope coils and slap them against your thigh (the thigh farthest away from the horse). If your horse does not respond by jogging, swing the lead behind your back, loosely aiming the popper at the forward spot on his hip.

EMPLOY ARDP   Tune into the four-step ARDP schema.

- The ASK stage is the trainer breaking into the jog; the horse sees you trot, so it trots.
- The cluck or kiss is the REQUEST.
- The rope slapping against your leg is the DEMAND phase.
- Throwing the rope behind at the forward spot near the hip is the PROMISE.

The slap of the lead rope on the horse's hip allows the trainer to keep his or her forward focus on the horizon while still being assured of applying enough chi to the hip to ensure forward motion. This maneuver works well. Sometimes beginners have a hard time figuring out how to throw the coil behind themselves to exert pressure on the forward spot without breaking their own focus, plus maintaining the jog, all at the same time.

It takes practice. Stick with it. Recall how difficult and cumbersome it was when you first learned to ride a bike? You thought you'd never be able to steer and pedal at the same time, but now it's second nature. Be patient. Go easy on yourself and your horse.

USE THE TRAINING WAND   When students are having difficulty coordinating the lead rope, it's easier to let them run with all the lead collected in their right hand and a training wand or whip in their left. It is simple for students to apply chi to the forward point of the hip by swinging a wand, or whip, behind their back, which doesn't interfere with the fixation of their gaze. Once the idea is mastered, the lead rope can be used instead.

The wand can always be used to overcome any rope-handling issues. It's a natural way to teach us how to concentrate and project chi. This automatically gives us focus and control, which can be more difficult to assemble in a long lead rope.

When it comes to speeding up the horse, don't insist the horse take up a canter or lope (I use the terms synonymously) next to you. First, it's hard for you to run fast enough to keep up. Second, before you take up the lope, make sure the horse is well-versed in picking up the proper lead. The last thing you want to do is encourage your horse to lope next to you and then have to stop and correct it for picking up the wrong lead. The term *lead* here does not refer to the lead rope. In the context of cantering, it relates to which front foot the horse lifts up first. The proper lead when a horse is circling is to pick up his inside front leg first.

The second reason the wand works for mastering new tasks is that it is safe. The wand allows you to direct chi from a safe distance. This is not only useful for beginners, who may lack experience or confidence, but it can also be helpful for experienced trainers when handling a potentially dangerous horse.

One of my favorite expressions is that it's unfair to pit a 150-pound human against a 1,200-pound horse. But the wand adds at least 500 pounds, making it a fairer contest. It's magical to watch students suddenly succeed because they have learned to urge their horses with a wand. They change from being frustrated and confused to wizards, like instant Harry Potters. Why? Because the wand seems to conduct our chi. It gives us a physical place to concentrate our chi. That simple transformation produces amazing results.

Jogging: Working with a Partner

■■■

THE SECOND WAY to teach your horse to accelerate his gait while remaining in proper position next to your ISL is to work with an additional partner — a human one. Your partner stands behind the horse and off to one side and helps drive your horse forward. This division of labor frees you up to take care of the lead and focus on the horizon.

This arrangement accustoms your horse to having you lead while your partner walks behind, opposite the inside hip. Let your horse move freely to the right and left while you and your partner learn to swing smoothly with the horse through each directional change.

Horses learn quickly with this double-team approach because it's easier to provide speed without losing direction. Double-teaming allows the horse to distinguish between directional cues and driving pressure, because the two are now managed by two physically distinct handlers.

Highlights

∎ ∎ ∎

It's easier to add chi than to remove it.

∎

Chi is elastic.

∎

*Reward the behaviors you want
rather than punishing the ones you don't.*

∎

You can never use too much praise.

∎

*A training wand or longe whip
focuses chi, but the handler is the source.*

MINDING YOUR MANNERS

Start by doing what's necessary, then what's possible,
and suddenly you're doing the impossible.

■ ■ ■

ST. FRANCIS OF ASSISI

FEW THINGS ARE MORE DISCONCERTING (or dangerous) than a horse without manners. In the wild, an ill-tempered, unruly horse is banned from the herd. When faced with the prospect of ejection from his family group, such a horse soon mends his ways. Being exiled from the herd is tantamount to a death sentence, so horses teach each other firmly and unequivocally how to behave. Explicit leadership requires that safe and clear boundaries be established.

The trainer, however, must distinguish between misbehavior and fright. Horses need to flee. It is a genetically imprinted part of their nature to become frightened. Teaching a horse to listen and to obey your instructions goes a long way toward helping him avoid panic. But there is no panacea — and no such thing as a bomb-proof horse.

Fearful as he may feel, a polite horse is distinguished by his ability to stop. So once we're confident our horse will hold his position at the ISA and adjust his pace to match ours, it's time to work on a solid stop. We can't work on "stop" until we've got the foundation of a solid "go."

Whoa!

...

FOR THE STOP, we'll need to differentiate between the "whoa" and the "quit it" commands. People often use *whoa* indiscriminately when they're around horses, when they actually mean "quit it," not "stop" or "halt." So let's clarify these commands.

The word *whoa* is reserved for instances when we expect our horse to *cease all forward motion*. *Whoa* means: "Hold all four of your feet still! Halt now!"

Quit it! — the ubiquitous bark of frustration — is reserved for a situation when the horse misbehaves, acts out, or does not carry out what he has been trained to do, with the emphasis on *trained*. We can ask a horse to *quit it* only when he's been well trained to *do it*. What we really mean is, "Hey, stop what you're doing."

Whoa is a command, *quit it* a rebuke. The former conveys a need to have the horse obey; the latter implies the horse knows better.

LEARNING HOW TO COMMAND   Since one of our central themes is impeccable intent, focus on giving the commands you mean to give. If you want your horse to stop moving, discipline yourself to use the command *whoa*. If you want your horse to stop pawing at the ground, then don't say *whoa*; use *quit it*. When trainers project a flustered or confused

14.1 A trainer in a *whoa* position, with an upheld hand, bringing the horse to a sudden stop

chi, the horse reacts in a similar fashion. So be clear-headed and present with your commands.

Use simple verbal commands with distinct sounds. If you use *whoa*, don't at other times use the command *go*. They sound too similar to a horse. Pair verbal commands with visual cues to assist your horse in learning them. For example, say *Whoa!* while you hold up your hand as though you're stopping traffic. Your upheld hand sends chi against the horse's muzzle to stop forward motion (*see figure 14.1*).

Once the horse has firmly established in his own mind what *whoa* means, you can work on ensuring an equal response to both visual and verbal cues. Practice, and then practice some more under distracting circumstances, until you're sure your horse responds automatically to your command.

WHOA ON THE LEAD   Teach your horse to stop on the lead by letting him move out at a moderate walk. Focus your chi on the horizon. Walk a dozen steps and pick out a spot three paces ahead, where you plan to stop.

When you reach your first mark, start counting aloud: "One... two...three — *Whoa!*" As you begin counting, your chi is preparing for the halt. It may not be something we can spot, but a horse can. By focusing on the spot ahead where you intend to stop, you automatically initiate a shift in your chi that sends subliminal signals to the horse to get ready to shift from a forward focus to a rearward one.

EMPLOY ARDP   When you first carry out this exercise, you'll use an abundance of cues to help your horse understand what *whoa* means. Employ the ARDP schema.

My grandfather frequently admonished me to "hope for the best, but prepare for the worst." The best is that our horse will stop on a dime, planting his feet. The worst? He runs you over!

The first level will be to Ask, which is the assembly of chi building up in your body during the three-count. The horse can tell something's going to happen. Arrive at the preselected spot, stop, and say *Whoa!*

Nothing happened? Go around the round pen another time. Pick another spot. This time use the REQUEST, the second cue. As you approach the preselected spot, inhale deeply. Puff out your chest and throw your shoulders back. Now come up to the spot, say *Whoa!* with authority, and come to an exaggerated parade rest with your feet.

Didn't work? Repeat the preliminaries. This time, for the DEMAND, you're going to actually stick your elbow out to build up a lot of chi in front of the horse's muzzle.

Still didn't work? Go back to the same sequence. Now when you arrive at your preselected spot, stop directly in your horse's path. Halt directly in front of your horse's nose, with so much force and insistence that he must stop! That's the PROMISE. There's nowhere he can go.

When a Horse Won't Whoa

■ ■ ■

WHAT IF THE WORST HAPPENS, and your horse won't stop? Maybe he even bowls you over. If so, dust yourself off and get ready to use some sure-fire techniques to halt him: (1) directional reversal and (2) substantial chi to his face.

DIRECTIONAL REVERSAL   We'll again use directional reversal, as we did earlier when we taught our horse not to rush ahead of the ISL. This situation is different, however, because we're not exploiting the horse's search for an energy-efficient solution to the problem. Instead, we're harnessing the moment he turns.

This time, count out: "Three…two…one — *Whoa!*" As soon as your horse seems to be edging ahead, reverse course 180 degrees. Take off in the opposite direction. Walk for three or four paces and then start counting again: "Three…two…one — *Whoa!*"

If your horse continues to try to walk past you, keep making reversals at a relatively fast pace until he tires. Each time, build up to the direction

The croup of the tail is closer to the ground as the horse brakes onto his hindquarters.

Keep an eye out for what I call "flying the flag." Watch your horse's tail (the flag) during the *whoa* command. The lower the croup, or base of the tail, the more your horse is responding to your halt. His body posture conveys a great deal about how genuine his intention to stop all forward movement of his feet is.

change with the same sequence of words. Timing is the reason for inserting the *whoa* at a special moment after the countdown.

As your horse fatigues, you'll see a great gift of directional reversal: a momentary stop. A horse cannot change directions without stopping, even if just for an instant. This presents our teachable moment.

Keep counting down. Eventually, your *whoa* will coincide with a moment when the horse actually stops moving his feet for an instant. That's precisely when you reach back and lavishly praise him for standing still. Make it seem like it's your idea to stop right there. If your horse starts to move, lead off immediately, making it seem like the departure was your idea too. Great trainers exploit mistakes, turning breakdowns into breakthroughs.

PRESSURE ON THE FACE: THE "CHOPPER"   A second way to bring your horse to a stop is to apply increasing amounts of chi in front of your horse, in zone 1. Walk your horse along a fence line. Carry out the halt, complete with parade rest, that you previously used as your Request. Now it is your ASK.

No stop? Fine. Come around again and halt, but this time swing the end of your lead rope in front of the horse's muzzle (*see figure 14.2*); use a subtle upward flick in the air (REQUEST).

No response? Make it an energetic twirl (DEMAND) — whatever it takes. Some horses may require so much chi, you have to start spinning

14.2 The handler is using the "chopper" maneuver to get her horse to stop.

14.3 A handler using a training wand to bring a horse to a halt.

your lead rope so quickly and noisily that it resembles the rotor of a helicopter buzzing (hence its nickname, the "chopper").

The rope is rotating so fast, it threatens to "buzz" your horse's nose off (PROMISE). The chopper never fails, if it's done right.

USING THE TRAINING WAND   The training wand also works with the same ARDP. As you come to your preselected stop spot, place the tip of the wand on the ground in front of your horse: the ASK. No? Next time, bring the tip up; that's the REQUEST. Still no response? Swing the wand back and forth (in a windshield-wiper action) in front of your horse's nose: the DEMAND. Inevitably, as surely as the sun rises, your horse will halt, or it will bump into the briskly moving wand (*see figure 14.3*).

By swinging the lead rope or wand in front of your horse, you have presented him with a dilemma: if he refuses to halt, he risks introducing his face into the path of the chopper or the windshield wiper. This is not something any horse is going to wish to pursue for long. That's the PROMISE. A reminder: try never to strike a horse anywhere around the face. The pressure is in front of the muzzle, out into zone 1. But if your horse needs a solid whack to understand that you and your wand (or lead rope) mean business, don't be afraid to deliver it, as promised.

Time-Tested Training Strategies

■■■

WHEN WE WORK in a close partnership with our horse, one of our objectives is obviously to teach or train him to carry out the tasks we set for him. But there's a second goal, too: to *learn* from our horse. To allow him to instruct us in the wisdom of his species, the secrets of the heart, and, most importantly, his innate talent to be connected, immersed in the natural world around him. Not to be *in* the world but *of* the world. Not to feel empowered as the master of the environment, but to be nurtured as one of its children. The horse has that secret but we must earn his trust and respect before he'll share it with us.

THINK LIKE A PREY ANIMAL   When it's time to enter the round pen, learn to leave your predatory nature behind. Instead, let the prey qualities of your horse's nature soak into you. Learn to see the world through the eyes of an animal that must live with the fear of pursuit, of isolation from its family, of a potentially grisly death by tooth or claw. There's a peace-loving innocence within the equine state of mind, where you wish no harm to any living creature. The patience of prey will improve you as a teacher, parent, spouse, and person. Horses learn best from trainers who see the world through their eyes and who seek to instruct by cooperation rather than intimidation.

I once attended a roping clinic in the Southwest given by two talented trainers, Brian Andersen and Harvey Jacobs. Harvey was working a yearling in the round pen. He had the horse circling at a good clip, and then he just stopped. He let the horse circle in from the rail and stand next to him at the center. A lady in the audience wanted to know why he had just abruptly given up working with the horse.

"I didn't give up," Harvey said. "I just figured I was feeling a little pooped and maybe this little filly might need a breather, too. At least, that's what I'd want if I were her.".

As if on cue, the filly stepped over and took her position behind Harvey. As he moved up to the rail, closer to the students, to converse, the filly followed, as if attached to him by an invisible lead.

His empathy had been rewarded by loyalty. The shortest route to getting that horse to listen to him was to think like her, to see things from her perspective.

SAVOR THE JOURNEY   Don't get too hung up on having your horse perform. If your horse gives a decent attempt at a halt, remember he is learning. It's a process, not a destination. Often students coach their horses to accomplish 70 or 80 percent of a particular task, but then they persist in their training session far beyond the horse's attention span, striving way too hard to get 100 percent completion during the first day. How well your horse learns, not how fast, is the best measure of how good a trainer you are.

Maybe it takes 100 days of practice until the horse halts perfectly. So what? As long as the horse tries and makes progress, the two of you are doing fine. Constantly remind yourself to reward effort — in your horse *and* yourself.

Also, know when to quit. Look for the right moment to help your horse feel the sweet rush of achievement. When he leaves the round pen on a high note, you both feel calmer and more peaceful than at the beginning of the training session. This is a great lesson for your horse, your parenting, or any situation where you are effectively serving as a teacher: let 'em leave feeling like champs.

Remember the great teachers in your life, the ones who recognized your efforts and gave you a gold star for trying? Well, that kind of teacher — one who rewards effort — is especially successful with horses. Effort counts. Trying matters. Never underestimate the heart every horse brings to the task.

RELY ON YOUR HORSE'S MEMORY   Change your pace as you're leading, halting, and jogging with your horse. Quit working on tasks when you feel your horse getting stale. Horses are endowed with keen memories that persist, even if the task is not practiced again for months. Experiments have shown that once a horse is taught to distinguish one pattern out of a series of paired ones, he remembers that correct pattern, intact, for 12 months, without repeating the task. When retested after a year, horses have a practically perfect recall. By comparison, human abilities are puny. They begin to measurably degrade within a few days! Predators do not require such durable memories because, as hunters, they exploit new opportunities and scenarios. The latest ambush is yesterday's news.

The prey animal, on the other hand, survives by having an enduring memory. Horses learn from experience, based on mistakes and bad choices. Remembering a fatal error that took the life of a herd member is vital. For prey, there is often no second chance. For example, if a particular type of ground cover (like tall buffalo grass) allows predators to sneak up close to the herd, then each horse must always remember to be wary of it, to have the best chance of staying alive. Lasting memory gets a prey animal's genes into the next generation.

LEADING OUT AND MIXING IT UP   Instead of always training in the round pen, move into the arena or the pasture, where there's plenty of open space and trees. Weave in and out among the tree trunks. Jog, halt, and walk your horse around them in figure 8s. Go up and down slopes and jump over low-lying branches. (*See figure 14.4.*)

Variable terrain engages a horse's curiosity and sense of play. Never underestimate these wonderful qualities in your horse. Let the child in you run free. The horse will never tell.

An extreme variant of this game is to lead your horse into recreational parks and conservation areas. Be sure to scout the terrain first. When you find a suitable path, take your horse for a walk. It will get both of you out into nature. Remember, of course, to respect the land, first and foremost. Nature is full of beauty, but it is also full of surprises that may frighten your horse — like the great blue heron. What? Never heard of it?

14.4 This trainer is using an array of obstacles to create a more lively, creative game out of leading her horse.

THE GREAT BLUE HERON SPOOK   I took one of my three-year-old geldings for a walk. I had him on a lead rope, and we were strolling down one of the paths in a bird sanctuary near my ranch. I thought it might give me an opportunity to work on introducing him to some novel stimuli. Little did I know....

We turned up the main path into a section of the forest, and we ascended around a sharp bend. There, planted front and center about 20 yards ahead of us, filling the entire trail, was a great blue heron, erect on its tall, stilt-like legs (*see figure 14.5*). It stared at us benignly for a moment with its long, extended beak and then shifted its enormous wings.

My horse took one look at that creature and decided this had to be the legendary horse-devouring Heron from Hell! He reared up on his hind legs and swung violently around in one swift movement. It happened so fast, I barely had enough time to register what had caused his fright before I had to worry that he might land on top of me. He planted his hind feet and was getting ready to engage his after-burners and blast back to the barn at Mach 3.

Fortunately for me, the gelding had spun only about halfway around at that point. He was still turning, half in the air and off-balance, so I had some mechanical leverage with the lead rope. A split second's more rotation and I would have been yanked off my feet to become a doormat for my horse on his way home.

I was able to bring the horse's front legs back to the ground, and I started circling him. This kept his hindquarters side-stepping in a tight circle around me. Gradually, I let our little circle drift so we put some distance between ourselves and the heron. The fright (and pressure) my horse was feeling from the bird diminished. When his fear decreased enough, his feet stopped moving entirely.

We then stood together and safely contemplated the heron. The gelding didn't even flinch when the bird eventually fully extended his immense wings and lifted off out of sight.

As this episode illustrates, nature can be full of surprises. We want our training to be able to rise to the demands of such surprises. Regular practice generates learned responses that can become habitual, reliable habits, even under duress.

LEADING OVER GROUND POLES   Teaching horses to lead over obstacles also helps instill confidence. Don't start with a 5-foot-high obstacle or a stack of 50-gallon drums; choose something much less daunting: 12- to 15-foot-long poles on the ground.

It reassures young horses if they can watch you, their leader, walk back and forth across the ground poles first. Don't be shy about demonstrating.

The horse-devouring, fire-breathing character known as the great blue heron

14.6 Leading your horse over ground poles can improve confidence, foot placement, and muscle memory for collection later in training.

For most horses, watching a couple of times and then quietly being led alongside you is all it takes. Alternatively, take a seasoned veteran horse over the poles a few times to give a younger, less experienced horse a little dose of confidence. Eventually ask your horse to vary his gait over the ground poles. Change the spacing between the ground poles if you ask your horse to trot or lope over them. (*See figure 14.6.*)

When you're confident your horse is secure striding over the poles, ask your horse to go back and forth in both directions. Continue to vary the pace at which your horse passes over the poles. Throw in a halt or two to reinforce all of the skills you've been teaching. The height of the poles can eventually be raised to help your horse elevate his gaits.

In the first few months of a horse's training, keep the obstacles low enough that you can easily step over them yourself. This will keep you from going jump crazy. Remember, you're not trying to teach your horse to jump in this phase of his training; you are trying to enhance your horse's posture and carriage while increasing his confidence.

THE PLATFORM   One of the best obstacles to use for training horses is a low-lying platform (*see figure 14.7*). Few things can build up a horse's surefootedness and confidence like the platform. A good-sized one should measure about 10 by 12 feet and be approximately 1 foot high. One side should have a ramp, with a step-off at the other end. The dimensions and shape are outlined in the figure on the next page.

The platform must be solidly built and reinforced so it can withstand the full weight of a horse and rider. Using a ramp trains the horse to maneuver up and down obstacles. The step-off end teaches a horse to

14.7 A sturdy platform is an invaluable adjunct to building a horse's confidence and surefootedness.

jump off a small ledge and gain confidence in placing his feet in a step-wise, deliberate fashion on command. In addition, it's a wonderful way to prepare a horse for loading in and out of a trailer (which we'll come to in a later chapter).

Again, avoid letting your practice become dull or repetitive. Think of fresh angles and approaches to keep your horse's mind engaged and his curiosity at peak intensity. Adding a ramp to the ground pole routine is a great method to work on foot placement. Obstacles build confidence and surefootedness.

Your Foundation

∎∎∎

UP TO THIS POINT, we've focused on skills related to leading the horse. We have emphasized intent, control, and patience. There's no point in proceeding further until we're sure we have built a strong foundation of leading together on the ground. Everything else to come is predicated upon the strength of the connection we have forged here with our horse.

CHAPTER FOURTEEN

Highlights

■ ■ ■

"Whoa!" means stop moving all four feet.

■

"Quit it!" means stop misbehaving.

■

*When your horse won't whoa,
add directional reversal.*

■

*How your horse is flying his flag
tells you how truly sincere his stop is.*

■

*When you enter the round pen
leave your predator nature at the gate.*

■

Effort counts and trying matters.

■

Never let a training goal become a chore.

■

*Know when to quit; leave your horse feeling
like a champion.*

CHAPTER FIFTEEN

SENDING OUT & BACKING UP

*The only approbation a rider should covet is
that of his horse.*

∎ ∎ ∎

ETIENNE, CAPTAIN BEUDANT

T to send a horse out, we must encourage him to depart, to leave our side, on cue. For some students this exercise can prove difficult in a fundamental, emotional way. It is easy to ask your horse to reunite with you, to come join up with you. Sending your horse away from your side means going through the motions of rejecting or being rejected, which can make handlers reluctant to tackle this task with their horse. But a horse that cannot be sent away is being short-changed — even if in the name of affection.

First Degree of Separation

■■■

WE NEED TO HELP our horse distinguish between stepping forward and departing. To obtain the first degree of separation, we ask our horse to take *one* step away from us. The send-out starts with pressure on the horse's shoulder, where it joins the chest.

Follow the ARDP schema; allow plenty of breathing between steps. The less energy you use, the more elegant your horse's response will be. ASK will be a simple glance, as usual. REQUEST is the wag of a finger or lead. DEMAND means a swing of the lead. And the PROMISE is an energetic twirl of the rope with a quick snap. From depart, ask your horse to walk straight ahead of you.

Straight Ahead

■■■

SENDING A HORSE OUT straight ahead requires three distinct applications of chi (*see figure 15.1*). First, urge your horse to leave your side (send chi to his shoulder, zone 2). Then ask your horse to step forward (chi to dock of tail, zone 5). Finally, apply chi obliquely forward through the girth line. Applying chi to zone 3, or obliquely forward through the girth line, drives the horse forward. This is how we are able to train a horse to walk ahead from the ground and later get the same result under saddle through our legs.

To start, you want a first few consecutive steps away from you; ignore any drifting right or left. Just encourage forward motion at this time.

Once your horse is readily moving two or three steps forward at a time, add length to your lead (20 feet) so he isn't tethered by too short a rope. Let your horse consistently travel out to the end of the lead, and practice until the training is solidified.

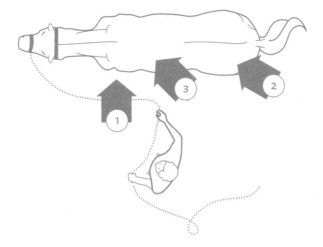

15.1 The applications of three vectors of chi required to send the horse ahead. First, chi is applied to the near shoulder (1), then the trainer allows his focus to slip back to the hip (2) to send the horse forward with impulsion; finally, a vector of chi is applied just behind the girth line (3).

After that, if the horse strays too far to the right (away from you, if you are located at the horse's left shoulder), you can nudge him back toward you by applying chi to his hips (equivalent to an inside turn). Too much chi at this site, however, will cause an overcorrection that turns the horse completely sideways (equivalent to a turn on the forehand) to bring him around in a circle to a stop (*see figure 15.2*). So the nudge should be light and pulsing.

If, on the other hand, the horse moves left toward you, aim your chi at the horse's shoulder. Again, light and less is best. Too much, and the horse accelerates away from you and may actually circle completely around, away from you. Your lead will then lay across the horse's shoulder, behind his head. You cannot correct him from this position unless you teach your horse how to neck rein (a task we won't tackle in this book). So avoid excessive chi. If it should happen, shrug it off. Get your horse straightened out and start over.

It takes a little trial and error to project the right amount of chi from the right and the left. Here's a little exercise that can help. With a stick, draw two parallel lines in the dirt, about four feet apart and forty feet or more in length. Allow your horse to walk ahead of you while you take up a position next to his hips. As you walk, correct your horse when he drifts out of the alley. Tug a bit on one side to pull him back; push on the other to keep your horse between the lines. Release your horse whenever

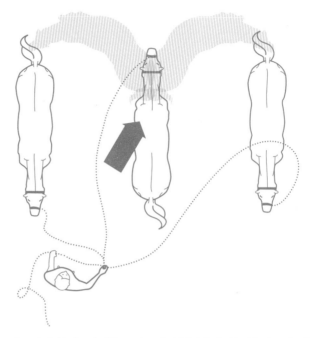

15.2 A horse moving straight ahead of the trainer (middle). Left side: The handler has over-corrected with a tug on the lead line, so the horse circles left and now faces the handler. Right side: The handler has overcorrected with excessive chi exerted on the left shoulder so the horse turns completely around to the right. The horse is now stopped, facing the handler, and the lead is across the horse's neck.

he's walking straight. It's wise to remember that some horses may need stimulation from behind to keep them stepping out ahead of the handler. The wand can be helpful for this part of the exercise.

Circle Ahead

■■■

TO GET YOUR HORSE TO CIRCLE, apply chi the way you did to move him forward. You'll check the horse with your lead so he begins to circle around you. At first, pay no attention to your feet. Just move your horse smoothly in a circle. Once he is circling reliably, slow your feet down. Let the circle traced by your feet on the ground grow smaller and smaller.

Ideally, the handler will eventually become the still center of a circle the horse is making along the rail. At first, use the fiberglass training wand (or longe whip) in combination with the lead so you can stimulate the horse from behind to move him forward; half-halts (or small, quick mini-tugs on the lead) will usually be all that's needed to encourage him to tip his head toward the center of the circle. If he tips his nose away from you, give a short, quick tug until his nose is pointed slightly back toward the center, toward you. If you have a horse that's a little weary or outright rude, he may try circling with his head carried far to the outside. Don't correct this with half-halts. With this horse you have to go back and practice yielding the hindquarters. He needs to understand that he must yield his hips, and then he'll automatically tip his nose toward you, at the center. Too heavy a hand with the lead, and the horse will simply fall out and frontally face up, and then just stop. As you learn to become quieter at the center of the circle, your horse orbits around you with greater ease and grace. By moving your feet less, your chi moves him for you instead.

FAR SIDE OF THE MOON   One universal problem when you're first teaching your horse to circle is that he will stop when he travels behind you (*see figure 15.3*); it's where your chi is least intense. While a few moms and teachers may have eyes in the back of their heads, the rest of us have

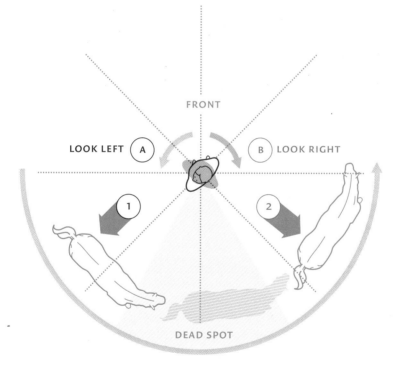

15.3 Here the horse is passing behind the trainer, where there is a space of low chi. It's important to help the horse keep up his impulsion until he learns to sustain his circling movement through this "dead spot."

to be content with our chi being most easily directed where we look. Your chi will push the horse around until he passes beyond your shoulder; then it fizzles out.

Reduce this patch of diminished chi by swiveling around on your hips. Take the horse as far behind you from one side as you can; then twist around quickly, so you pick the horse back up with your gaze on the other side as fast as possible.

The gap in chi behind us reminds me of what happened when the Apollo space capsules circled on the far side of the moon. For a brief phase of the orbit, the astronauts lost all radio contact with NASA. Back on Earth, there was a moment when everyone held a collective breath, till the spacecraft emerged on the other side and resumed communications. It's the same with your horse. You want him to pick up your signal as soon as possible, so limit how long your horse orbits behind you (on the far side of the moon) by quickly swiveling at the hips. Your horse will soon learn to pass behind you even with diminished reinforcement. As you work on this skill, you will need less chi to keep the horse circling; eventually you can stop turning all together.

A word of caution about using the 12-foot lead when circling horses. Most horses can slowly (but barely) lope in a circle with a 10- to 12-foot radius; a 14- or 20-foot lead is better suited for circling. Circling too fast on a short lead can put substantial stress on a horse's joints.

A variation on the circling game is to put ground poles at several points around the circumference of the round pen. This develops the horse's confidence and athleticism.

Circling at Different Gaits

■ ■ ■

CHANGING GAITS ADDS SPICE. As you accelerate, elevate. Swing the end of the lead upward to lift your horse's body while he increases the pace. Use vocal cues at the same time. *Walk*, *trot*, and *lope* all sound very different, and horses have no problem distinguishing among them. Let your voice enthusiastically rise when you ask your horse to accelerate. There should be a sharp, punctuated crescendo to the command *trot* when you ask your horse to speed up from a walk. When asking your horse to slow down to a trot from a lope, the command should be longer, lower, and slower (*trahhht*).

Chi is faithfully transmitted through your tone of voice. My horses can tell from one hundred paces if I'm approaching the barn wearing a grin or a frown simply by the tone of my voice when I call out their names.

Whether we project chi through our gaze or our tone of voice, each of us, knowingly or unwittingly, is engaged in a conversation with the Universe. To some extent, how eloquent that exchange becomes is a personal choice. We can be content to go through this life making inarticulate utterances, equivalent to grunts and whines, to the animals with whom we share this world; or we can be inspired by our fine interactions with the horse to tune our personal sensibilities. We can fashion ourselves into instruments. We can hope to add our individual music to the chorus of all living things.

ASPIRING TO A HIGHER LEVEL While it is fun to have our horses perform at high levels of sophistication, I see that as a less significant aspect of training and working with horses. Training horses allows us, as humans, to awaken to *what horses feel*. The round pen opens our ears and, eventually, our hearts.

We were all born into a flow of infinite energy. Our horse will be a horse, with or without our participation. But without our horse, we are less. We will be less able to give voice to the deepest parts of our soul — those parts that move us without words. Our horse has taught us that the experience of consciousness is the essence of self-awareness.

There is some danger that we pursue training exercises more for the sake of seeing enhanced performance rather than deepening the awareness within ourselves. Trust your heart. Your deepening mindfulness will engender greater trust and partnership from your horse. Your horse will perform at a higher level because his kinship with you will grow.

Backing Up

∎∎∎

A PERSON COULD SPEND an entire lifetime studying the variations and subtleties of backing up, one of the most important building blocks in the foundation of any horse's training. Horses are built to be forward-moving creatures. They're built for speed, like an automobile with six forward gears and a relatively paltry one for reverse. Given the choice, a horse will instinctively move forward or sideways rather than backward. He'll hop, jump, or vault to get around an obstacle or an unexpected surprise (like a rattlesnake) but rarely move backward. Why? Because horses want to use that huge, one-horsepower engine under the hood to get moving.

Backing up is broken down into a number of related maneuvers, based on whether horse and trainer are facing in the opposite or the same direction. It can be further subdivided by the method we use to apply chi to push our horse in reverse: lead rope, longe whip, or manual pressure. (A training wand with a rope can be substituted for a longe whip. The training wand is a more compact, manageable variant of the full-size longe whip.)

BACKING UP: LEAD ROPE   The lead rope is the simplest way to send chi against the front of the horse's chest and forelegs to get backward movement in his feet.

USING THE LEAD ROPE FROM ALONGSIDE   Earlier, we explored the variations of leading and then stopping our horse. We're going to start with the same maneuver we used to halt our horse. This time, when we stop him, we will send substantially greater amounts of chi out behind us to encourage him to back up. Think of it this way: we can lead a horse forward. When we decide to back him up, the horse has to stop. If our chi dies quickly, we get only a stop. If we keep up sustained chi that projects rearward, the horse continues from the stop to the back-up. The more intense the chi, the quicker and shorter the stop and the faster the horse throws himself into reverse.

You'll again want to implement a four-step ARDP process. The first step, the Ask, is to simply give the verbal command *back*, while slightly stiffening your spine and focusing your chi as it emerges from between your

DIRECTING CHI

Aiming your chi low is important for backing up. Focus your chi behind you, which requires greater intensity than does a direct forward gaze. You need to aim your chi low on the forelegs of your horse.

If you aim too high — say, at his neck or face — he will back up with his head held high. That will create a problem once you get him under saddle: he will tend to throw his head up to initiate a back-up. High-headedness makes a horse ungainly and out of balance, so avoid this complication.

Rearward chi when trainer is facing away from horse.

shoulder blades against the horse's front legs. Aim your chi deliberately *(see box, previous page)*. Note: pairing the verbal command with each step of the ARDP paradigm is reviewed in more detail in chapter 10.

For the next phase, the REQUEST, inflate your chest to make your trunk broader and more imposing; pair this with the command *back*. In the DEMAND phase, stick out your elbows and exaggerate your foot fall — stomp loudly — as you take a step backward. For the PROMISE, back right into your horse, again in conjunction with the verbal cue *back*. You have to be willing to physically ram your horse and even put a little elbow into your horse's chest or front shoulder to be sure that you get the desired response of one step backward.

Once you have received a response, begin to decrease the amount of chi applied to your horse. Again, obtaining any response backward is the important first step. Once the response is given, however, you must change gears. Now you need to work on subtlety. For a horse to back up elegantly, he must be relaxed. His neck must be bowed, with his head suspended well out over his front legs. His face should be vertical. All of these factors require your horse to be calm. For that to occur, your chi must evolve into a quiet, precise application aimed at or below the horse's chest. This will earn you a trusting, quiet response with a relaxed poll and neck.

It helps if you visualize your chi hitting the front of the horse's legs. It's common for horses to look down at the ground where your chi is focused. As the horse gazes down, guess what? The neck gradually becomes elegantly flexed, and the horse's face becomes vertical. So learning to handle and manipulate your chi lightly engenders an elegant response from your horse. As a general rule, grace creates grace. Nowhere is this physically translated as readily as in the world of horses.

Work progressively from a single step to multiple steps by keeping your chi rhythmic and pulsing. The horse can cue off the serial pulses to figure out how many steps to take. The rhythm of the pulses tells him how fast to go. As your horse becomes more comfortable with adding speed to the back-up, you'll notice his hind legs shift dramatically under his body.

USING THE LEAD ROPE WHILE FACING THE HORSE   It is important for your horse to back away on cue when you assume a squared-up position, facing him. To get this exercise under way, drop your horse's lead rope and simply do whatever it takes to get him to take one step backward. You'll figure out how to send out enough chi to ensure your horse will back up.

Usually this requires you to exaggerate your body size, with your shoulders out and your chest expanded. Emphasize your foot fall. If necessary, hang on to the lead instead, so you can add some wiggle into the rope to

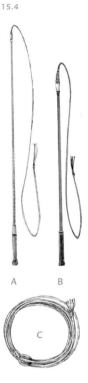

15.4

Longe whips (A), training wands (B), and lariats (C) are all training aids that amplify and focus the trainer's chi while working with horses.

help your horse get the point as you step forward. Focus your chi on his lower chest and forelegs. Once your horse is stepping backward with each cue, you will be able to turn down the amount of chi. Visualize your chi rising, getting bigger like a wave, then crashing on the front legs of your horse, and then dying out. Send another wave to get another step.

Once you are seeing a reliable response with each wave, work on fine-tuning your chi until you only need a simple, quiet body movement to ask your horse to back up. You can add more challenge by teaching your horse to negotiate backward through gates, in and out of stalls, and around obstacles such as tree trunks.

VIBRATING THE LEAD ROPE   Instead of asking your horse to back up as you walk back, you also want to ask him to step back away from you while you stand stationary, facing him. This approach is borrowed from Pat Parelli's "yo-yo" game; readers can refer to Pat's book, *Natural Horsemanship*, listed in the bibliography, for more details.

Employ the ARDP process. Start by slightly vibrating the lead rope to and fro a bit: Ask. Give the verbal command *back*. Repeat the verbal command in each phase of ARDP to help the horse make the association in his mind between the verbal command and the physical movement of taking a step back. In this Ask phase, the horse is capable of feeling the smallest vibrations and can easily choose to step back (*see figure 15.5*).

If the horse does not step back in response to a low-amplitude shaking of the rope, infuse more chi. Shake your lead more rhythmically: Request. Still no response? Follow up with vigorous, forceful shaking: Demand. Still no? Add a dramatic, darting, downward snap to your lead rope as you vigorously shake: Promise.

15.5 Vibrating the lead rope

Once your horse gets the idea to step back when the lead rope vibrates, work on using smaller amounts of chi until it's little more than shaking your finger back and forth. Play with longer lengths of lead: 20, 40, even 60 feet. Then for a little spice, see if you can get your horse to back up over obstacles or uneven terrain.

BACKING UP: LONGE WHIP   Whenever we're working with a longe whip, it is wise to move slowly. I liken longe whips to a microphone hooked up to a gigantic amp at a rock concert. All of sudden a quiet little whisper booms at high decibels. Whips, training wands, leads, lariats — all amplify chi, sometimes tremendously (*see figure 15.4*).

Full-size longe whips have an eight-foot stalk with a flexible ten-foot lash on the end. They can produce a loud snap. A trainer can set herself back quite a spell if things are overdone with the longe whip. So, to desensitize our horse to the longe whip, we're going fly fishing.

FLY FISHING   You want your horse completely comfortable around the longe whip. To avoid him flinching or hesitating, begin by lightly touching your horse all over with the whip end. Simply stroke your horse. Be sure to convey absolutely no chi — zero — through the whip. Take all the life out of the whip. Gradually increase the length of your stroke and the number of strokes. Once the horse is sure and steady, pass the flexible stringlike lash over the horse's back (*see figure 15.6*). Start softly; pull it from the far side back to the near side. This should be comforting and reassuring to the horse. Practice pulling the lash back and forth. Place it around the horse's neck and even his extremities. Then it's time to go "fishing."

15.6 "Fly fishing" — a method of desensitizing your horse to the longe whip

This is a good way to learn to control your chi. Draining all of the chi out of the whip permits you to cast the end of the whip back and forth over your horse's back. As your horse gets used to this maneuver, experimenting can become a lot of fun. First, help flick some flies away. Then work your way up till you can really start casting the longe whip as if you were fly fishing.

Go through this ritual with every horse you train. You want to completely abolish any dread or fear related to the whip. In this way, the horse soon learns the whip is merely an extension of your fingers. You put life into the longe whip. Your chi runs through it.

USING THE LONGE WHIP (OR WAND) FACING THE HORSE   Once your horse is at ease with the longe whip, you're ready to start backing him up using it. Start by facing your horse; use the ARDP process. Face your horse squarely from four or five feet away and verbally ask for a back-up: ASK. Next, elevate your chi by jiggling the longe whip (or wand) about four to six feet in front of the horse's forelegs: REQUEST. Increase the amplitude of the longe whip's movements where the horse's hooves meet the ground: DEMAND. Tap the horse across the forelegs: PROMISE.

USING THE LONGE WHIP (OR WAND) FACING AWAY FROM THE HORSE   Use the same ARDP process with the longe whip while standing alongside your horse. Stiffen your body and verbally ask for a back-up: ASK. Next, elevate your chi by jiggling your longe whip about three or four feet in front of your horse's forelegs: REQUEST. This jiggling in the Request phase is smaller in amplitude to when you were facing your horse. Increase the amplitude of the longe whip's movements where the horse's hooves meet the ground: DEMAND. Again, use less energy than when you were facing the horse. Tap the horse across the foreleg: the PROMISE.

MANUAL PRESSURE   The final method for getting your horse to back up is manual pressure (*see figure 15.9*). This is a convenient technique for backing up your horse in tight spaces. There are two techniques you'll employ: manual pressure on the nose and manual pressure behind the shoulder.

For the former, you will apply enough pressure on the bridge of your horse's nose to encourage him to take a step back. As soon as he responds by starting to lift his leg, remove the pressure. In fact, your hand should become soft and soothing.

The simple ARDP schema goes like this: simply put your hand on the bridge of your horse's nose and give the verbal command *back* to ASK. Add slight backward pressure from your hand: REQUEST. A firm grip and

15.7 Backing up with the training wand while facing the horse

15.8 Backing up with the longe whip while facing away from the horse

moderate backward pressure is the DEMAND. Squeeze across the nose to the point of pinching: the PROMISE. Release immediately with every step back.

Manual pressure applied to the girth line (*see figure 15.10*) can also be useful to back up your horse in tight spots (e.g., inside a trailer). Face the horse's hindquarters. Place the four fingers of your hand (if you are on the horse's left) behind his shoulder, approximately where the girth would lie. Start backing the horse up (you can use one of the earlier methods above to get the horse started backing up). Each time your horse prepares to lift his left hoof up to take a step back, put a little rearward pressure behind the shoulder. The vector of the chi you're applying should be aimed from the near shoulder to the far hip.

Release as soon as the horse's foot lifts off the ground. Repeat when the near foot is ready to rise again. Perform this on the right and left sides until your horse can cue off the pressure of your hand to back up. Begin to vary the pace at which you ask your horse to back up. Use the rhythm of your finger pressure to establish the pace. This will set the stage later (*see chapter 21, Stopping & Spooking*) for backing up under saddle.

Head Position and Resistance

■ ■ ■

A CRITICAL FACET of EQUINE behavior is "what resists persists." Nowhere is this more obvious than in how a horse holds his head. When a horse understands and accepts a situation, his head drops and his neck flexes. He relaxes. But when a horse is anxious or resistant, his head lifts and his neck stiffens.

Why? Because when a horse is unwilling or confused, he feels the need to flee. By raising his head, the horse is initiating the first phase of

WATCH WHERE YOU PUT YOUR CHI

You always need to be aware of where your chi is directed. Working with horses opens your eyes to the depth of the energetic connections you can modulate. Our brains were once better tuned to those energies, but we all have the ability to reawaken those latent abilities. Backing up in all its infinite variations, but especially with a longe whip or wand, really makes you focus on where you're directing your chi. With backing up, you can see even minute changes in your horse's responses.

15.9 Pressure applied to the nose to encourage the horse to back up

15.10 Manual pressure applied at the girth line to teach the horse to back up

preparing to leave. A rigidly fixed head and neck provides the horse with a long counterweight to help him spin around and depart. It can be a ballistic, explosive start, if need be.

When a horse's head goes up, it is a bad prognostic sign. The horse is not absorbing whatever you are trying to teach. You're messing up. Rethink what you are doing. A relaxed head position is the essence of backing up. It's worth focusing on how to get your horse to assume that flexed poll.

Carefully separate your releases: one for when the horse drops his head and a second one for backing up. Practice these two maneuvers at different times. First, work on your horse dropping his head. Exert downward pressure on the poll with the halter. When your horse flexes his neck down and drops his head, release. Work separately on your horse backing up: focus your chi onto the horse's legs and feet. Whenever he takes a step backward, release. When the two tasks are thoroughly learned with independent cues, then you can combine them.

Looking for the Relaxed Poll

···

RELAXATION OF THE POLL is the cornerstone for developing a horse that is soft, pliable, and calmly collected under saddle. Collection is the elevation of the horse's trunk, with his legs centered deeply beneath the rider.

It's similar to the difference between when you're simply standing erect in place and when you are getting ready to hop upward on both feet from a standing start. There's more power, spring, and collection — upward thrust — already imbued in your trunk. Collection is accompanied by the relaxation of the horse's neck and the rounding of his back, as the horse bears more weight than normal on his rear legs, to bring them closer to the horse's center of gravity.

A word of caution here: it takes time for a horse to develop the musculature to carry himself with both *impulsion* and *collection*. Such physical development can require months — years for maneuvers such as airs above the ground. Proceed with a thorough exercise regimen to build up solid muscle.

We can't cut corners when it comes to encouraging our horse to flex (or "break") properly at the poll. Furthermore, a wise trainer begins to incorporate this relaxed posture into everything a horse learns, because a stress-free horse is the best learner.

So many of the practices and rituals encoded in the world's great cultures and religions are aimed at achieving a state of physical relaxation. It is understood that this release of physical tension serves as a prerequisite to personal transformation. So it is with our horse. Relaxation of the poll — that great sweep of the neck, bowing like a branch heavy with fruit — is the hallmark of piercing equine intellect. It evokes not just a state of grace but also of intellectual keenness and spiritual eagerness.

The great spiritual traditions provide physical invocations — the chanting of monks, the postures of yoga, the sitting postures of *zazen*, the spinning ceremonies of the whirling dervishes — to bring about spiritual readiness. The horse's relaxation of the poll reminds us that only when we bow before the world do we truly open ourselves to its effect. The trainer who nurtures the lowering of the horse's head is paying homage to his or her partner's need to feel safe in the world before he can learn from it. As Nuño Oliveira reminded us: we must all strive "to awaken curiosity by the tenderness of... [our] aids."

15.11 This horse, with its sweeping neck and relaxed poll, was rendered by Leonardo da Vinci in 1480.

SENDING OUT & BACKING UP

213

Highlights

■ ■ ■

Rejoice in the first step.

■

Never lope on a short lead.

■

Use your voice as
a cue for your horse to speed up or slow down.

■

A low head carriage and relaxed poll are
the hallmarks of a horse with a
prepared mind.

TENDING TO HORSES

Fear is the main source of superstition, and one of the main sources of cruelty. To conquer fear is the beginning of wisdom.

• • •

BERTRAND RUSSELL

I N THE MID-1980S, I worked as a neurosurgical resident at Boston Children's Hospital. On my second day there, I spotted a group of children — none of them more than five years old — walking down the hallway. All were dressed in surgical garb, complete with caps and masks. A nurse was leading them around like a Pied Piper.

Out of curiosity, I followed them around the next corner to find out what was going on. Midget interns? Head Start program for cardiac surgeons? It turned out the children were scheduled to have their tonsils removed in a week's time. They were all part of an orientation tour so they would be more familiar with their surroundings on the actual day they would undergo their tonsillectomies.

The idea behind decking the children out in surgical gowns and masks was to reduce their fears about coming into the operating room, where everyone would be wearing the same apparel. I thought to myself: *What a great idea! We should do that for everybody who's scheduled for surgery — even adults.* Everyone feels trepidation being rolled into the operating room.

I was struck by how the staff exerted themselves to get the children accustomed to the feel of the surgical suite. Simulating the strange, foreign aspects of an encounter in the operating room reduced much of the fear and anxiety the kids would experience.

We all encounter the unexpected. The more sudden and novel the change, the greater the anxiety we experience. We need to practice for change. Simulation is one way that we can learn to anticipate the uneasiness and diminish anxiety. For example, take an upcoming job interview. It makes us nervous. So we might ask a friend to sit behind a desk and pretend to be the tough new boss who's going to grill us. We try to immerse ourselves in the circumstances that might make us uneasy. The greater lengths we go to faithfully reproduce the scenario, the more our level of reluctance dissipates.

Meeting the Farrier

■ ■ ■

THE FARRIER'S VISIT can produce stress in our horses, if we fail to prepare for it. In chapter 6, we reviewed many of the unusual elements farriers introduce when they arrive. It's a universe of sounds, smells, and sensations that, at first, may be overwhelming for a horse to grasp. I like Monty Robert's approach to training horses to stand politely for the farrier: reproduce all the sights and sounds that he may produce.

Getting Ready for the Vet

• • •

WE ALSO NEED to set the stage for when the vet comes for a couple of reasons. First, it puts the horses at ease. Second, there just aren't enough veterinarians to go around, so I'd rather none of them gets hurt.

I suggest four common veterinary tasks that we can train our horses to readily tolerate:

- Immunizations
- Deworming
- Examination of the mouth
- Insertion of a rectal thermometer

GIVING INJECTIONS   Obviously, horses need sedation for procedures like a pelvic examination or castration. I don't believe there's a lot of training we can do to prepare a horse for an actual surgical procedure. But most horses can be taught to stand steadily and quietly for shots. On the grand scale of what happens to horses (such as bites, kicks, and thorns) a little poke with a hypodermic needle probably is not too big a deal; nevertheless, we can make it easier for them.

For example, you can do many preparatory steps to get your horse ready for injections. You can practice tapping with the heel of the hand and darting an orange with the needle to get a good feel for the maneuver and coordinate your movements. But the practice that really counts is to just do it: start giving some immunizations, one or two at a time, to your horse. If you're not feeling confident, team up with a friend or a trainer who's comfortable doing injections. That way there's someone to talk you through your first few vaccinations. Finally, if all this stuff about needles and injections is freaking you out, call the vet and let a professional do it.

PREPARATION   First, use the smallest-diameter needle possible. Consider this: during acupuncture, the practitioner can place dozens of needles into the skin, and the patient experiences no pain because the needles are so thin. Hence the reason we want to use a small-diameter needle. But be prepared: there is a trade-off. The smaller the needle, the more time you will need to inject the contents of the syringe. The larger the diameter of the needle, the faster you will be able to discharge the contents of the syringe.

Remember: as the width of the needle goes up, the number of the gauge goes down. A 22-gauge needle (outer diameter 0.711 mm) is much easier to insert through the skin than a 14-gauge (outer diameter 2.108 mm). A 14-gauge needle is three times bigger. (Ouch!) Use a reasonably long needle; 1½ inches is fine. It needs a sharp bevel (tip) so it pierces the skin with little pressure.

Two rules help decide what size needle to use: first, the jumpier the horse, the larger the needle, because there will presumably be less time to give an injection if the horse won't stand still. Second, the more viscous, or thick, the liquid (like many antibiotics) to be injected, the bigger the diameter of the needle should be. Thick materials do not flow well through small-diameter needles (just as maple syrup is harder to sip through a straw than soda pop).

So my guidelines are as follows:

Gentle, steady horse $\longrightarrow$ **22 gauge**
Average, "may jump a bit" horse $\longrightarrow$ **20 gauge**
Jumpy and skittish horse $\longrightarrow$ **16 to 18 gauge**

The SYRINGE (the plastic part with the plunger that holds the injectable medicine) should also have a Luer Lock, because it ensures your needle is firmly attached to the syringe and the contents will not leak when you inject.

THE PROCEDURE STEP 1. Once you've decided on the injection site, rub it vigorously with an alcohol wipe. Not only does this scrub and remove dirt, but it also reduces the skin sensitivity by momentarily overstimulating the nerve endings.

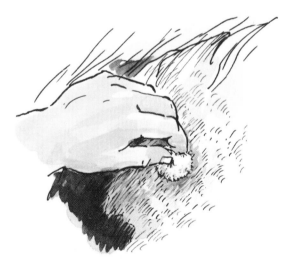

16.1 Wiping with alcohol

STEP 2. With the syringe still off the needle, pinch the skin up quickly with your nondominant hand. While holding the needle in your dominant hand as you would a dart, gently tap the site four or five times in rapid succession with the heel of that hand. This desensitizes the area.

STEP 3. On the final tap, stick the needle through the skin in one swift jab. Don't count. Don't hyperventilate. Just do it.

16.2 Inserting the needle

STEP 4. Now attach and lock the syringe to the needle by rotating the syringe onto the hub of the needle. Pull back on the plunger to ensure the needle is properly positioned (*see box on page 220*).

16.3 Attaching the syringe

PULLING BACK ON THE PLUNGER (ASPIRATING)

A critical piece of advice: always, always, *always* pull back on the plunger of the syringe before injecting, to be sure the needle is in the appropriate place.

If it's a **subcutaneous** (SQ, just under the skin) or **intramuscular** (IM, deep in a big muscle) injection, meaning the medication isn't going directly into a vein, pull back the plunger to be certain you have not accidentally hit a blood vessel. There should be no return of blood when you pull back on the syringe in this case.

If you want to give a medication **intravenously** (IV, meaning directly into the bloodstream), you must be sure you do see a strong return of blood in the syringe, and then you can inject smoothly into the vein (usually the jugular vein is the largest and most accessible for horses). Bottom line: no matter which way you plan to inject, *always* pull back on the plunger right before you're ready to inject.

To review:
- **SQ or IM:** If *NO* blood return, then inject.
- **IV:** If *YES* blood return, then inject.

STEP 5. Inject the contents of the syringe by pushing down on the plunger until all of the medication has been delivered. Withdraw the needle; cleanse and rub the site one more time. If it bleeds a little, usually all that's needed to stop it is to apply some pressure to it with a piece of gauze.

16.4 Pushing the plunger home

SPACE THE INJECTIONS   Don't try to give all seven seasonal immunizations to your horse at one time. Space out the injections. You wouldn't sit still for seven consecutive bee stings; don't expect any more from your horse. Give one or two at a time, spacing them out over several days and rotating injection sites.

DEWORMING Most horses don't need to be dewormed more than a couple of times a year. You can schedule deworming at your convenience.

The biggest problem with dewormers is we don't think about them until it's time to give them.

STEP 1. About a week before you are ready, get a couple of large jars of applesauce. Each day, load the applesauce into a squeeze bulb or 20- to 30- milliliter syringe (without a needle!). Tuck it in the corner of your horse's mouth, and squirt the applesauce in. Do this for one week just before deworming.

STEP 2. Your horse will begin to anticipate your arrival with a yummy syringe full of applesauce (*see figure 16.5*), so stick to a regular time of day, every day.

STEP 3. On the day you're ready to give the dewormer, just slip the deworming syringe into the horse's mouth and deliver deworming paste. Follow it up *immediately* with an applesauce chaser.

STEP 4. The real trick is to give the horse a taste of applesauce for a few days *after* you are have dewormed. Stick to the same daily schedule for three to four days. Your horse will soon put the unpleasant taste of the deworming paste behind him.

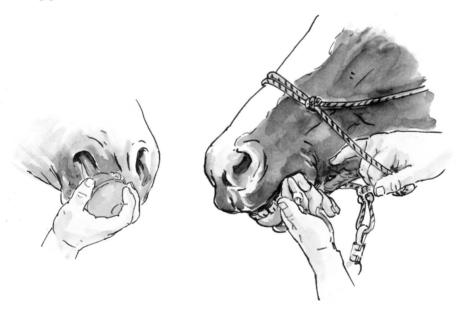

16.5 A bulb with applesauce as a precursor for worming paste (left); worming paste being administered (right)

EXAMINING THE MOUTH   Don't expect any horse to willingly allow a veterinarian to insert a large retractor between his jaws and rasp it on his teeth. That's what sedatives were made for. What we're discussing here is training your horse to allow you to look into his mouth. You want your horse to stand quietly and allow you to look at his teeth and tongue for a reasonable interval without throwing his head back.

START WITH THE LIPS   Start with small steps. First, get your horse accustomed to having his lips handled, by lightly picking up the edges. Every time your horse stands still and lets you play with his lips, stop, and let him have a momentary break. Then resume until he's comfortable with your handling his lips. Gradually increase the time you hold his lips apart (*see figure 16.6*).

Don't be tempted to let go when your horse shakes his head or throws it back. Hang on and make your horse realize that standing quietly will be the fastest way to get you to leave him alone. And don't overdo it. Do two or three trials and move on to something else.

ON TO TEETH AND TONGUE   After lifting the lips, inspect the teeth. Put your hand into the horse's mouth, placing two fingers between the bars of the mandible and maxilla, where there are no teeth (*see figure 16.7*).

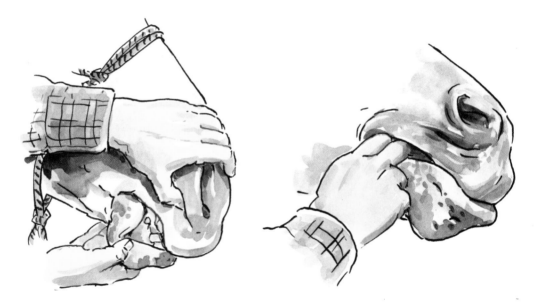

16.6 Holding the lips apart to begin examining the mouth

16.7 Placement of the fingers safely in the area between the "bars" of the mandible and maxilla

This is a safe place for your fingers. Let the horse get accustomed to your fingers exerting pressure on his tongue. Most horses will move their tongues to expel your fingers. Look for your horse to show the slightest yield — a fraction of a second when his tongue stops squirming. Help your horse find that instant, quickly remove your hand, and praise lavishly. Keep repeating these maneuvers until your fingers lying on the tongue between the bars of the mouth are almost second nature to him.

Once your horse calmly accepts your fingers in his mouth, start gently moving your fingers around a bit. Run your fingers along the outside of the teeth. Be attentive once you move your hands away from the relatively safe area between the bars of the mouth. Eventually, get the horse comfortable with his tongue being handled and gently held off to one side.

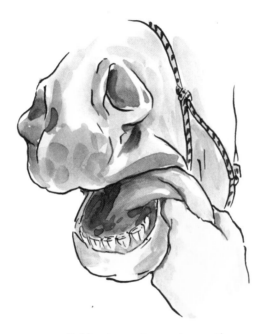

16.8 Holding tongue to examine mouth

BENEFITS   Aside from detecting oral health issues, there are other pay-offs. Your horse will be much calmer about taking a bit into his mouth if you have prefaced that experience by helping him be at ease with having his mouth manipulated. Accepting your fingers is a vital preparatory step to a horse calmly accepting the bit (*see chapter 20, A Leg Up*). The horse learns to open his mouth readily, and the metal bit can be gently slid between the upper and lower teeth.

TAKING A RECTAL TEMPERATURE   Horses don't like having their rear ends manipulated any more than we do — especially without sufficient warning. Before you stick a thermometer in your horse's rectum, it's worth educating your horse on what to expect.

- Start by raising and lowering his tail. Release the tail only when the horse relaxes it. Gradually hold the tail up for longer intervals.

- Practice taking his rectal temperature with a digital probe (the days of the old mercury thermometers are over, my friend).

- Practice when your horse is feeling well. Don't wait for him to be sick.

- A horse's temperature should run between 99° and 101°F. When a horse's temperature is 102°F or higher, it's time to call the vet.

- Always keep a firm grasp on the end of the rectal thermometer!

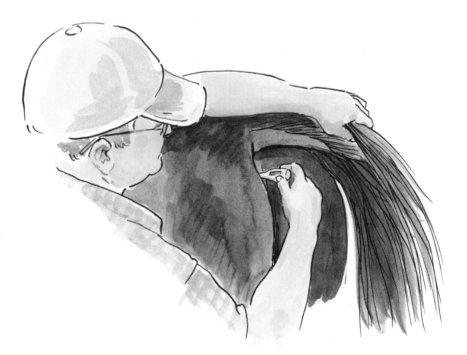

16.9 Taking rectal temperature

Closing Thoughts about Tending to Horses

■ ■ ■

I'M STRUCK BY HOW HORSES seem to be able to cue into when a human being is trying to treat them rather than hurt them. Several years back, we had a troublesome gelding at the ranch. Wild-eyed and disheveled, he looked as if he was waiting to pick a fight with any one of the handlers. As soon as a person entered his stall, he would swing around and line himself up so his hindquarters were cocked and loaded, ready to fire at the first individual who came too close. To most of us, he seemed "meaner than a junkyard dog."

Then he developed a bad case of the strangles, a streptococcal infection that causes huge, abscessed lymph nodes in the neck, often so large they choke off the windpipe (hence the name). Obviously, the development of such a condition is a life-threatening event. Antibiotics must be administered. Abscesses must be lanced, drained, and flushed. Warm compresses and heating pads must be applied diligently to the neck. Strangles means a lot of up-close work. So when it came to this gelding, we were just shaking our heads. There seemed to be no way we would ever be able to get that close to the animal, let alone carry out all those ministrations at multiple intervals during the day. But if we did nothing, he would perish. We decided to go into his stall and at least try. I expected that the first time I went into his stall, I was going to get my head knocked off by two ballistic blows from the hindquarters.

Even though many of the procedures and maneuvers to lance and drain the boils were painful, the gelding was placid and tranquil. I was dumbfounded. Two or three times a day, for ten days in a row, I would irrigate abscesses, pack open wounds, give antibiotic injections, and wrap his neck in layers of warm packs and towels. He never offered so much as a grunt, a flinch, or a hint of fearful reaction.

For me, taking care of that horse was a magical turning point. First, it reminded me that we exhibit different aspects of our characters under different circumstances. In some situations, our compassionate intent seems to shine from within and tame the most savage heart. The experience emphasized a point: don't rush to judgment about someone's deep, inner persona — equine or human. Obviously, there was a horse with a great heart in there, one that could bond and form a special relationship with his caretaker. I suspect he somehow knew that we were trying to save his life — trying hard. He sensed we meant him no harm and were genuinely worried about the pain and suffering he was enduring.

The combination of compassion emanating from all of the handlers and the horse's personal sense of vulnerability created within him an eagerness to bond. To this day, he remains one of the friendliest, most social horses in our stable.

How different things might have been, I think, had he not developed a case of the strangles. I might never have grown to love him, and he might never been given the chance to become the cherished member of our barnyard family that he is today.

Sometimes the right hemisphere connects, while the left side stands by, dumbfounded. The latter reviews its rationalizations, explanations, and strategic plans, suffering from paralysis through analysis. The right shows us a clear path to action, drawn by intuition, based on a hunch, and, usually, illuminated by passion, too.

Highlights

■ ■ ■

Simulate ahead of time
as many as possible of the farrier's
and vet's activities.

■

Use the smallest needle
and the fewest sites you can for injections.

■

Always pull back on the syringe plunger to
check on blood before injecting.

■

Worming calls for applesauce.

■

Tending to your sick horse
is the opportunity of a lifetime to
bond with him.

SIDE-PASSING & JUMPING

There is something about jumping a horse over a fence,
something that makes you feel good. Perhaps it is the risk,
the gamble. In any event it's a thing I need.

● ● ●
WILLIAM FAULKNER

S IDEPASSING AND JUMPING may seem to belong in an advanced set of drills, like dressage or hunter-jumper classes. Under saddle, there may be some truth to that, but on the ground they represent essential skills that call on us to fine-tune our abilities to use and understand chi.

Teaching your horse to sidepass (called a *leg-yield* under saddle), requires you to exert chi against the entire side of the horse. You've already mastered getting your horse to move his hindquarters and forequarters separately. For the sidepass, you'll simply combine them together. The sidepass is a requisite piece of groundwork training to teach your horse to be coordinated and agile in his footwork. It also puts elegance into the horse's lateral movements, improves strength in the legs, and ultimately yields a horse with better muscle strength and coordination for events like jumping and steeple chase, trail rides and working cattle.

Sidepassing

■ ■ ■

MAKE THINGS EASY FOR YOURSELF by beginning to train your horse to sidepass while facing the rail (*see figure 17.1*), to block forward movement. Most horses will readily move either their forequarters or hindquarters but, at first, rarely both together. You will help the horse by sending your chi to whatever part of the body is lagging behind. If he moves with his head farther away from you than his hips, then you need to pressure the

17.1 Sidepassing against the rail

hindquarters to catch up. On the other hand, if his head is closer to you, then apply chi to the forequarters and neck.

A longe whip (or training wand) comes in handy here. The length of the longe whip (or wand) allows you to easily apply chi in three directions: pivoting the tip horizontally toward the forehand moves the shoulder away from you, while tipping the handle toward the hips moves the hindquarters away. Moving the full length of the whip up and down vertically, parallel to the horse's flank, creates pure sideways movement.

Also teach your horse to sidepass away from the railing. Move your horse to the center of the round pen and ask for lateral movement. Check any tendency for your horse to step forward by using small half-halts (easy, brief, tapping pressure) on your lead rope. If the horse tries to step back, shift the chi behind the horse with the lead or wand to help correct the mistake.

It's fun to ask your horse to sidepass along the length of a ground pole, a railroad tie, or even a full-fledged log. Ask him to step sideways through a large gate opening, and for a real challenge, ask him to sidepass back and forth over uneven terrain and obstacles.

EFFORT AND REWARD   This is a tough endeavor for the horse, and we must look for the slightest momentary successes. Students sometimes apply additional pressure on their horses because the sidepass wasn't executed perfectly. In the process, they overlook a thousand little efforts that could and should have been rewarded.

Jumping

...

IN EARLIER SECTIONS, we sent our horse out over obstacles. In the round pen, we can introduce our horse to several jumps that have been placed radially along the circumference of the pen.

To start, walk your horse over these obstacles. Then encourage him to circle around, taking the jumps in succession. In the beginning, many horses will try to evade the jumps, often trying to skirt to the inside. Patiently insist that he tackle the jumps. Assume an attitude of insistence and inevitability. Your body language and application of chi gently inspire the horse to understand: "It is already written that you will make this jump. I must simply show you the way to accomplish this."

Again, in the end it boils down to the trainer's mindset: he or she must search for a way that the horse can *pass* over the jump before he is required to *face* it. This means letting him get over the jump before he turns it into a psychological obstacle.

For example, your horse might balk at a three-foot-high jump, but he will hardly notice a pole lying on the ground; he will walk over it dozens of times. If you then raise the pole in small enough increments, the issue of confronting the jump will never arise in your horse's mind. If you sense significant psychic resistance when you increase the height of the jump, then go back and set the jump low enough to not trigger an anxious, faltering reaction in your horse.

This is the essence of the art of training: to thoughtfully melt away the obstacle in the horse's mind, so that his action can blossom without interference.

JUMP CONSTRUCTION

When working a horse over jumps, gradually build up both the height of the jump and its mass. Start with jumps made of relatively small two-inch diameter polyvinyl chloride (PVC) pipe.

Once the horse can easily and calmly clear a certain height, switch to wider six-inch diameter PVC pipe, so the horse perceives more visual mass and picks up his feet.

PVC pipe is light and flexible and poses no risk to the horse's legs. Eventually, jumps can be constructed out of anything, including wooden planks, poles, and fifty-gallon plastic drums.

HEADING OFF HESITATION   As you gradually increase the height of the jump, use a longer lead line. Your horse will need more room to build up the necessary speed and impulsion. As he collects himself, approaching the jump, there is usually an instant when you can see him deciding whether to balk or jump. Scrupulously avoid letting your horse develop any habit of dwelling in that moment of hesitation. Look for that first sign that he might hesitate, stop him before he balks, and lower the jump. Don't create a scenario where your horse learns the habit of balking.

CONCENTRATING THE CHI   Your horse needs to coil like a spring, concentrate his chi, and then launch into an explosive release over the jump. It is up to you as the trainer to help him with the timing and feel of this build-up of chi. The concentration of chi in the horse right before a jump can be prodigious, especially in animals with a natural proclivity for jumping.

The best jumpers have an innate ability to pause for a fraction of a second before they launch themselves, as their kinetic energy builds. If you get a chance to watch great riders in competitive jumping, you will see how much forethought and strategy the rider applies to pacing his or her horse to allow him to build up, launch, and release his energy through the jump.

MUSCLE AND MIND   Let your horse gradually build his muscles and improve his conditioning for jumping. Teaching a horse to jump with a rider on his back requires a whole new layer of training, but the entire foundation is established on the ground before the rider swings a leg up on the horse.

The obstacles a horse confronts in jumping are only as big as he perceives them to be. The trainer must operate within the animal's innate abilities yet also create new opportunities for him to learn and apply those abilities. Some horses break out in a sweat at the lowest of jumps; others exalt at the opportunity to jump higher. Much of such jumping ability is genetic. If the parents are great jumpers, there's a high likelihood the offspring will take to it.

The greatest jumpers are born with a fearless, almost defiant quality in the face of jumps. There's no holding back such a horse. The trainer's task is to patiently improve that horse's conditioning without ever damaging his enthusiasm. But for all horses, jumping is always more an issue of mind than muscle.

QUIETING OUR FEET We can create loop after loop and switch directions doing figure-8 exercises around 50-gallon drums (*see box, below*). This exercise helps us focus on our footwork. We want to gradually diminish how much we shift our feet.

As we work on quieting our feet, our visceral connection with our chi becomes fluid. Energy streams between us and our horse. Your feet no longer move at all. Then your horse sweeps within inches around you, with a thrilling sense of his tremendous power. You experience the same excitement a matador feels when the bull rushes past the sweeping cape.

PUTTING IT ALL TOGETHER WITH FIGURE-8s

We all have favorite drills. Figure-8s around two barrels are one of mine. A good figure-8 requires grace and flow from both horse and trainer, with chi shifting seamlessly between them. The eventual goal is to do the exercise without moving your feet.

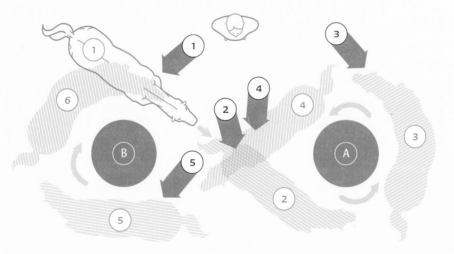

1. If you send your horse in a counterclockwise direction around barrel A, you'll apply chi to the left shoulder first (see position 1 in the drawing above).

2. You'll next apply chi behind the horse's rump (position 2).

3. As the horse comes around barrel A and returns toward you (position 3), you'll need to quickly shift hands so the lead is in your right hand.

4. Push the horse across by applying chi to his right shoulder (position 4).

5. Apply chi again to the horse's rump as he circles clockwise around barrel B (position 5).

6. In position 6, the horse prepares to begin the cycle all over again.

Highlights

■ ■ ■

*Sidepass using the rail to
block the horse's forward movement.*

■

*Control all three points for sidepassing:
shoulder, flank, and hindquarters.*

■

*Inexperienced horses need smaller, lighter,
and lower jumps.*

■

*A jump should never become a
psychological obstacle for your horse.*

■

*In a perfect figure-8 maneuver,
your feet never move.*

CHAPTER EIGHTEEN

COME TO ME

If you have it, it is for life. It is a disease for which there is no cure. You will go on riding even after they have to haul you onto a comfortable wise old cob, with feet like inverted buckets and a back like a fireside chair.

■ ■ ■

Monica Dickens

FEW THINGS CAN MAKE YOU feel as foolish as walking up to the pasture gate, halter in hand, calling out your horse's name with warmth and affection, and seeing him take off in the opposite direction. At first, you reassure yourself, *Oh, he probably ran off because he just didn't recognize me!* It must be a case of mistaken identity. Just so your horse can get a better look, you amble across the entire length of the pasture. Now he gets an even better look at you and runs off again. You resort to chasing him, but you tire long before he does. He looks back at you, as if to say, "Silly human, did you think you could catch me?"

Few things make an equine aficionado's heart soar higher than when our horse jogs up to greet us, and there's little that disappoints us more than when he rejects us. But, in the final analysis, as handlers and trainers, we're not seeking popularity as much as teamwork. One of the hallmarks of teamwork is responsiveness. So we need to train our horse to come to us when we call — not because it means he likes us but because he respects us.

The Twin Principles

■ ■ ■

ADHERING TO TWO PRINCIPLES will ensure your horse comes to you on command:

1. Never ask him to come unless you're certain you can get the response you're looking for.

2. The less sure you are of his response, the less space you give for an answer.

Another way of putting this is: when you're confident your horse will come to you, you can give him more space and freedom to roam than when you are not confident. When you have little or no faith he will come to you on command, you must have the ability to compel him to do so by confining him to a smaller space.

You want to reinforce a strong habit within your horse of always coming when you call. At first glance this may sound stern, but it is not meant to be. You don't teach your child how to ride a bicycle by enrolling her or him in the Tour de France. You start out on a quiet street, with your hand firmly on the back of the bicycle seat. It is the same for getting your horse to come up to you.

Both Eyes on Me

• • •

With that in mind, you'll start testing if your horse will return to you in the round pen, not in the Gobi Desert. First, you need to establish that he focuses on you with both eyes. This is the critical first step in getting your horse to come to you.

Step 1. As he circles the round pen on the rail, move your body and — most importantly your stare — in front of him, to get your chi focused in front of his ISL (intrascapular line; *see chapter 13, Picking Up the Pace*).

Step 2. Slow your horse down by applying chi in front of his ISL (*see figure 18.1*). Apply the chi at low intensity, or obliquely to the direction of travel, until he slows down. If you increase the level of chi directly against the horse's face and chest, you'll get a full stop.

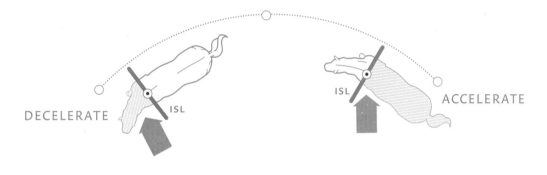

18.1 Chi applied behind the horse's ISL ⟶ forward progress or acceleration
Chi applied ahead of the ISL ⟶ deceleration

Step 3. Once your horse comes to a stop, diminish the intensity of your chi enough to hold him in place on the rail with your stare. Too much, though, and he will start to turn away (making an outside turn toward the rail, showing you his rear end in the process — a definite no-no).

Step 4. Let your chi diminish in its intensity a slight bit more. Lowering your gaze to the ground is usually enough to encourage the horse to move off the rail and look toward you (*see figure 18.2*).

If you want to speed things up or if your horse's focus (i.e., looking at you with both eyes) begins to drift, you can accomplish this by putting pressure on the hindquarters, sending him a cue to turn his rear end away from you. Clinton Anderson, the famous Australian horse trainer,

Breathe in deeply through both nostrils. Do not expand your lungs to their limits but rather let them fill, almost sagging open like a bucket. Pause.

Now let the air seep out of you, almost of its own accord. Let it escape through your mouth. Press the tip of your tongue against the roof of your mouth.

Make the air pass around it with the slightest whistling noise as you exhale. This ensures that your chi falls dramatically in intensity.

18.2 Just shifting your gaze to the ground will decrease the amount of chi applied to the horse so he will turn off the rail toward you.

always reminds his students that the fastest way to get a horse to give you his head is to pressure his hips. He likes to say, "Two eyes are better than two hooves."

STEP 5. Create a vacuum of chi at the center of the round pen to draw the horse to you. There are two ways to diminish the chi at the center. The first is to reduce your chi by breathing deeply and gently.

Use intentional breathing (*see box, above*) method to enter a state of surrender, of humility. This is the kind of breathing Lillian used to calm Romeo down, as described in the introduction of this book.

Chi Sinking into the Ground

■ ■ ■

THE SECOND WAY you can quickly reduce the amplitude of your chi is to send it into the earth, snaking into the ground beneath your feet. Visualization is critical to this maneuver. Much as the earth is a sink or ground for electricity (whether household current or lightning), it can also absorb an infinite amount of the chi we generate as individuals. By picturing your chi exiting through the soles of your feet and sinking deep into the layers

18.3 A horse relaxing at the center of the round pen with the handler: the essence of the peaceful bond between horse and human.

below, you cause it to leave, emptying the space around you so it becomes devoid of chi.

The center then becomes a zone of zero or negligible energy that attracts your horse (*see figure 18.3*). It becomes a very tranquil, unperturbed space — with one significant proviso. We regenerate chi with every thought, heartbeat, or blink of an eye, so we must guard ourselves from *reaccumulating* chi. We must constantly breathe our chi down and keep relinquishing it into the planet below.

If you are vigilant about attending to shedding your chi, your horse will inevitably move toward you, as if drawn by a magnet. He will feel rewarded by your allowing him to stand quietly near you, basking in the peace of the limpid epicenter without chi.

Inviting Your Horse In

■ ■ ■

To bring your horse to you, stand at an angle of approximately 45 degrees behind his ISL. This provides an obvious, inviting space for your horse to enter. You have opened an energetic door; your body position invites him to come through it.

This position also allows you to apply chi to the horse's hip to help the hindquarters move over and drive him forward. Think back to the earlier exercise, when moving behind the ISL encouraged the horse to circle inward toward the handler. Here we're doing the same thing: inviting the horse to circle in toward us from the outside rail to the center of the round pen.

It's best to first try out these exercises and practice them when your horse has worked a bit and is somewhat fatigued, eager to find a place in

18.4 Using the long longe line to help teach the horse to turn inward and come off the rail.

the training program to rest and catch his breath. This enhances his motivation to seek relief by standing beside you.

What should you do if your horse doesn't turn in and come to you? The answer requires a bit of judgment on your part. If he doesn't immediately turn and start moving toward you, send him off to make a couple more circuits around the round pen. Then try to reel him back in toward you. If that doesn't work, send him back on the rail for a few more laps around the pen. Finally, you can use a long longe line to help guide your horse to turn away from the rail toward you (*see figure 18.4*).

COLLECTING WITH "SUGAR"   Earlier in the book, we discussed the fact that typical food rewards do not work well with prey animals. A dog can be motivated to run toward you by a bit of dog biscuit. It's difficult to use a piece of a carrot or apple to make your horse move more quickly. The main objection to rewarding a horse with tidbits is that he starts getting "mouthy," constantly poking and prodding (and violating personal space) when he detects the smell of a treat in your pocket.

Try to overcome this tendency with a little reverse psychology. Remind yourself: as *otancan*, you have the right to carry a treat in your pocket and to give or withhold it as you choose. You can carry snacks around all the time; it does not mean you are inviting encroachment into your space. But you can also exercise the option of giving a treat — at your invitation and on your terms — for a job well done. Finally, never give a treat to your horse when he asks for one. That just invites more requests. A treat is your gift, so make it entirely your choice.

There are plenty of good hands at my ranch, and we all get along well. But we are also not above competing against each other. One of our best

It is your job as trainer and *otancan* to remind your horse he has a choice to make: come stand peacefully next to you, or keep moving. That said, be on the lookout for even the tiniest flinch — it may be little more than an imperceptible feint — in your direction. Reward the try instantly. In short, you wait patiently, stalking the moment when you can immediately reward.

trainers used to tease me about my horse jogging off when I went to collect him in his pasture. Well, I got tired of the ribbing, so I worked secretly to train my horse to always come to me when I went out to collect him.

It took me about two weeks, but pretty soon my horse was running over to greet me whenever I appeared at the pasture gate with a halter and lead rope in my hand. The secret was that every time I walked out in the pasture, my horse received a treat after the halter was on. Pretty soon, my horse would duck his nose into the halter, trying to earn that treat each time. After a while, I was the one teasing my colleague about how slow and sluggish *his* horse was to greet him when he went to collect him.

"Yeah," he said, "how do you get them to come a-runnin' like that?"

Well, a little treat works wonders.

The Horse Who Resists

■ ■ ■

WHILE YOU CAN USE TREATS, don't tolerate a horse that resists being collected. Ignoring a signal from the *otancan* is disrespectful. If you get the cold shoulder when you walk out into the pasture to collect him, don't try to bribe your horse! There's a world of difference between a reward and a bribe.

GO BACK TO THE CERTAIN OUTCOME   If your horse refuses to be collected, walk away. Gather your thoughts. This is where it pays to think rather than act. If he is in a five-acre open pasture, it is not the time or place for you to remind him about being collected. We discussed earlier that you need to virtually *guarantee* he will respond to you. Well, you can't be very certain of the outcome if he has five acres in which to evade you.

Next time, turn your horse out in a small pasture or the round pen. You need a small enough space so that you can remain confident about keeping him circling at liberty until you've impressed upon him that he has to make a choice: keep moving or come to you. You're going to use the conservation of energy principle to make your point. When you've succeeded and your horse walks up to you to be collected, be magnanimous, not vindictive. Step back. Make room for him to step into a quiet place next to you.

If he balks and refuses to be caught, then "it's time for a few more laps," as football coaches say. Nine times out of ten, he has only shown a small slip in judgment. It usually will take only a lap or two to remind him about how to respond properly to his training.

Once your horse is responding consistently to being collected, turn him into a larger pasture. Try collecting again. Problem? Back to the smaller enclosure. Success? Back to a bigger turn-out area.

Try *not* to invest your ego in this exercise. Restrain yourself if you feel compelled to teach your horse a lesson. This rule pertains as much to people as it does to horses: when you're trying to teach someone (or some creature) a lesson, it's probably going to send a very different message from the one you intended. That's because when you're intent on proving you're in charge, you're not.

Don't lose your cool with horses. Remind yourself: this is a creature with a brain less than a tenth the size and complexity of yours. Do you really believe it's a fair contest to match wits with a horse? You want to remind him of how he *should* behave, not punish him for how he *did* behave.

Removing the Halter
the Polite Way

■ ■ ■

REMEMBER: WHENEVER YOU'RE INTERACTING with your horse, you're either teaching him something or being taught by him. Taking the halter off is a perfect example of that principle. Many owners put up with rude and surly behavior when they remove the halter from their horse and prepare to turn him loose. This is especially true around dinnertime, when the horses are being released into their stalls. They're anxious to get to their grain and hay, and they may throw their heads back, jerk free from the halter, spin around, and make a bee-line for their food.

Not only is such behavior disrespectful, but it's also dangerous. Teach your horse to stand quietly while you take off his halter and to wait until he is dismissed. A treat right after you remove the halter can perform wonders: he will stand there waiting for it. Gradually increase the interval you make him stand before you give the treat. You will be gratified by your horse's polite patience.

Highlights

■ ■ ■

*Never ask your horse to come
unless you're sure he will.*

■

*One judicious treat
can save a month of training.*

■

*Treats in your pocket should never
make your horse nosey.*

■

*Your horse should always
stand quietly after you remove
his halter.*

FROM SACK TO SADDLE

Things are in the saddle, And ride mankind.

■ ■ ■

RALPH WALDO EMERSON

S ACKING OUT IS PRACTICALLY a lost art — a pity, because it holds the key to preparing your horse for being saddled and, more importantly, to resolving any tendency he may have to spook. It is the most essential ingredient to make your horse safe.

Sacking Out

■ ■ ■

THE TERM *SACKING OUT* refers to a process of systematic desensitization. A piece of cloth (initially a burlap sack, hence the name) is used to rub down the flanks of a horse until he becomes gradually less nervous and skittish about being touched, handled, and eventually saddled.

START WITH A WASHCLOTH   For this process, always have your horse on a loose lead. Don't hitch him up; instead, give him plenty of room to move around and, if necessary, to spook in place. To begin, you'll need a grooming brush, a washcloth, and a coiled lead rope.

First brush out your horse's coat as you would during your usual grooming routine. Let your mind seep into the brush. Imagine the fibers passing to and fro with each breath. Brush to acquire a mind-set of profound patience.

As you breathe and brush, your horse will enter a deeper state of relaxation, visibly sagging into your touch. When this happens, cover the brush with the washcloth. Use gradually more cloth and less brush for each stroke. Let the brush fade, and allow the washcloth to gradually "blossom" — to unfurl. Let it flap back and forth more energetically.

Always check that the horse remains within the bounds of his comfort zone. This is not an exercise in subterfuge but in persuasion. You've already painlessly, imperceptibly guided your equine companion across the first bridge in the journey: he's now comfortable with a flapping washcloth, something that would have spooked him earlier. Some call this process bombproofing, but it really is about desensitizing the horse to sensory and auditory stimuli. We managed to make a flapping washcloth replace a familiar brush — without trauma or coercion.

HANDLING THE HORSE'S AGITATION   Occasionally, a horse will come out of his reverie and startle when he suddenly perceives the washcloth. Relax: the battle is already won. You need to remind him it was just the same washcloth passing over again. Reduce the size of the cloth to fist-size and go back to stroking with it. Return your horse to a peaceful state of

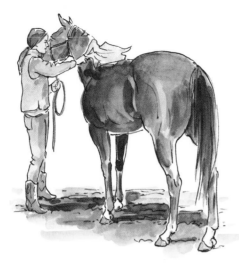

19.1 Sacking out with a washcloth

19.2 Sacking out with a lead rope

19.3 Sacking out with a saddle blanket

19.4 Sacking out with a plastic bag. This is one of the best training tools to help your horse develop a calm demeanor.

mind and then allow the cloth to resume its expanded size. Remove the washcloth when the horse is standing still.

This point is key: do not stop sacking out when the horse gets agitated. Stopping would teach your horse that his reaction — panicking, spooking, getting jumpy — makes you withdraw the scary object. You want the opposite mentality to sink in: you want to encourage calming down, relaxing, and assimilating. When the horse becomes quiet and calm, that is when the scary object is withdrawn.

The more the horse assumes a calm demeanor, the more quickly the object or experience evaporates. You want your horse to use this principle to think his way out of scary situations rather than blindly react to them. To the extent that you can teach this to your horse, you can replace instinct with habit.

TRANSFORMING THE MONSTER

There's something approaching sorcery in those good training moments when you can help slay a monster for your horse. The potentially dangerous serpent that could have come to life within the lead rope is slain. Patience, persistence, and love have helped you transform the serpent into nothing more than a simple rope.

THE SERPENT IN THE LEAD ROPE   We progress from sacking out with a washcloth to using a lead rope. Second verse, same as the first. Breathe the horse down. Introduce the coiled lead over the washcloth. Start in those areas where he feels most secure: the shoulders, neck, flank. The horse seem relaxed? Great.

Now focus your attention on the coiled lead. Now begin "brushing" the horse with the coiled rope in your hands. Gradually loosen your grips on the loops of rope. Eventually the loops become longer, the free ends begin flopping back and forth. The lead becomes more and more like a snake that can wiggle back and forth across your horse. Ultimately you want to accustom your horse to having the lead rope flopping and bumping along any part of his body. We want him to feel perfectly at ease if that lead rope swings all the way under his belly and between his legs.

Once the rope is uncoiled to its full length, swing it to touch the more ticklish or sensitive areas. Ultimately, there should be no area on your horse that cannot be touched with the lead. You can let it flop anywhere and your horse remains calm and at peace. That's magic.

THE TERRIBLE TOWEL AND OTHER PREDATORS   Then travel from one bridge to the next. Take your horse from the loathsome lead to the terrible towel. Then cross the bridge to the predatory plastic bag (*see figure 19.4*) and on to the behemoth beach blanket. Next, the terrifying tarp. Eventually you'll get the horse accustomed to being touched everywhere, especially his legs and belly, by the saddle itself. You're on a hero's epic journey, slaying monsters along the way.

EXPANDING THE COMFORT ZONE   You name it, you can desensitize your horse to it. The overarching principle is: never proceed to a new challenge until you have completely desensitized your horse to the preceding one. And never proceed beyond what your horse finds comfortable. I hesitate to use the word *comfortable* in this context because, by definition, you are asking the horse to expand his comfort zone, and that can only happen when you help him stretch emotionally in the face of new stimuli.

19.5 Sacking can never start too early. This six-week-old foal is standing at ease on a tarp with loops of lariat dangling about his back and legs. A safe, confident horse emerges from such experiences.

19.6

Mounted police officers in a crowd. These horses have learned to handle random noise, and even jostling, without overreacting — a testament to both trainers and horses.

The more you push your horse to allow new objects and experiences into his world, the more faith in you he will express by inserting learned responses in place of instinctual ones (*see figure 19.6*).

No creature, human or equine, can ever afford to completely sever its connections to innate survival reflexes. And prey animals, including horses, are hardwired by millions of years of evolutionary pressure to quickly access those primitive responses.

BENEFITS OF BOMBPROOFING In terms of bombproofing your horse, of helping him learn to squelch some of his flight responses in exchange for learned ones, the benefits of sacking out are infinite. And, one day, these lessons could save a life.

One of the most frightening episodes I ever experienced came on an idyllic Saturday morning. My ten-year-old daughter Tessa and I went horseback riding in an *arroyo* near my ranch. It was one of those fresh mornings when the air crackled, and, in our rush to ride out, I forgot to recheck the girth on her pony's saddle — a terrible oversight on my part.

As happens so often, the girth loosened as the pony warmed up during the ride. We began dropping into the sandy bottom of a wash. The pony braced his front shoulders as he began to descend the embankment, and I watched in horror as my daughter and the saddle suddenly slid off to one side. She dropped to the ground, her foot stuck fast in the stirrup, while the saddle slid all the way around and hung off the pony's flank. His hind hooves stood inches away from my daughter's head on the ground.

My heart stopped. I cannot imagine what might have unfolded if that pony panicked. But I had worked months earlier to sack out this pony with a saddle. Part of that process involved letting the saddle slide off to one side, with ropes and burlap sacks hung down among his legs. And now the pony, bless his little heart, stood stock-still like a statue. Not a twitch.

I lifted my daughter out of the way and gave a silent prayer of thanks for that pony's sterling character. Since that episode, I sack out every horse I train with a saddle. I work my way up to letting the saddle flop all over: off the rump, off the withers, and, most importantly, hanging from a loose girth. Oh, yes, I also developed a "pre-flight' checklist before heading out on the trail to ensure I always, always double-check the girths.

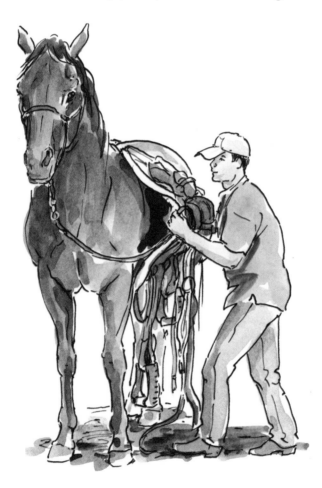

19.7 Sacking out with a loose saddle

Taking the Bit

■ ■ ■

INSTALLING THE BIT needs to be done respectfully and gently. Start with the head and neck if you want to end up in the mouth. Teach your horse to readily lower its head and tip its nose toward you; the bit will be easier to install after that. Earlier in the book (*see chapter 15, Sending Out & Backing Up*) where we covered backing our horse up, we used the lead rope and halter to teach our horse to flex at the poll and lower his head. Now we want our horse to tip his nose toward us. There are two ways to do this. The first is to use the lead rope and give it a series of half-halts or tugs to bring the horse's face and nose toward you. The second approach is to reach around, either under the horse's jaw or over his poll and put pressure on the far cheek. When the horse moves away from the pressure, the nose will start to get closer and closer to you. Every time the horse moves his nose closer to you release the pressure and pet him. Gradually he'll learn that your hand being on that cheek is a cue to tip is nose toward you.

FIRST REVIEW THE BASICS   Ask yourself this series of questions:

1. IS YOUR HORSE COMFORTABLE HAVING HIS FACE AND EARS HANDLED FOR GROOMING? If not, go back and teach him to get over headshyness first. If your horse is headshy, you must essentially start a "sacking out" process just for his head alone. If he won't let you touch him around his head or ears, then you start by petting his head and ears so quickly that he simply can't react to it. You swipe your hand past his ears or eye or whatever part of the head you need to address as fast as you can. Gradually you then slow the speed of the petting down. As long as your horse accepts it, continue to lower the speed of the petting. If he balks, speed up your hand-swiping back to a level so he can't react. Is he calming back down again? Then try slowing your hand speed down again.

Once your horse is comfortable with your petting and stroking all over his face, return to the sacking out process. As you pet your horse's face, put a balled up washcloth in there. Gradually increase its size by unfurling it. Use exactly the same process and strategies we on sacking out. We need to be sure our horse is past any issues of headshyness before we move on to placing the bit properly because it requires fitting the bridle crownpiece around the ears. Any unresolved headshyness will turn those adjustments into a bitter, senseless struggle.

2. WILL YOUR HORSE WILLINGLY YIELD HIS HEAD? If not, go back to leading, turning, and backing up. You need a horse that will let you easily shift his head up, down, right, and left.

3. IS YOUR HORSE COMFORTABLE WITH HAVING HIS LIPS, MOUTH, AND TONGUE HANDLED? He must feel at ease and allow your hand to float in his mouth. By *float*, I mean that your hand can be placed in his mouth, slightly supported by the tongue, and he does not try to forcibly expel it. (*See chapter 17, Sidepassing & Jumping.*)

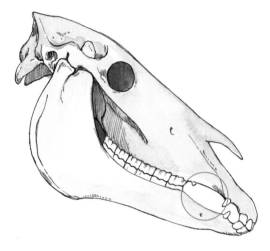

19.8 The open space between the incisors and the molars is known as the **bars**.

4. CAN YOU OBSERVE THE HORSE'S BITE, WHERE THE INCISORS MEET, BEFORE INTRODUCING THE BIT INTO THE MOUTH? This point is the only way (as emphasized by John Lyons) you can be sure the bit is being introduced into the open space between the upper and lower incisors (*see figure 19.8*). Feeling around or pushing the bit itself to locate the gap between incisors can create uncomfortable pressure from the metal against teeth and gums, which can make a horse shy away from the bit even more.

BEST BIT MATERIALS I am a big fan of copper-coated bits. Copper oxidizes well and sets up a chemical reaction that causes the horse to salivate. The more saliva produced, the moister the bit and the less likely it is to pinch his lips.

I also like bits made from so-called sweet iron, which is simply iron that contains between 10 and 15 percent carbon, making it prone to oxidization. To match a type to your horse, gauge his reactions. If he is among the lucky ones that produce abundant saliva, the bit will always be well

19.9

A horse salivates abundantly around a quality bit.

lubricated and will slide comfortably in the space between the upper and lower bars. Novices in clinics will often see a horse that is slobbering and producing abundant saliva and ask, "What is the matter with him? Has he got rabies?" No! He's just blessed with the ability to make a lot of spit.

HEADSHYNESS AND TAKING THE BIT   Once I was asked to make a "horse call" at a nearby stable for a bit problem. A boarder reported that her horse constantly tossed his head whenever she tried to bridle him. When I arrived, a frustrated-looking woman came up to me wearing the largest pair of sunglasses I've ever seen, the sort a Hollywood starlet uses to stave off the paparazzi. Underneath them was a huge shiner. She admitted that when she tried to bridle her horse he had tossed his head and hit her in the face.

I asked her to show me what was happening and she hesitated, screwing up her courage before she unhitched her horse. A petite woman, she couldn't reach over the top of his poll. Instead she took the bit and laid it flat in the palm of her hand. Her horse visibly tensed as she started pushing the bit against his teeth. Then he jerked his head back, tipping so far rearward I thought he might fall over backwards. It looked as though she would be more seriously injured if this situation were not addressed.

We needed to focus first on what was most dangerous: the head tossing. In a nearby round pen we worked on getting her horse to yield and drop his head when he experienced pressure on his poll. The horse began to yield naturally and softly. We still had to convince him that having a bit in his mouth was not a bad proposition.

For this, I had a sneaky approach: molasses. Before I put my two fingers into his mouth, I dipped them into a jar of molasses. Pretty soon, that horse seemed to think I had the sweetest fingers he had ever tasted, and he looked forward to my hand sitting on his tongue, safely in his mouth between the bars.

Finally it was time for him to take the bit. I coated it with molasses and let him play with it on his tongue to get as much of the sweet flavor as he could. Pretty soon he was oblivious to everything except his next chance to taste that bit. Eventually we had a horse that was compliant, relaxed, and willing. Our determination to rewrite his personal history with regards to the bit was critical to our success.

We cannot allow past experiences to restrict our future opportunities nor to hold us in a dysfunctional or restricted state of mind. Before we can express our full potential, whatever might be holding us back must be resolved. Because horses have such a ready capacity for forgiveness, they can show us how and why revisiting the past can resolve earlier mistakes or nullify bad impressions. By doing so, we can open the door to a much wider future. Horses allow us to understand an invaluable lesson: *just because something was written in the past doesn't mean it can't be corrected for the future.*

Yielding to the Bit on the Ground

■■■

OWNERS COMPLAIN THE MOST about the problems they see when their horse is under saddle. For example, as we just saw, problems with the bit arise in the context of saddling and bridling a horse for a trail ride. But *the root of the problem is on the ground*: the horse is not comfortable yielding his head, so the bit cannot go smoothly in the mouth, and so on. On the ground is where we are able to observe and resolve our horse's needs.

BIT BY BIT   To get a horse to develop a soft, responsive mouth, we need to evaluate the mechanics of how pressure is exerted by the bit — on the ground. I'll use the snaffle bit as an example, for the purposes of discussion. The snaffle is the most humane bit because it depends purely

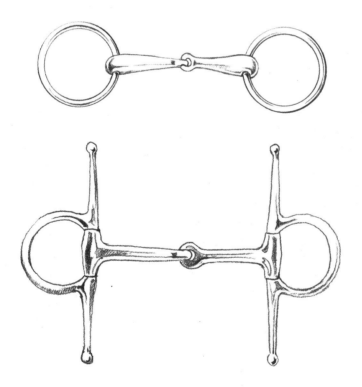

19.10 Comparing a simple snaffle (top) and a snaffle with cheekpiece

on pressure and does not require any curb, a bit that employs a pinching, painful component of its action. And, frankly, the snaffle is the only bit we ever need.

My bit of choice is a snaffle with cheekpieces. I learned from John Lyons to appreciate the addition of cheekpieces because they keep the bit from shifting from side to side in the horse's mouth, and they also reduce the risk of pinching the corners of the lips. Cheek pressure is an important component of how a bit functions, because more than 90 percent of the time we use the reins to apply asymmetrical pressure — that is, we exert more pressure on one side of the mouth than the other. The cheekpiece reinforces pressure on the side of the horse's face rather than focusing it at the sensitive edges of the horse's mouth.

When we ask our horse to tip his nose to the *right* and yield his neck and poll in a long relaxed arc in the same direction, we are actually asking him to respond to the pressure on the *left* side of his face that is exerted by the snaffle bit and cheekpiece. By turning toward the right, our horse seeks to relieve the pressure on the left side of his face by turning away from it. We do this training in increments: first we teach the horse to tip his nose and, later, include the whole headset and relaxation of the poll, the neck, and the shoulders in one fluid response to bit pressure. The trick, however, is to get things right with the bit on the ground before ever going under saddle.

19.11 A horse learns to yield the head, neck, poll, and shoulders to the bit on the ground before going under saddle.

THE PROCEDURE   The best format for practicing yielding to the bit usually begins with a longe whip (or wand) held in one hand and the inside rein in the other (*see figure 19.11*). Standing next to the horse's shoulder, use the longe whip to stimulate him to walk in a straight line ahead and give the near rein a light, pulsing squeeze. As soon as he yields, relinquish tension on the rein. Practice between two to four yields on one side and then switch over to the other. As your horse learns to give to the bit pressure, add nuances such as dropping the head, flexing the neck, and relaxing at the poll.

Eventually, you will be able to ask your horse to yield and turn with the most feather-light of touches on the reins, by literally picking the rein up or closing your fingers around it. Then you can move on to practicing serpentine maneuvers between cones, then figure-8s, and, finally, full-blown obstacle courses.

BENEFITS FROM THE GROUND UP   Teaching your horse to yield to the bit from the ground offers a hidden bonus feature: you learn to ride with soft hands and a slack rein because you avoid the bad habit of balancing on the reins (which many riders unconsciously do in the saddle). It never happens when you are working the reins on the ground. So not only will you develop a more responsive horse by working on yielding to the bit on the ground, but you'll also become a better rider in the process. When the ground work is all in place, then you can think about getting astride your horse.

CHAPTER NINETEEN

Highlights

■ ■ ■

*Sacking out is vital to
your horse's safety.*

■

*Sack out your horse with everything —
including the saddle.*

■

The better the bit, the greater the amount of saliva.

■

*Just because something was written in the past
doesn't mean it can't be changed
in the future.*

■

*Every problem under saddle
took root on the ground first.*

■

*A feather-light touch on the reins
is learned on the ground,
not under saddle.*

CHAPTER TWENTY

A LEG UP

*Of all animals kept for the recreation of mankind
the horse is alone capable of exciting a passion that
shall be absolutely hopeless.*

■ ■ ■

BRET HARTE

OUR FINAL CHAPTERS ON ground work will address how to get your leg up and start your horse under saddle, how to teach your horse to stop and spook in place, and how to trailer. Remember: this is *not* a book about riding. It's a book about gaining insight into yourself through training. The ground work we have laid out in this manual can lead anyone to begin riding safely. But the *beginning* is as far as this book goes, because the nature of the partnership changes when you begin to ride.

The Transformational Moment

■ ■ ■

RIDING TOGETHER is the most momentous transition you'll experience in your lifelong partnership with your horse. When you climb up in the saddle, you cross a symbolic threshold. Until that moment, you and your horse have moved on the ground together, on a single, level plane — eyeball to eyeball and shoulder to shoulder. But once you climb into the saddle, you'll experience a new, undeniably intoxicating sense of power. It comes, however, with a certain loss of innocence.

Ground work is not necessarily better than horseback riding. But the purity of purpose on the ground does become somewhat obscured when we ride. Our self-awareness is not as thoroughly engaged under saddle. Astride a horse, we attend to different details.

From the saddle, the perspective is radically changed. We no longer directly observe the horse's facial expressions or body posture. From the saddle, we extrapolate a lot about him by sensing his body through our own. He is carrying us — an act utterly foreign to any horse in the wild. Riding is the culmination of domestication, the merging of the human and equine species. It is the stuff of *our* deepest animal dreams, but we can't help but wonder: is it of theirs?

The introduction of the bit is the prelude to this metamorphosis. It is part of a general method we must teach our horse so we can use our hands, along with our seat and legs, to transmit chi while we are on his back. We provide the horse with new cues and tools. We change the conduits for our chi to get him ready for life under saddle.

Sacking out, covered in chapter 19, is a prerequisite for getting your leg over a horse. If your horse demonstrates the slightest hesitancy when the burlap bag touches his flanks, he is not ready for your leg.

For saddle work, teaching your horse to stand parallel to the fence is important. With halter and lead, show him how to align himself alongside the fence and stand there quietly. The horse may feel claustrophobic.

20.1 Desensitization with a leg over the horse's back

Many horses begin shuffling their feet. Coax your horse to stand as still as a Sphinx for ten minutes.

SACKING OUT FROM ABOVE When the horse is comfortable standing alongside the fence for ten minutes, accustom him to having you above him as you sit on the highest rung of the rail. Look over his head and back. Some horses take a while before they become comfortable with a human peering down at them. It's natural for horses to be leery of a creature hovering above them, as this is often the preferred angle of attack for a predator lying in wait. Try to turn your chi way down by breathing your horse down. Persist until he will stand quietly.

You'll occasionally need to move your horse around from your position atop the fence to reposition him parallel to the rail. Using a wand or longe whip from the top of the rail can be helpful for touching his far hip or flank to shift him next to the fence. From your position above him on the fence, rub your horse's back, flanks, withers, and rump with your wand, your boot, or your calf.

As with everything else, devote five times more training time than you think you'll need. Start light and soft. Let your horse shudder if he must, and always wait till he is calm before you remove your boot or whatever is touching him. Avoid the temptation to shift your weight off the rail. For maximum safety, the leg (usually the right) that is sacking out the horse should not be supporting you in any way (*see figure 20.1*).

Swing your non-weight–bearing leg out and behind your horse, because if he should bolt he will inevitably shoot forward. Don't let your leg hang so far over the horse that you risk being carried off the fence if the animal spooks. Remain vigilant about keeping your weight solidly anchored to one of the lower rungs on the fence.

PUTTING A LEG ACROSS   Now put your leg across your horse's back, with no weight on your horse. That's coming. As soon as your leg is over, lift it off immediately. Do this dozens of times. When your horse can sit quietly with your leg over his back for five minutes, it's time to consider not just the correct way to get a leg over the horse but also all the wrong ways. For example, what will happen if you swing your leg up and the heel of your boot accidentally hits the horse's rump? What if there's a spur on the end of that boot? Rather than hope such moments never happen, anticipate they will. Bump your horse in every conceivable way. Tap his rump. Graze him with your spur. Once you're sure there's nothing in your arsenal left undone, you know your horse is ready for you to step up and over and put yourself into the saddle.

Carrying Weight

■■■

ONCE YOUR HORSE IS accustomed to having you parked above his back, it's time to gradually transfer your weight from the foot that's on the rail onto the saddle. The shift pushes down onto the bars of the saddle, increasing saddle contact with the horse's back. Repeat this weight shift dozens of times until you are thoroughly convinced your horse will stand comfortably and quietly while supporting all of your body weight. Then — and only then — are you ready to give up your secure hold on the rail and transfer all your weight onto your saddle. Slide your feet into the stirrups.

Naturally, everyone's first impulse once they're in the saddle is to prod the horse into walking. No! You want him to stand still. You don't want to go anywhere. After a couple of seconds, you're going to climb back onto the fence. Then you're going to repeat the process, each time lengthening the interval in the saddle.

Each time you lower yourself into the saddle, you're going to send the same message through your peaceful breathing and the relaxed muscle tone in your legs and seat: you are content to just sit here. Work on teaching your horse to maintain this tranquil state until you're sure you could head over to the drive-in movie theater, sit in the saddle, and watch a full-length feature without your horse objecting.

We want to isolate each new thing we introduce into the horse's environment, so we separate just sitting in the saddle and going nowhere from the very different task of sitting in the saddle and walking around. Before we go anywhere, we need to teach our horse about climbing in and out of

20.2 Placing weight into and out of the stirrups from the ground familiarizes the horse not only with weight shifts but also with the movement and creaking of the fenders.

MANY WAYS TO MOUNT

For a good idea of the myriad ways riders can get on and off their horses, you need only turn to the rodeo. Look at the pick-up men: the cowboys who pluck contestants off the saddle broncs. Cowboys will be jumping on and off the backs of the pick-up horse from every imaginable angle (*see figure 20.3*). You'll also see cowboys slide halfway down the side of their horses at a dead run while getting ready to grab a steer and wrestle it to the ground (*see figure 20.4*). All these horses had to be trained to become accustomed to these extreme saddle positions and weight variations.

the saddle. Up until now, you have been moving into the saddle from high up on the side rail. Now you have to get your horse accustomed to you stepping up into the saddle from the ground.

MOUNTING AWAY FROM THE FENCE   Move your horse to the center of the round pen (*see figure 20.2*). Before you put your foot into the stirrup, get your horse familiar with how the feel of the saddle will change when you're using a stirrup to mount. The fenders move. The leather creaks. The rider holds onto the horse's mane and horn while putting a toe into the stirrup. Suddenly the saddle pulls to one side. All of these effects can represent new sensations to the horse, especially when he's first becoming saddle-broke.

Devote time and energy to each intermediary step. Swing fenders, shift stirrups back and forth, and make the saddle creak and slap. Pull down on the horn of the saddle and hang off it so the horse gets used to the saddle being pulled sideways. Pull yourself up in the stirrup and then lower yourself back to the ground. Up. Down. Swing a leg over and then get off again. Do it from the left. And then the right.

WALK ON   Once you've managed to make your horse comfortable when you climb into the saddle, it's time to go somewhere — but not far. Walk around the round pen. Don't direct your horse at all. Let him wander on a loose rein for a minute or two, stop, then praise your horse and climb down. In another minute, climb back up and go for another stroll around the round pen. Do this until your horse accepts having you on his back almost as second nature. Remember: his first nature remains a flight animal.

Because you've already taken the time to train your horse to yield to the bit on the ground, you can begin to gently exert directional control on the horse's head and neck and reverse directions or carry out a few turns. Later, throw in a jog or slow lope.

20.3 Rodeo pick-up men at work. Note the odd angles and weight shifts horses must become accustomed to for demanding rodeo work.

20.4 Steer wrestling requires the horse to accommodate huge shifts in the rider's weight.

Backing Up under Saddle

•••

Your horse already knows how to back up. Now we're asking for it from the saddle. Horses don't need a bit in their mouth or someone yanking back on reins to teach them how to move in reverse.

To take your horse from the walk to backing up requires the horse to carry out four steps (*see figure 20.5*):

1. Stopping
2. Shifting his weight from the forequarters to the hindquarters
3. Dropping his head
4. Providing impulsion in reverse

First, use your bit to provide your horse with a cue to stop moving forward. You will also use other cues to help your horse to stop. While you put slight braking pressure on the bit, shift your weight rearward so the horse feels your center of gravity shift toward his hindquarters. Also press your heels down in the stirrups. Round out your lower back to fill the

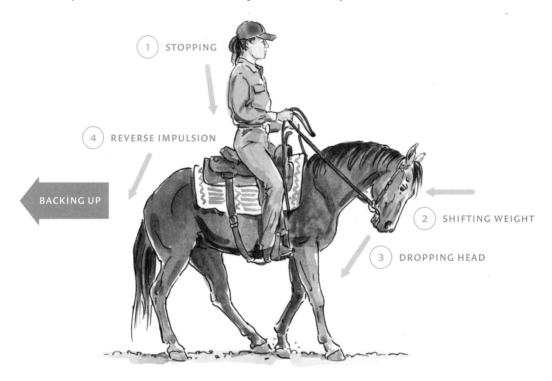

20.5 The four components of teaching a horse an elegant back-up

cantle (the back of the seat) of your saddle. Drop your shoulders and tuck your elbows into your flanks. All of these are cues for your horse to stop, and they help him to shift his weight to the rear.

The next step is for your horse to learn to drop his head. The most common mistake is to continue exerting rearward pressure on the horse's mouth through the bit after he stops. Early in the process of training your horse to back up, you can use the bit to help him to understand he needs to stop walking. Very quickly, however, you want him to cue off the shifts in your body to stop, not the bit. If you continue using the bit to stop your horse through the mouth, you'll begin to create some bad habits. Most horses will lift or jerk their heads upward in an attempt to reduce the backward pressure from the bit.

Try a little experiment on yourself. Stand and back up about four or five steps with your neck extended and your nose and jaw thrust up high in the air, looking at the ceiling. Now try it again with your head flexed slightly down (i.e., chin down toward your chest and eyes on the floor). Which of these was easiest? Did you feel the difference in the soles of your feet and how they made contact with the ground? Undoubtedly, you found the task easier to do with your head flexed downward, and your feel of the ground was improved in the relaxed, flexed position. Your horse agrees! This is why he looks more elegant and more natural backing up with his head lowered rather than raised (*see figure 20.5*).

The only time you regularly use the bit while backing up is to help your horse understand *where you expect his head to be*. Put light pressure on the bit when he moves his head out of the desired position. Release the reins whenever the horse's head is in the proper position; i.e., his forehead is perpendicular to the ground.

The final ingredient to backing up is impulsion. You've set your horse up for rearward impulsion by shifting your weight back and sinking down into the seat of your saddle. To start backing up, press with your calves and heels against his flank. We start him walking backwards by squeezing the flanks between our legs; calves and heels are against his side. Squeeze just forward of the girth. As soon as he begins to stride backwards, you will ease up on your grip on both sides. Then, you'll begin to pulse him to back up by first pressing on one side and alternating that with the other. The cue will be for the horse to pick up his foot; then you'll release the squeezing on that side and get ready to pulse him rearward on the other (*see figure 20.6*).

The faster you pulse with your legs, the faster your horse should move. You want him to get all the cues and training worked out in his mind at a slow speed (at the walk) before you try it at a faster pace. Confine your early trials to asking your horse to back up just a few paces. Later, you can ask him to back up the length of the arena and even around obstacles.

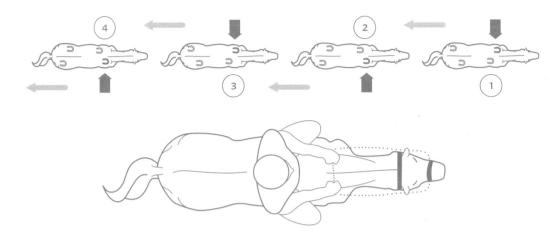

20.6 Alternating pulses of chi delivered just in front of the girth line produce vectors of chi, identical to those used earlier for ground work. This gives the horse the cue to back up one step at a time. The faster the pulses, the faster the horse's pace.

Riders often are not patient or persistent enough to ensure their horses fully master the task at hand. This is probably most riders' weakest point: they do not work diligently enough to let their horse see a task through to an elegant finish. They become too impatient and move on to more complicated tasks before a solid foundation is in place. Pat Parelli writes in *Natural Horsemanship*:

> .... *Generally speaking it takes about 1,100 hours for the horse to become true blue — to be a solid, dependable partner.... I've found that it takes the human about 1,000 hours before he or she is comfortable with being in the saddle. It takes that long before a rider is used to horses and the way they think, act, feel, do, etc. Everything the rider learns after that initial 1,000 hours is what really counts.* [pp. 54–55]

Trainers at the famous Spanish Riding School in Vienna start dressage training with their horses at three to four years of age. Typically, the horsemaster does not make a decision about whether a Lipizzan stallion will join the performance team until the horse reaches approximately his eighth year. The average stallion may have received as many as 4,000 hours of training before the riders and staff make their ultimate decision (*see figure 20.7*).

Be patient, and polish the training until the results are refined, elegant, and effortless. See it through.

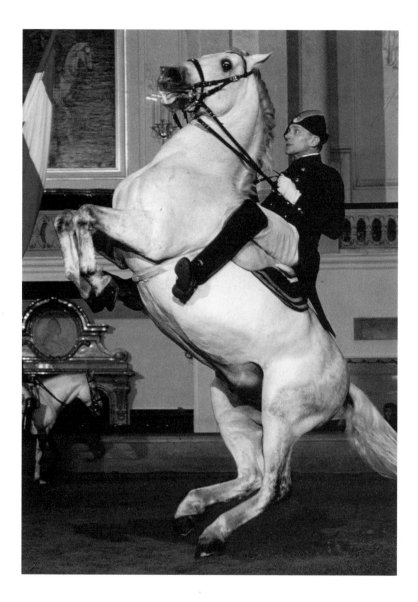

20.7 A Lipizzan stallion of the Spanish Riding School in Vienna. It takes years of training before a stallion is finally selected to participate in public exhibitions of classical dressage.

Highlights

∎ ∎ ∎

Teach your horse to stand forever.

∎

When you first sit in the saddle, be still.

∎

*A good back-up
is the key ingredient to teaching your
horse to relax.*

CHAPTER TWENTY-ONE

STOPPING & SPOOKING

A man's mind will very gradually refuse to make itself up until it is driven and compelled by emergency.

◼ ◼ ◼

ANTHONY TROLLOPE

I N AN EARLIER CHAPTER we explored the broad category of *whoa* on the ground. Under saddle, we want to confirm two types of stops: the casual and the emergency versions. These are two of the vital skills you'll ask your horse to learn under saddle, to safeguard himself and, more importantly, you.

To keep a horse's mind finely tuned with respect to stopping, you must regularly practice backing up. It also important to teach your horse to consistently include a back-up step with every stop. This helps him to balance his weight more squarely over his hind legs. By incorporating a back-up step into every stop, over the course of thousands of repetitions your horse will automatically set himself back onto his hind legs whenever he comes to a halt.

The Casual Stop

■ ■ ■

THE CASUAL STOP is meant for situations where we *anticipate* stopping: to allow a fellow rider to catch up, to look at a view, or before getting off to adjust equipment. The casual stop will flow as a natural consequence from teaching your horse to back up.

The casual stop uses the first set of cues employed in the back-up sequence. Sit deeply into the saddle and round your back against the cantle

21.1 The advanced reining stop, a deeper, more powerful exaggeration of the casual version

while you pick up your reins, without adding any backward pressure. This should be enough not just to initiate the stop but also to incorporate a mini-back–up step into every stop. Your horse will stop his forward impulsion, bring his feet to a halt, and, finally, shift his center of gravity rearward.

While this stop is casual, it is definitely a full stop, not a pause. You should get the feeling your horse's feet are glued to the ground, and he will be content, if necessary, to stand still for hours. Eliminate any idea that he can begin moving again unless you give him a specific signal. He must understand his job is to stand still until he receives new directives. This is not recess.

The Emergency Stop

∎∎∎

THERE IS NOTHING CASUAL about the emergency stop. It has a very different context than the casual stop. We use it when we absolutely *must* stop — no matter what.

Imagine for a moment the worst scenario: your horse spooks and takes off at a dead run, frightened for his life, pulling at the ground with every muscle fiber at his command. Under such circumstances, your horse is in no frame of mind to recall or respond to subtle weight shifts or leg pressures. No, an emergency is often a life-threatening situation. You need to hit the "kill power" button on your horse to save everyone on board (*see figure 21.2*).

You can't take chances that your horse will not respond. In an emergency, you have to work *with* his flight-drive forward motion, since you don't have much of a chance against it. So you're going to bring him to a stop by making him circle back in a reasonably sharp turn.

There are two important provisos about the turn. First, pick a spot where there's sufficient room. Secondly, don't make the turn so sudden and sharp you risk flipping your horse over. As hard as it may be for you to think clearly during such a panicked moment, you have to. The horse is bolting; thus he's going to take a stride or two strides before you can assess where you're headed and that you're still reasonably, securely seated in the saddle.

Now focus on slowing down your horse. Sit deep in the saddle. Lean back. Pull back on the reins to make contact. As soon as there's enough room — in the middle of the trail or a space between trees — start circling him. You're going to do this by pulling hard and steadfastly on the inside rein, bringing your horse's nose as far back toward you as you can. You'll

21.2 An emergency stop. Circling becomes a tight turn on the forehand to disengage the hindquarters.

hold that pressure resolutely — no matter what — until your horse has begun circling and circling around on himself. You will also want to use your inside heel (or spur) to put pressure on his inside flank so he's encouraged to side-step with his hindquarters (*see page 161*).

At this point, you have attained two vital results. The first is that your horse is going nowhere. He is circling over and over again in the same small piece of real estate. The second consequence is that as he steps over with his hindquarters, the one horsepower engine in his rear legs is put into neutral. Just hold your rein tightly over until all four legs come to a complete stop. Then release him and give him a reassuring stroke. Once your horse begins to first turn, start slowly making tighter and tighter circles until he simply must shift his hindquarters over.

Remember, as long as he is going around in circles, he's not going anywhere; he's just covering ground. In essence, your turns will become ever tighter until he has to pivot on the forehand. He simply must disengage his hindquarters under such circumstances. So make small circles until he comes to a stop, and *voila!* You have your emergency brakes. You need to know that they are always there, ready to be used, and that you can count on them.

KEEP THIS TOOL SHARP This maneuver is not something you'll wait to try when you need it. As the saying goes: "How do you get to Carnegie Hall? Practice. Practice. Practice." Well, it is no different with the emergency stop. Practice it regularly. Circle your horse around until he yields his hindquarters. Don't release your horse until those rear hooves stop creating any traction! When the legs are standing stock still — and not an instant before — then release and reward.

Also test this maneuver in practice situations that closely mimic the emergency situations you might encounter out in the real world. Flap a flag. Have someone shake a tarp as you pass on your horse. Create situations to test his brakes. Ride him up to a quick lope and then ride him down to an emergency stop. Get this right well before you ever need it!

Spooking in Place: Facing Our Fears

■ ■ ■

ALL HORSES SPOOK. But a safe horse spooks safely — in place. Nothing distinguishes a smart, well-trained horse more than how well he overcomes his instincts to flee. No one can train a horse not to be frightened. But you can teach your horse to dissipate his urge to escape by circling and then disengaging the hindquarters, eventually coming to a stop.

When something suddenly frightens your horse, he will spook. Let him slip into a slow retreat. Create some safe space between the frightening object (great blue heron) or event (lawn sprinkler pops up) and the horse. Allow him to circle to a safe distance.

Circling is like slipping the clutch a little on a manual transmission so not all the power is delivered to the hind end. Your horse puts some distance between himself and his fear. Circling does not let him beat a retreat in a straight line, but it's a chance for him to move and dissipate some adrenaline. Then it's time for him to square up and face whatever spooked him — but from a safe distance.

Back your horse up farther if necessary. Find the distance where his need to flee is low. His ears should be up but not locked too rigidly forward. His head should be down and his nostrils flared, taking in a deep whiff. Got the picture? Now you're ready to face some fears. As we practice helping our horse to face his fears, we have the opportunity to face some of our own.

Facing Fear

■ ■ ■

THREE ESSENTIAL POINTS will help your horse confront something fearful:

- Direct your horse's head as little as possible
- Distract your horse as much as possible
- Let your horse stand still and soak it in

1. DIRECT YOUR HORSE'S HEAD AS LITTLE AS POSSIBLE. Leave the reins long and soft, especially any time your horse drops his head. Horses have an instinctive need to investigate a potentially dangerous object or situation. They do so by shifting their heads up and down. Ensure that he has the freedom to do so.

Raising and lowering the head allows a horse to alternate between his near, stereoscopic vision, and the more distant, monocular view of the object. Dropping his head also lets him get a good sniff to pick up any dangerous telltale scent. Often you will hear horses snort when they are alarmed. This is an instinctive reaction to notify any nearby horses: "Hey, I'm on high alert. You'd better get yourself ready, too, in case something is really out there!"

2. FOCUS ON LETTING YOUR HORSE SLIP AROUND IN CIRCLES. Let him slow down, relax, and come to a stop. Bring him back to a spot where he can see whatever spooked him. The circling distracts your horse. It also keeps him cued on you, not his fears.

The more your horse thinks about you, the less he worries. Give him a task. Walk over a log. Sidepass. Walk in a circle. If he can't focus on you, then make wider circles away from the source of the scare. The farther back you go, the easier it will be for him to concentrate on you. Remember to offer a loose rein, because at some point your horse will drop his head (*see figure 21.3*). That's when his mind is back on you!

3. LET YOUR HORSE STAND UNTIL THE TENSION FLOWS OUT OF HIS BODY. Get him to relax. Let him just breathe. You breathe, too. Allow the stress to drain out of his body. Now you've found a way for him to feel more confident, emboldened, and, yes, even curious about what scared him.

Search for opportunities (and they seem to abound) where your horse feels uncomfortable. Parts of the human brain are specifically designed to be triggered by empathy. Strive to see the world as it must appear to him.

21.3 This horse drops his head to investigate an unfamiliar object of curiosity that suddenly appeared in his pasture.

Don't lose your temper when your horse is spooked; help him instead. Apply your penetrating predator insight. View anything that makes him jumpy or stand-offish as something you want to investigate on his behalf. I cannot recall a single trail ride when I have not found something to work on: a spot, a new object, a new perspective that makes my horse uneasy.

An interesting dividend of this strategy is that horses seem to anticipate it. They realize that as soon as something surprises or scares them, you're going to investigate it. They also learn there is a safe, acceptable alternative to being frightened. Best of all, you have a safer partner to ride. The more experiences and challenges your horse has, the more his mind engages in working mode and the safer he becomes. More hours of working and training mean increased safety.

A good way to visualize this is that your horse is born with an instinctive mind. Training pours learning into that instinctive mind. Soon, instinct is displaced by learning. You will never completely replace all of your horse's instinct, but the more learning you load into him, the less room there is for instinct to seize his attention. You alone will make the biggest contribution to your horse's safety.

COURAGE THROUGH COOPERATION   It is unrealistic to expect never to feel fear. Eleanor Roosevelt said, "You gain strength, courage, and confidence by every experience where you really stop to look fear in the face. You must do the thing which you think you cannot do." You're asking your horse to face fear — with you. In the process, you also teach yourself something about fear. You see that even a creature who is primed to explode into flight can be persuaded by loving guidance and reassurance to choose, instead, a response that runs contrary to his very nature.

The horse offers us living proof that fear can be overcome by cooperative endeavor. Fear's power lies in its ability to make us believe we are alone, abandoned to the mercy of monsters, beasts, and demons. To the extent that we discover strategies to overcome that sense of isolation, we find courage.

There's a certain irony in this partnership forged between horses and humans: we seek to improve them by supplanting their instincts with training, while they inspire us to expand our thinking through intuition (*see figure 21.4*).

21.4 Horses help us to grasp the larger spiritual truths
that are our instinctive birthright.

CHAPTER TWENTY-ONE

Highlights

■ ■ ■

A casual stop begins with a good back-up.

■

*An emergency stop requires
total disengagement of the hindquarters.*

■

*The only useful
emergency stop is one that is infallible.*

■

*Let your horse circle or
back up from whatever is frightening him.*

■

*Let your horse have his head to
investigate what's spooking him.*

■

*Teaching your horse to spook in place
requires that you replace his fright
with curiosity.*

■

A scared horse can't learn.

■

*How safe your horse becomes
is a measure of how much you've replaced his
instincts with experience.*

TRAILERING (OR NOT)

A true horseman does not look at the horse with his eyes;
he looks at his horse with his heart.

■■■

AUTHOR UNKNOWN

OUR FINAL CHAPTER will return to getting our horse loaded in the trailer, ready to head out into the wide world with us, on the road to adventure. Again, to tackle the problem of trailering we need to turn it on its head by *not* trying to trailer our horse at all.

One of our big problems when we're trying to help our horse master the task of trailering is that we focus too much on the trailer itself. We're thinking about getting the horse inside the constrained space and closing the doors. As we've been discussing throughout the book, when we confront a problem, the solutions we can see are predetermined by the way we frame the question. Trailering is a perfect example.

Entitling this chapter "How to Get Our Horse Out of the Trailer" might be more accurate. Instead of focusing on the problems of teaching our horse to trailer, let's concentrate on the solutions we already have. To do that we'll combine three tasks we've have already worked on and fold them into our final objective of trailering:

- Coaxing our horses onto a platform
- Getting our horse to step forward and backward
- Getting our horse to pass through a gate (a constrained space) straight ahead of us

Hitch onto the Herd Instinct

∎∎∎

FIRST, LET'S HITCH OUR HORSE near the trailer so he can watch a more senior, seasoned horse go in and out of it easily and calmly. Let the young horse see how it's done. *Horses are herd animals.* They go where the herd goes. They do what herd members do. So why not use that instinctual trait?

22.1 Team an anxious horse with a veteran who feels more confident about entering the trailer.

We will take our seasoned, senior horse and lead him up and into the trailer several times (*see figure 22.1*).

Don't underestimate the significance of the impression on a horse to watch another veteran horse loading without fear or mishap. It will not teach a novice horse the task, but it delivers the image that nothing bad happens. Now you'll lead your young horse up to the door of the trailer and let him stand there quietly. Then simply back your horse away. Maybe go around a tree; maybe walk a few paces up and down, away from the trailer. Then come back.

Step by Step

■ ■ ■

NEXT, YOU WANT TO CONVINCE your horse — to coax him — to put a single hoof up on the ramp or floor of the trailer (*see figure 22.2*). When that's done, walk away from the trailer and go onto a new task, a new distraction. Then return again and ask for one hoof on the ramp. Do that for a while. Throw in some other tasks and, intermittently, break things up by loading your veteran senior horse in and out of the trailer.

22.2 The first foot in the trailer

22.3 Both front feet in the trailer

Trailers can come with a ramp or not. There are advantages and disadvantages to both configurations. Personally, I like a trailer with a ramp because my horse gets to step up and down out of the trailer without worrying about a huge step *up* when climbing into the trailer, and, more importantly, a huge step *down* when backing out of it. When some horses are backing out of a trailer, they are literally backing up into their visual blind spot. From watching them, it's obvious they're reaching out with their rear hoof to find out when it will encounter and land on solid ground. With a ramp, the horse has the physical reassurance of being able to feel the ramp sloping away behind him as he steps backward.

The disadvantage of a ramp is that the horse learns to depend on it; i.e., they learn to expect a gradual slope down from the trailer to the ground. So if a horse inadvertently steps off the ramp, they have no expectation of encountering a drop-off. When they do encounter such a drop, the horse will usually panic, often thrashing around in the doorway of the trailer where there's a higher likelihood of an injury. On the other hand, stepping up and back from the trailer gets the horse accustomed to a very large step-off as part of its experience. But it can make the horse very leery of that

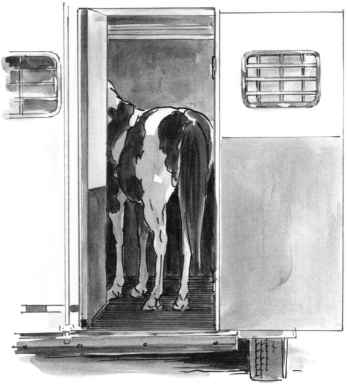

22.4 All four feet in the trailer

initial step out of the trailer. In the final analysis, it's truly dealer's choice, in my opinion. I've done it both ways but I usually prefer a ramp.

Next, ask him to place both forefeet onto the floor of the trailer (*see figure 22.3*). Add more distractions. Load the senior horse in and out. Then ask for three feet in the trailer. You'll notice tension building in your horse. On his own, he will feel a drive to get that fourth foot inside the trailer. Be patient; allow the tension to build on its own. It helps if your veteran horse is standing, tied, inside the trailer, to send your novice horse the message "it is safe for a horse inside this trailer." Eventually, you will see him give in to the irresistible force; your novice horse will be standing with all four feet inside the trailer (*see figure 22.4*).

TRAILERING WITH A HAPPY HEART

The first few times you leave a horse in a trailer, feed him a little grain or hay: a kind of snack break in the trailer. Load another horse in there to keep him company. Trailering is persuasion, not a contest; it's systematic desensitization. The tortoise always wins that race.

Key Moment: Getting Back Out

• • •

THAT MOMENT, when your horse has all four feet in the trailer, is critical: now you back him out! Emphasize *backing out* of the trailer, not *climbing in*. Praise your horse when he steps out. Distract him with some unrelated task and then return to the trailer. Every time your horse steps into the trailer have him step right back out. Work on controlling the backing out. Get his feet moving slowly, one foot at a time.

Keep in mind that trailering does not need to be taught in a single session. If your horse is doing well stepping in and out of the trailer, find a good place to stop. Praise your horse. Come back to the task the next day. The key to trailering is this: there's no point to trailering a horse until he backs out of the trailer calmly, quietly, and slowly. That's why I said the focus is getting your horse *out* of the trailer.

Doors

• • •

TRAILERS HAVE LOW CEILINGS, and the frame around the door leading into the trailer is even lower. When a horse panics, his first reaction is to throw his head up and back (remember: what resists, persists). It's important to avoid letting that happen while the horse is in the doorway because he can receive a significant blow to the head, something he may not easily forget.

It's for this reason that Monty Roberts likes to place a protective skull-cap on horses when he first teaches them to trailer. It's a wise precaution. But some horses react negatively to the cap being in place, too. Again, dealer's choice.

Avoid at all costs letting your horse traumatize his poll against the roof or frame. Spend lots of time coaxing your horse backward when only his nose and face, not his head, neck, and shoulders, are in the doorway. If the horse is going to yank or jerk back, you want the top of his head to clear.

Never slam a trailer door shut behind a horse. The first few times the horse is in the trailer, leave the doors *wide* open. Let the horse go in an out several dozen times before even thinking about the doors. When you do close the doors, close only one side first, and then just for an instant. Then close the other. Do this several times. Then close both for a second (literally) and immediately reopen them.

Always take your horse in and out dozens of times between opening and closing the doors. We want the horse to understand we have no desire to trap him in the trailer. The trick is to go slowly. Leave the doors closed for one second. Two seconds. Three seconds. Gradually increase the intervals. Have someone feed the horse a carrot through the window to distract him while the doors are being closed.

Time to Travel . . . a Few Yards

ONCE YOUR HORSE is accustomed to standing inside the trailer and munching contentedly with the doors closed, it's time to hit the road. Pull up your ramp. Double check your hitch. Make the first few trips in the trailer short — maybe a few yards or a few hundred. Then, gradually increase the length of the trips. You want your horse's approval and confidence before you proceed to the next level. The secret to successfully trailering your horse is reassurance that he is not trapped. Never rush to the next step (*see figure 22.5*).

22.5 With the right training, every horse can look forward to trailering
with a happy heart.

Highlights

■ ■ ■

*A horse who is new to trailering
should always have the benefit of watching
a veteran horse do it first.*

■

*To keep your horse in the trailer,
don't close the doors.*

■

*The more you feed your horse in the trailer,
the faster he'll climb in.*

■

*Backing your horse out of his trailer
is the key to getting him into it.*

EPILOGUE

Black care rarely sits behind a rider whose
pace is fast enough.

■ ■ ■

ORSES DO NOT HAVE as much to gain from our training them
as we do from their teaching us. They can help us commit to our
spiritual development and motivate us to acknowledge or change
our personal values. The quiet, gentle way of the horse encourages us to
hear the music that follows after we learn to silence our ego's voice.

Effective horse training poses an implicit challenge: it does not require us
to demonstrate ingenuity, but it demands we express integrity — especially
to ourselves. Horses have no concept of what deceit is. It does not exist in
the equine world. No horse sidles up to another, pretending to be its friend,
so it can steal the other's feed. If they covet a bucket of grain, they state
it unequivocally; they go over and immediately try to claim it. If a horse
wants a rival to leave, there's no excuse or white lie. There is simply action:
chase the usurper out. There's a great honesty linking intent and action.

For humans, the absolute, unwavering honesty demonstrated by horses
can be a terrible threat. That's because as humans, we're born liars. We
learn to lie early in childhood. We learn to lie to our parents, sibs, friends,
colleagues, our spouses — and even ourselves. In fact, police investigators
often have a hard time telling when a suspect is lying to hide a crime or
just lying out of habit.

But the fact that humans are such consummate liars doesn't mean we
are evil. A friend of mine once attended a seminar presented by a famous
Hindu guru. This small, brown, bearded sage spoke of the joy each person
holds in his heart. He pronounced: "All human beings represent the perfection of the Universe. They are all beautiful."

A man stood up in the audience and yelled: "Yeah, maybe. But
they lie."

The wise man answered: "Yes, that is true. They are all beautiful — and they lie too."

Lying is just our human nature. But training horses allows us to see how equine-style honesty can work for us. Our fear to reveal ourselves is our burden alone. Horses come with no agenda; the only expectations are those we impose on ourselves.

Our equine companions help us believe there's no need to lie. It's okay to be no more and no less than the complete truth of who we are. Dare we awaken to that?

As Gangaji writes: "...the truest teaching is like a bird flying across the sky; it leaves no tracks that can be followed, yet its presence cannot be denied." The horse's presence also cannot be denied. He begs us to open ourselves to the mystical power of intuition and emotion. He asks us to harness our chi, to depend on it, and to channel it.

So much of our daily energy is consumed maintaining personal stories, fueling the postures we have convinced ourselves we must sustain. Fictions about being successful. About being envied. About feeling powerful. Looking rich and beautiful. All of these facades collapse in the presence of a horse.

Horses do not see us as our collective stories but simply as we are, standing in front of them. We grasp that recalling the past is meaningless and reaching for the future futile when we are presented with this creature that holds itself so perfectly in the moment, in the now. The horse brings us its uncanny ability to peel our egos back, to strip the layers away like an onion, until we find ourselves awkwardly naked and vulnerable. But the horse also shows us the joy that comes from living with the bare truth of our selves. What a gift that is.

How do you get comfortable with who you truly are? By giving up everything that isn't you. How do you know what isn't you? The horse responds to you while you are *not* an impostor. The horse calls us out, daring us to just *be*. Being truthful and honest is a very low-energy state. It needs no chi to feed it. It is a zone of perfect release — a refuge of sincerity. We arrive at complete release; we enter a space of unadorned honesty.

We learn the full measure of patience from horses. How much better would we be as friends, parents, spouses, or bosses if we could practice more patience, exhibit more forgiveness? Horses also help us learn to listen actively. To see that speaking too much means growing deaf.

Horses see worth. They forgive our trespasses and try to see instead the goodness of our intentions.

Finally, horses demonstrate to us, directly and tangibly, that Nature is able to read our hearts and to lend its suport to our lives. It never left us. We simply lost the habit of seeing it clearly.

In all these ways, horses rescue us. The horse is tethered to our soul. The lead that binds us to our horse also belays us to bedrock so we can ascend to spiritual discovery.

I hope I have been able to pay homage in some small way to these fleet-footed messengers, who demonstrate such forgiveness and kindness toward the human race. The drumming of their hoofbeats is the pulse of the Universe's overflowing, generous heart. I live in awe and gratitude for all the boundless blessings that horses represent.

TWENTY EXERCISES

Expand Your Spiritual Awareness
with Your Horse

1. IT'S SHOWTIME!

DEVOTE A BLOCK OF several hours to grooming your horse down to the last and finest detail. Imagine you have been asked to show him in front of royalty or a head of state. Your horse alone will represent all the horses of your nation. Groom to perfection. Give him a shampoo from head to toe. Brush out the mane and tail. Braid the mane. Clean the eyes and nose. Trim ear and chin hair. Give him a pedicure. Oil and brush the hooves. Put a coat sheen product into his hide.

Focus your mind on each task in sequence. Absorb yourself in every detail. Imagine you have become the conduit for all the love in the Universe to be showered on your horse. Rejoice in how it feels to do something good for a fellow creature, how the world grows when we allow ourselves to serve others.

2. HERD HIKE

TAKE OUT A TRAIL guide for a wilderness area of park near your home. Scout an interesting location with engaging landscapes, terrains, and vistas, and pick a trail that also has ready access to water. Select a destination for your horse, somewhere you think he would especially enjoy. Now trailer him to the trailhead and take him for a walk (not a ride) in the woods. Enjoy strolling next to each other as fellow herd members. Imagine you are crossing this landscape as prey animals, looking for browse, cover, or ambushes. Let your horse take in all the new sensations and smells. Don't be afraid to take on challenging trails. Remember, horses have been covering treacherous ground for millions of years.

Watch how he moves. Look at the footwork. For some of the trail you can lead; on other segments let him go first and you follow. Enjoy the hike as a herd.

STORMS, ESPECIALLY HIGH WINDS, really spook prey animals like horses. The reasons for this reaction are simple. First, there's a lot more ruckus: limbs blowing, branches snapping, shutters slapping, and things flying around. More importantly, with high winds and lots of noise, there are just so many more distractions that could cover up the advance of a potential predator. Thus, as a storm approaches, you'll notice that horses get energized and often will start running around, sometimes quite frantically.

This can be a dangerous undertaking so I recommend that, if you're a novice, you do this activity with someone who is very experienced with horses. When it's time to get the horses in from the elements, take advantage of this situation in which you must work with a horse under very distracting circumstances. Use all the techniques we reviewed under Stopping & Spooking (*see page 269*).

Try to get your horse to focus on you despite the commotion the storm is making. Give him some simple task, like circling around you or backing up. Then walk for a bit. Then another task. Soothe him. Breathe him down and calm him. Then another task. Try to use weather as a circumstance in which you can demonstrate your leadership skills to the horse by showing him you can make him feel better.

There are few things more gratifying than getting your horse to safety and knowing you have managed to make him feel more secure. Sometimes, in a big lightning or rain storm, I'll stand in the stall with my horse, and we'll look out at the elements and just enjoy being safe in the rain together.

4. GIMME SHELTER

LOOK FOR A SPOT to build your horse a shelter. It can be to upgrade the stall or barn where you currently house him or to provide shelter in turn-out pastures. Think about the view, protection from the elements, the availability of potable water. Retaining body warmth and at the same time permitting adequate circulation of air. There's something therapeutic about building something with your own hands, about picking up a hammer and saw and making a home for the horse you love.

Somewhere on the structure create a dedication of some kind. Carve your initials. Write your horse's name and the date. For a horse, there is no greater gift than security.

5. EYE OF THE BEHOLDER

THIS IS ANOTHER EXERCISE where you take a walk with your horse, only this time you will bring along a camera (still or video). What you shoot is whatever you believe your horse would shoot if he could. Grass. Another horse. A good-looking stock tank. This is your opportunity to try to see things from his point of view. When you are done, put together a montage of your walk, from start to finish, as your horse saw it.

6. HIDE AND SEEK

HORSES LIKE TO PLAY when they feel safe and at ease. One game you can teach your horse is hide and seek. You can do this in a field or create a series of obstacles in an arena.

Use a pocketful of treats and try to tease him into following you. Then "hide" behind a tree or a bush. The point is not to actually hide but to get him to come looking for you. Whenever he puts his head around the corner and touches you with his muzzle, give him a treat. Get up and run to another hiding place. Make it close enough that he will follow.

Your horse will quickly get the point of the game, and then you'd better be prepared to have a rambunctious playmate on your hand. But how great to be playing together!

7. CROSS A TARP

HORSES HAVE A NATURAL, protective instinct to avoid putting their feet on a surface where they do not know what lies underneath. A tarp lying on the ground is, thus, a profound challenge to a horse's confidence. Your job is to patiently show your horse that it is safe to walk across the tarp. You need to exhibit great patience and gentleness. Never push him beyond his comfort zone, but be constantly aware of expanding that space. You will be rewarded with a horse that will stand quietly with you in the middle of the tarp, showing you the depths of trust.

8. SLEEP OVER

HEAD OUT INTO A PASTURE. Build a small campfire. Put out your bedroll. Sleep under the stars. Share the night with your equine roommate. You will be surprised to find your horse nosing around as you get your dinner under way. And once you climb into your roll... well, there's nothing like that warm breath on the back of your neck.

As PREY ANIMALS, horses are endowed with wonderfully enhanced senses of smell, hearing, and vision. While they possess poor visual acuity — the clarity with which they see can see fine detail — and they're unable to see colors, the equine eye has enormous power for detecting objects, movement, and landscape in little or no light. Those equine eyes — large and soulful — have enormous retinal surfaces that are richly embedded with rod cells, exquisitely sensitive to even starlight. Horses are equipped with the ability to detect light about five times more sensitively than humans can. (Cited in: www.horsechannel.com/media/horse-health/how-horses-see-the-world.aspx.pdf) This gives our equine partners the equivalent of night vision.

While your horse may usually look to you for leadership, at night, as a human, you're at a distinct disadvantage trying to navigate over unfamiliar terrain. So this exercise is aimed at a little role reversal.

Wait for a night where there's a full moon. Trailer your horse out to a wooded area. Make sure this is a park or plot of land you've been to before but that is far removed from artificial light. Be sure to have completely scouted the area out during daylight hours! You need to be sure it is safe (i.e., no cliffs, open mine shafts, swamps, and other hazards). This is meant to be an experience, not a survival exercise.

Once night has fallen, get your horse haltered up while you allow your eyes to adjust to the darkness. Lead your horse at a walk in some open or broken terrain, where you can get accustomed to the low light and the shadows.

When you're ready, head into the deeper woods. Deep into the shadows. You will begin to falter as you lose the moonlight but your horse will not. This is where you have to give up some control and walk closely by him as he leads you through the darkness. Try to accomplish this in small "patches." By this, I mean try out 20 or 30 yards and then loop back into open ground.

Build up your confidence in small, progressive steps (baby steps, remember). The goal is to allow yourself to remain the leader while you depend on your horse's physiologically superior powers to help you "own" the night — together.

I also recommend a moonlight trail ride, but don't get overly aggressive in your riding style. An acquaintance went out on a trail ride under a bright full moon. He decided to show off and took off down a dry wash at a full gallop. Suddenly, the party heard a painful screech. He had run at full tilt right into an overhanging saguaro cactus limb. He made a very slow and painful recovery thereafter. His horse was unscathed — not a single cactus spine in him. By contrast, my friend stopped counting after the Emergency Room staff extracted two hundred cactus prickers out of some very tender anatomy!

10. MOTHER AND CHILD

ASK AROUND the neighboring barns if there is any mare due to foal. Bring your camera. Tell the mare's owners you want to document the first twenty-four hours in the life of a newborn. Then just strap your battery pack on your camera and let 'er rip. You will see a thousand touching, tender moments. You will see pure *Equus* spoken here.

11. MASSAGE

NEXT TIME YOU COME back from a trail ride, let your horse cool down. Now, start rubbing and gently kneading those large, sore muscles. Go slow. You will be surprised how quickly your horse's body begins to relax, almost sagging beneath your hands. If you have any concerns about how to proceed, ask a professional equine massage therapist. Stand back and watch your horse turn to putty. Watch and learn how to relax your horse.

12. BUILD YOUR HORSE AN OBSTACLE COURSE

PLAN A LAYOUT OF a small area on your property that can serve as an obstacle course. This can be as elaborate or as simple as you want. Use logs or poles to lay out parts of the course. Don't be afraid to include obstacles that challenge your horse, such as floating helium balloons, flapping plastic bags, and inflatable beach balls. Include as wide a variety of terrain as possible. Try to build up jumps and small trenches that compel your horse to trust not only his own footwork but also your leadership through these areas. Include plenty of claustrophobic gateways to help him gain confidence negotiating them.

13. MEET NEW FRIENDS

OWNERS ARE OFTEN HESITANT to introduce horses to one another, due to underlying fears that injury may occur. Certainly whenever horses get together and try to establish dominance injury is one possible outcome, but, in fact, 99 percent of encounters between horses end nonviolently. Take your horse to a friend's place where there is plenty of open space, like a pasture. Turn him out with a new horse, one of roughly the same age. This will give your horse a chance to romp and play and to socialize. Watch and learn about your horse's personality.

14. INTRODUCE NEW HUMANS

WE FORGET THAT HORSES become very accustomed to our presence, focusing on those of us who take care of them and feed them as part of the daily routine. It is important to introduce new experiences into a horse's life so, on occasion, we should allow a new person to meet him and greet him. We should let that individual groom the horse and then carry out some ground work exercises with him. Not only is it good for the horse to cue in to different body language and chi but it is also useful to allow the person (if they are qualified and confident) to take that horse out.

Watching someone else work with your horse can produce valuable insights. Not only do you see how the horse responds to another individual but you may also detect the differences between the other person's technique and your own. This exercise will also prevent your horse from becoming overly fixated on just you as his handler and rider.

15. EDUCATE YOURSELF

NO MATTER HOW GOOD a rider you are and how well trained your horse is, you can always learn more. If a reputable and professional trainer visits your area, sign up for a clinic. There is always something new to be learned. You'll find there is no single right method for training horses. Very often a roadblock in our spiritual development is overcome when we apply a completely new technique in our ground work with our horse.

16. WATERWORKS

MANY OF OUR HORSES have problems negotiating water. This has to do with the fact that the water offers a reflective surface and horses are unsure of where they are putting their feet. As prey animals, they depend exclusively on their feet to deliver them from danger and therefore water represents an unusual hazard in their minds. For these reasons, training horses to overcome their fear of water can be a wonderful exercise.

For this training technique, you will need to dig a trench or hole that is approximately twelve feet in length or diameter and 2 to 3 feet deep. Line it with a tarp and weigh down the edges with dirt. Before you do this exercise, be sure to have trained your horse to walk across a tarp (*see exercise #7*).

Once your horse is comfortable crossing the tarp, use a garden hose to introduce a small amount of water onto the bottom — no more than an inch. Coax your horse through the water, back and forth across the tarp. As he gains confidence and calms himself, allow your hose to slowly accumulate more water on the tarp. Gradually the water will deepen and your horse will grow more and more accustomed to walking back and forth through the water, ultimately overcoming his fear.

Another benefit: if you ever need to soak all four of your horse's feet for medical treatment, this tarp technique can help prepare him for the experience.

17. HANG OUT WITH YOUR FARRIER

MANY OF US SIMPLY turn over our horse to the farrier and then pay the bills. However, there are lots of interactions that go on with your farrier, and many of these should be studied. Often you will discover things in your horse's training that need to be improved to make him calmer and more willing to stand patiently for the farrier's ministrations. In addition, you can learn a lot about horses' feet from your farrier.

Don't be afraid to ask questions. More importantly, don't be afraid to make requests. I've been struck by how often you will discover things that you see that can be improved in your horse's shoeing. It's important to look at the frog and the hoof wall and see how the heel is trimmed. Schedule your farrier's appointment in such a way that you can be present for the entire process. It not only enriches your horse's life but improves your knowledge about his feet as well.

18. TAKE A VACATION

THERE ARE DIRECTORIES that list outfits offering overnight boarding for horses and accommodations for the horse owners as well. These can range from a hotel to a bed and breakfast, from a recreational vehicle hookup to simple camping facilities. Something wonderful can be gained by traveling across the country, visiting different areas to ride, and meeting different horse owners in different locales. Not only does this give you an opportunity to introduce your horse to new terrain and new surroundings but it also allows you to devote a significant block of time to him. Many of us don't put aside enough time for our horse enjoyment and training. When we book an equine vacation, we guarantee that we will spend quality time with our horse.

19. SUPPORT A CHARITY

THESE DAYS SO MANY CHARITIES are committed to the welfare of horses. From therapeutic riding programs to adopting abandoned horses or captured mustangs, there really is no reason why every horse lover cannot be involved in some charitable undertaking. Not only is it important for the long-term welfare of horses, but it is one more technique for forcing ourselves to make time in our schedule for the things that we are passionate about. If we are passionate about horses, then we need to put our time and our money to advancing those causes.

20. BLESSING CEREMONY

THIS IS YOUR CHANCE to express your gratitude. Go buy some water-based finger paints. Make your own symbols. Look up some of the emblematic decorations Native Americans used, such as circles around the eyes (to see better), thunder stripes, hail stones (to confound the enemy), and handprints (for courage) on the hips. Make up your own. Decorate your horse. Take a lock of your hair and braid it into its mane. Then write a personal prayer to express your gratitude directly to your equine partner. Bring your horse out underneath the broad heavens. Let your horse hear your thanks for being the gift from the Universe to you.

As part of the blessing ceremony, you can include a smudge ceremony. This involves preparing a blend of sage and herbs (or purchase a readymade smudge stick). You can include cedar leaves, bear root, tobacco (considered an offering), sweet grass, and mint. Light the herb mixture and allow it to smolder in a small ovenproof dish or the more traditional abalone shell. Before starting the smudge, you must purify the surroundings and yourself. First pass your feather fan four times through the purifying smoke from the sage. Then make an offering of the smoke to the four directions and father sky and mother earth. Then use the fan to blow the smudge over yourself and then pass it along and over your horse to bless him.

Acknowledgments

■ ■ ■

THIS BOOK IS DEDICATED TO MY GRANDFATHER, MY OPA. He epitomized everything that was heroic and, in his youth, was the very image of the dashing, romantic cavalry officer. He distinguished himself for his brave actions numerous times on the battlefield.

My grandfather passed on to me so many values that I cannot single out one as more important than another. He also recognized that horses moved me the way they did him. That love of horses brought us closer, creating an enormous bond between us. He taught me that insight could be achieved by seeing the world through the eyes of those gentle creatures. Hardly an hour goes by that I do not think of him and how much I owe him. When I am around horses, not a minute goes by that he is not on my mind.

I next need to thank my wife, Jane, and my three children, Joshua, Luke, and Tessa. No one in my family ever really loved horses the way I did. The four of them could have lived perfectly normal, happy lives without them. They all seemed to understand that I could not, though, and they always supported me in my equine endeavors even if it meant that we had less money for other things. There is no higher expression of love than sacrificing so the people you love can feel fulfilled. I am eternally grateful to my wonderful family for the gift of letting a second family, an equine one, into their hearts.

To Jane, there is a higher level of gratitude. She supported this book project with countless hours of reading manuscript drafts and poring over collations of figures. Without her faith in this endeavor, I would never have undertaken it. As a doctor in clinical psychology, Jane has always astonished me with her grasp of how horses and humans connect and her magical abilities, as a psychotherapist, to help people process the insights that emerge from those interactions. As a horse professional, I have been blessed with being partnered with one of the most gifted psychologists in the country. That is a large part of why I've been privileged to see so many personal insights and breakthroughs with clients working with horses. The equine clinics and seminars Jane and I have run together number among the happiest days of my life.

In any field we are indebted to our teachers and mentors. It is simply not possible to claim any insight into the world and mind of horses without paying homage to my pantheon of heroes, trainers, clinicians, and authors who have cherished horses and were moved to try to teach others, including myself, about them.

The first are my riding counselors at Camp Lincoln: Lance, Lucia, Jim, and so many others. I am forever in their debt for their calm, patient instruction and all the equine adventures they managed to lead us campers on. They never missed an occasion to get out on the trail and make us feel like we were the first mountain men, exploring new territories.

The next noteworthy person must be Ray Hunt, who changed the whole world of horsemanship by advocating a new partnership with horses based on harmony. Ray showed everyone how much of a *gentle* man a real master of horsemanship could be. It is a great honor to have met him.

Then there is Monty Roberts. There will only be one Monty because he showed the entire world that training a horse meant first having to learn a new language, *Equus*. Monty proved that not only did horses speak in an eloquent tongue but also that humanity could be taught how to hear it. Monty also taught by example, by inspiration. He demonstrated in his personal life and values that learning to understand horsemanship could make you a better, kinder human being, and that, in turn, helped the world to be a better place.

John Lyons inspired me by showing me that horsemanship was accessible to anyone and did not have to be seen as a magical process. Instead, he persistently demonstrated its logical progression of discrete steps that can be mastered by anyone willing to take the time and patience to practice and refine technique. Every step of that process was built upon mutual respect between horse and human.

I must also extend a special thanks to Pat Parelli and his wife Linda. Pat not only invented the seven fundamental games that are so essential to training horses but also established a systematic approach that every student could use to gain mastery of horsemanship. He personally showed me that training horses means playing with horses. That has served as a transformational paradigm for me and thousands of other horse lovers around the world. For all of Pat's qualities as an expert trainer and showman, he remains one of the most humble and earnest men I have ever met.

Mark Devereaux, who worked for a while at Pat's place in Pagosa Springs, became one of the outstanding local trainers here in the Southwest. He often used my ranch for holding his clinics and always spared a moment to show me a new trick or twist to training a horse. I had never had such an opportunity to converse in such detail about the habits of horses. Those conversations with Mark will echo forever for me.

"Cricket" Metz was my riding teacher for years after I arrived in Tucson. Even when I thought I had hit a wall in my riding skills, Cricket always seemed to find an alternate strategy for getting over the hump. I will never forget her thumping on a drum to help me get the rhythm of my horse's diagonals. Bless her heart.

Brian Anderson and Harvey Jacobs were another pair of local horse trainers who always took the time to show me the ropes, literally — how to use a lariat. For both Brian and Harvey, there simply is no greater compliment a hand can be paid than to be called a "horseman." Like Monty Roberts, they impressed upon me that horsemanship was a set of values rather than techniques.

Lanny Leach is another of the Southwest's outstanding horsemen who is generous to a fault about sharing his wisdom, techniques, and insight in the most humble and generous formats.

I must thank Dr. Robert Miller, who has served the world of horsemanship as both its conscience and its scholar. He popularized foal imprinting and made it a standard technique for most horsemen and horsewomen. He has also made invaluable contributions to the literature on horsemanship.

I must acknowledge the inspiration of GaWaNi Pony Boy because he not only opened the world's eyes to the great gifts Native American horsemanship has given us but also understood the sea-change that women helped bring to the world of horse training.

I owe an enormous debt of gratitude to Lynn Thomas and Greg Kersten, the cofounders of the Equine-Assisted Growth and Learning Association in Santaquin, Utah. They have done both horses and clients a great service by seeing just how far horses and human beings can help each other through equine-assisted learning and therapy.

A special thanks to Kevin and Rosaleen Smith and the Healing Energy Alleviates Life's Scars (HEALS) who believe so much in what equine-assisted programs can bring to the horses and people of the Republic of Ireland. Jane and I have been honored by their friendship and inspired by their passion and love for horses.

I have to thank my great ranch staff, including Stace Hines-Holdcraft, Lex Deines, Gabriel Negrete, and the inimitable Samantha Biffar. They are my second family — the ones that love horses. Sharing horses, clinics, and clients with them has been one of the great honors of my life. My thanks to Lex, who epitomizes what it means to be "a good hand." Lex's exterior may be as tough as nails but there is a huge heart of gold underneath. Sam, who's helped me with calving, running clinics, doctoring horses, and looking for lost cattle in the dark, is the embodiment of a true, good character. In other words, she is the kind of person who does the right thing — no matter what. Her integrity and devotion to the welfare of every animal, large and small, inspire me every day. To Stace, who is always there, from running the Department of Surgery at the University of Arizona in years past, to coming, in the last few years, to take over running the ranch. If you look up "cool-headed competency" in the dictionary, Stace's picture is there. She worked tirelessly on the edits (which I notoriously and endlessly elaborate) for this manuscript. No one multitasks the way Stace does, going from brand inspector on line one to book editor on line two while editing a manuscript on the computer screen and keeping it all organized. She takes chaos and makes it orderly and calms the storms into navigable seas.

I have been blessed to work in the Tucson area. This is the heart of horse country and I've been exposed to some of the leaders in the movement to evaluate the deeper emotional and spiritual connections between horses and humans. Barbara Rector, who has worked on behalf of the Therapeutic Riding of Tucson and developed the equine-assisted program at Sierra Tucson, has been a leader in pioneering programs to heighten personal awareness through interactions with horses. She has touched everyone with her horse-size heart in Tucson. Linda Kohanov, the author of *The Tao of Equus*, has also been a huge inspiration. Her writings and her Epona Equestrian Services have introduced thousands of individuals to the transformational potential of horses.

My thanks to Mike Larsen and Elizabeth Pomada for being not just great literary agents but also great friends. Thanks to Rebecca Salome for reading, editing, correcting, and commenting on so many different aspects and versions of this manuscript. Thanks to Kris Spinning for creative photography, ideas, and encouragement and to Paul Dumbauld for working so tirelessly to translate concepts into eloquent illustrations and diagrams. Thanks to Lynn Wiese for always being there to push me into doing the interviews and talks I'd be too shy to do otherwise.

My deepest thanks to Deb Burns, who not only deeply believed in this project, but who approached its design and editing with a keen eye for the details of horsemanship, the sharp but sensitive talents of a great editor, and the support and enthusiasm of a close friend.

I also want to thank Pam Art, Jennifer Travis, and the incredible staff at Storey Publishing: I am eternally grateful for their support of a greater mission in this book that inspired all of us who worked together on it. Kudos to Dan Williams, our book designer; to Jennie Jepson Smith, our book builder; to Elayne Sears, our freelance artist; to Mars Vilaubi, our photo editor; and to Ilona Sherratt, our illustration editor.

Then there are all the horses. All the beautiful, wonderful horses. Thunder. Bubbles. Uncle. Andy. Ace. Bruce. Chiquita. Peanuts. Nanny. Thor. Y Tu. Hanna. Binker. Nicky. Sonny. Mahto. Romeo. Santana. Briana. My newest and most beautiful Lipizzan baby: Teddy. And so many beautiful equine souls I've met along the way and, I hope and expect, many more still to greet. To me, a world without horses would have been an unbearably impoverished creation.

Many of the horses and individuals in the stories in this book are based on real events, but I have taken liberties, much as I would when cooking up a good pot of chili, to combine or customize the ingredients to maximize the zest of the dish served up. Homemade cornbread on the side.

Blessings.

PHOTO CREDITS

© AF Archive/Alamy: 13

© Allan Hamilton: 15, 16, 21, 173, 174, 296

© Alexander Crispin/Getty Images: viii

The Art Archive/Bibliothèque des Arts Décoratifs Paris/Gianni Dagli Orti: 34

© Bob Langrish: 275, 284

© Christopher Dydyk: 38

Courtesy of Camp Lincoln, North Country Camps: 19

© Dawn Nichols/iStockphoto: 193

© Dennis Hallinan/Alamy: 213

© Dusty Perin: 78, 104, 252

© Erik deGraaf/iStockphoto: 132

© franzfoto.com/Alamy: 96

© Frederic Chehu/www.arnd.nl

© Getty Images, Jamie Grill: 121

© Getty Images, Majid Saheed: 94 top

© Getty Images, Paul Popper/Popperfoto: 6

The Granger Collection, NYC–All rights reserved: 40

© The Guardian/Alamy: 263 bottom

© Ian Davidson Photographic/Alamy: 14

© Jonathan Larsen/Diadem Images/Alamy: 263 top

© Juniors Bildarchiv/Alamy: 18

Library of Congress, Prints & Photographs Division, Edward S. Curtis Collection: 94 bottom, 276

© Lucca Tettoni/age fotostock: 41

Mansell Collection: 113

© National Geographic/Getty Images: 267

© Nik Wheeler/Alamy: 109

© Peter Adams/age fotostock: 93

© Peter Holmes/age fotostock: 86

© 2011 Photo Researchers, Inc., Neil Borden: 30

© Radius Images/Alamy: 37

© Sports Illustrated/Getty Images, Manny Millan: 44

© Tracy Tucker/iStockphoto.com: 45

Wikimedia Commons: 42, 73, 91, 106, 115, 148, 248

© World History Archive/Alamy: 114

BIBLIOGRAPHY

Abbey, Harlan C. *Showing Your Horse.* Arco Publishing, 1970.

Ainslie, Tom and Bonnie Ledbetter. *The Body Language of Horses.* William Morrow, 1980.

Albrecht, Kurt. *Principles of Dressage.* J. A. Allen, 1993.

Anderson, Clinton and Ami Hendrickson. *Clinton Anderson's Downunder Horsemanship.* Trafalgar Square, 2004.

Anderson, Clinton and Melinda Kaitcer. *Lessons Well Learned.* Tralfalgar Square, 2009.

Baskins, Don. *Well-Shod.* Western Horseman, 1997.

Bayley, Lesley. *What is My Horse Thinking?* Hamlyn, 2002.

Bayley, Leseley and Caroline Davis. *The Less Than Perfect Rider.* Howell, 1994.

Blazer, Don and Cathy Hanson. *Natural Western Riding,* rev. ed. Success is Easy, 2001.

Bloom, Lydia. *Fitting & Showing the Halter Horse.* Prentice Hall, 1987.

Boiselle, Gabrielle. *Horses: Their Temperament and Elegance.* White Star Publishers, 2006.

Boy, GaWaNi Pony. *Horse, Follow Closely.* BowTie Press, 1998.

———. *Out of the Saddle.* Bowtie Press, 1998.

Brannaman, Buck. *Groundwork.* Rancho Deluxe Design, 1997.

Brannaman, Buck and William Reynolds. *The Faraway Horses.* Lyons Press. 2001.

Budiansky, Stephen. *The Nature of Horses.* Free Press, 1997.

———. *The World According to Horses.* H. Holt, 2000.

Bürger, Udo. *The Way to Perfect Horsemanship.* Trafalgar Square, 1998.

Burkhardt, Barbara. *Dressage from A to X,* rev ed. Trafalgar Square, 2004.

Camp, Joe. *The Soul of a Horse.* Harmony Books, 2008.

Cavendish, William. *A General System of Horsemanship.* Trafalgar Square Publishing, 2000.

Chappell, Mike. *British Cavalry Equipments, 1800–1941,* rev ed. Osprey, 2002.

Charny, Geoffroi de. *Jousts and Tournaments.* Translated by Steven Muhlberger. Chivalry Bookshelf, 2002.

Coates, Margrit. *Connecting with Horses.* Ulysses Press, 2008.

Daly, H. W. *Manual of Pack Transportation.* Long Riders' Guide Press, 2001.

Davis, Francis W. *Horse Packing In Pictures,* 2nd ed. Scribners, Howell, 1991.

Dietz, Alfons J. *Training the Horse In Hand.* Lyons Press, 2004.

Dorrance, Bill and Leslie Desmond. *True Horsemanship Through Feel.* Lyons Press, 2001.

Dorrance, Tom. *True Unity: Willing Communication Between Horse and Human.* Give-It-A-Go Enterprises, 2009.

Dougall, Neil. *Stallions: Their Management and Handling.* J.A. Allen, 1973.

Dratfield, Jim. *The Quotable Equine.* Clarkson Potter, 2003.

Duarte, Dom. *The Royal Book of Horsemanship, Jousting and Knightly Combat.* Translated by Antonio Franco

Preto and edited by Steven Muhlberger. Chivalry Bookshelf, 2005.

Dunning, Al. *Reining*, rev ed. Western Horseman, 1996.

Edwards, Elwyn Hartley. *Ultimate Horse Book*, rev ed. DK Publishing, 2002.

Elser, Smoke and Bill Brown. *Packin' In On Mules and Horses*. Mountain Press Publishing, 1980.

d'Endrödy, A. L. *Give Your Horse a Chance*. J. A. Allen, 1999.

Equine Travelers of America. *Nationwide Overnight Stabling Directory & Equestrian Vacation Guide*. Equine Travelers of America, Inc., updated frequently.

Evans, Nicholas. *The Horse Whisperer*. Delacorte Press, 1995.

Exley, Helen. *Horse Quotations*. Exley Publishers, 1991.

Fletcher, C. *Trickonometry: The Secrets of Teaching Your Horse Tricks*. Singin' Saddles Press, 2008 .

Kahn, Cynthia M. and Scott Line, eds. *The Merck Veterinary Manual*, 10th ed. Merck, 2010.

Gonzaga, Paulo Gaviäo. *A History of the Horse*. Vol. 1, *The Iberian Horse from Ice Age to Antiquity*. J. A. Allen, 2004.

Green, Ben K. *Horse Conformation As to Soundness and Performance*, rev ed. Northland Publishing, 1991.

Guérinière, Francois Robichon de la. *École de Cavalerie*. Xenophon Press, 1992.

———. *School of Horsemanship*. London, England: J. A. Allen, 1994.

Harris, Charles. *Workbooks from the Spanish School*. J.A. Allen, 2004.

Harris, Susan E. *Grooming to Win*, 3rd ed. Howell Book House, 2008.

Hassler, Jill Keiser. *Beyond The Mirrors*. Goals Unlimited, 1993.

Hassler-Scoop, Jill K. *Equestrian Instruction*. Goals Unlimited, 2000.

Hausman, Gerald and Loretta Hausman. *The Mythology of Horses*. Three Rivers Press, 2003.

Haworth, Josephine. *The Horsemasters*. Methuen, 1983.

Hayes, M. Horace. *Points of the Horse*, 7th ed. Arco Publishing, 1969.

———. *Illustrated Horse Breaking*, 3rd ed. Hurst & Blackett, 1908.

———. *Veterinary Notes for Horse Owners*, 18th ed. Simon & Schuster, 2002.

———. *Stable Management and Exercise*, 5th ed. Hurst & Blackett, 1947.

Heaberlin, Sandra and Melody Hull. *The America Lipizzan: A Pictorial History*. Lipizzan Association of North America, 1999.

Hempfling, Klaus Ferdinand. *Dancing with Horses*. Trafalgar Square, 2001.

Henriquet, Michel. *Henriquet on Dressage*. J.A. Allen, 2004.

Henry, Marguerite. *White Stallion of Lipizza*. Chicago: Rand McNally, 1964.

Hill, Cherry. *How to Think Like a Horse*. Storey Publishing, 2006.

Hillenbrand, Laura. *Seabiscuit*. Random House, 2001.

Hills, R. J. T. *The Royal Horse Guards*. Leo Cooper Ltd., 1970.

Hinrichs, Richard. *Schooling Horses In Hand*. Trafalgar Square, 2001.

Hopkins, Frank T. *Hidalgo and Other Stories*. Long Riders' Guild Press, 2003.

Hoverson, Bob. *The Packer's Field Manual*. Stoneydale Press Publishing, 2005.

Hunt, Ray. *Think Harmony With Horses*. Pioneer Publishing, 1978.

Hyland, Ann. *The Medieval Warhorse*. Sutton Publishing, 1996.

———. *The Horse in The Ancient World*. Praeger Publishers, 2003.

Irwin, Chris and Bob Weber. *Horses Don't Lie*. Marlowe & Co., 2001

James, Ruth B. *How to be Your Own Veterinarian (Sometimes)*, 2nd ed. Alpine Press, 2007.

Johnson, Dusty. *Saddle Savvy*, 2nd ed. Saddleman Press, 2006.

———. *Horse Packing Illustrated*. Saddleman Press, 2000.

Johnson, Jackie. *Step by Step Trick Training*. Jackie Johnson, 2003.

Jordan, Theresa J. Peter E. De Michele. *Overcoming the Fear of Riding*. Breakthrough Publications, 1996.

Kane, Beverly. *The Manual of Medicine and Horsemanship*. AuthorHouse, 2007.

Karrasch, Shawna and Vinton Karrasch. *You Can Train Your Horse To Do Anything!* Trafalgar Square, 2000.

Kathrens, Ginger. *Cloud's Legacy: The Wild Stallion Returns*. BowTie Press, 2003.

Kersten, G. and Thomas, L. *Equine Assisted Psychotherapy and Learning: Untraining Manual*. EAGALA, 2004.

Kimball, Cheryl. *Mindful Horsemanship*. Carriage House Pub., 2002.

Klimke, Ingrid and Reiner Klimke. *Cavalletti: The Schooling of Horse and Rider Over Ground Poles*. Lyons Press, 2000.

Kohanov, Linda. *The Tao of Equus*. New World Library, 2001.

———. *Riding Between the Worlds*. New World Library, 2003.

Korda, Michael. *Horse People: Scenes from the Riding Life*. HarperCollins, 2004.

Krolick, David. *Shoeing Right*. Breakthrough Publications, 1991.

Dolenc, Milan. *Lipizzaner: The Story of the Horses of Lipica*. Control Data Arts, 1981.

Kunffy, Charles de. *The Athletic Development of the Dressage Horse*. Howell Book House, 1992.

———. *Dressage Principles Illuminated*. Trafalgar Square, 2002.

Kurland, Alexandra. *Clicker Training For Your Horse*. Sunshine Books, 1998.

Loch, Sylvia. *The Classical Rider: Being at One with Your Horse*. Trafalgar Square, 1997.

———. *Dressage: the Art of Classical Riding*. Trafalgar Square, 1990.

———. *Dressage in Lightness: Speaking the Horse's Language*. Trafalgar Square, 2000.

Loving, Nancy S. *Conformation and Performance*. Breakthrough Publications, 1997.

Lyons, John. *Lyons on Horses*. Skyhorse Publishing, 2009.

———. *Communicating with Cues: The Rider's Guide to Training and Problem Solving*. 3 parts. Belvoir Publications, 1998–99.

———. *Perfect Horsekeeping*. Belvoir Publications, 1999.

———. *Perfectly Practical Advice on Horsemanship*. Belvoir Publications, 1999.

———. *Raising & Feeding the Perfect Horse*. Belvoir Publications, 1999.

Mangum, A. J. *Ranch Roping with Buck Brannaman*. Western Horseman, 2000.

Mannis, Barbara and Catherine Lewis. *The Incredible Little Book of 10,001 Names for Horses*. Horse Hollow Press, 1999.

Marks, Kelly. *Creating a Bond with Your Horse*. J. A. Allen, 2000.

———. *Leading and Loading*. J. A. Allen, 2000.

———. *Teach Your Horse Perfect Manners*. Trafalgar Square, 2010

Marten, Marty. *Problem-Solving*. 2 vols. Western Horseman, 1998–2003.

McBride, Laura Harrison. *Teaching Your Horse to Overcome Fears*. A Storey Country Wisdom Bulletin, A-280. Storey Publishing, 2001.

McCall, James P. *The Stallion: A Breeding Guide for Owners and Handlers.* Howell Book House, 1995.

McCormick, Adele von Rüst, Marlena Deborah McCormick, and Thomas E. McCormick. *Horses and the Mystical Path.* New World Library, 2004.

McDonnell, Sue. *A Practical Field Guide to Horse Behavior.* Eclipse Press, 2003.

McGreevey, Paul. *Equine Behavior: A Guide for Veterinarians and Equine Scientists.* W. B. Saunders, 2004.

Meeder, Kim. *Hope Rising.* Multnomah, 2003.

Micklem, William. *Complete Horse Riding Manual.* DK Publishing, 2003.

Miller, Robert M. *Understanding the Ancient Secrets of the Horse's Mind.* Russell Meerdink Co., 1999.

———. *Imprint Training of the Newborn Foal.* Western Horseman, 1991.

Miller, Robert M. and Richard A. Lamb. *The Revolution in Horsemanship and What it Means to Mankind.* Lyons Press, 2005.

Mora, Joseph Jacinto. *Californios.* Doubleday, 1949.

Morpurgo, Michael. *War Horse.* Scholastic Press, 1982.

Morris, Desmond. *Horse Watching.* Crown, 1989.

Müseler, Wilhelm. *Riding Logic,* updated ed. Trafalgar Square, 2007.

Nolan, Louis Edward. *Cavalry: Its History and Tactics.* Westholme Publishing, 2007.

Oliveira, Nuño. *Reflections on Equestrian Art.* J. A. Allen, 1988.

Parelli, Pat. *Natural Horse-Man-Ship.* Western Horseman, 1993.

Pegasus Project. *Examples of Good Practice in Equine Therapy.* George Mann Publications, 2005.

Pelicano, Rick and Lauren Tjaden. *Bombproof Your Horse.* Trafalgar Square, 2004.

Pluvinel, Antoine de. *Le Maneige Royal.* J. A. Allen, 1989.

Podhajsky, Alois. *The White Stallions of Vienna.* Dutton, 1963.

———. *My Dancing White Horses.* G. G. Harrap, 1964.

———. *The Complete Training of Horse and Rider.* Doubleday, 1967.

———. *My Horses, My Teachers.* Doubleday, 1968.

———. *The Lipizzaners.* Doubleday, 1969.

———. *The Riding Teacher.* Doubleday, 1973.

Post, Charles Johnson. *Horse Packing.* Long Riders' Guide Press, 2000.

Price, Steven D., ed. *The Quotable Horse Lover.* Lyons Press, 1999.

Rashid, Mark. *Considering the Horse,* 2nd ed. Skyhorse Publishing, 2010.

———. *A Good Horse is Never a Bad Color.* Johnson Printing, 1996.

———. *Whole Heart, Whole Horse.* Skyhorse Publishing, 2009.

Reuter, Wolfgang. *The Lipizzaners and the Spanish Riding School.* Wilshire Books, 1969.

Rivas, Mim Eichler. *Beautiful Jim Key.* William Morrow, 2005.

Roberts, Monty. *The Man Who Listens to Horses,* rev ed. Ballantine Books, 2009.

———. *Shy Boy: The Horse That Came In From The Wild.* HarperCollins, 1999.

———. *Horse Sense for People.* HarperCollins, 2001.

Roberts, Monty and Jean Abernathy. *From My Hands to Yours.* Monty and Pat Roberts, 2002.

Ryden, Hope. *America's Last Wild Horses,* 13th anniversary ed. Lyon's Press, 1999.

Savoie, Jane. *More Cross-Training,* book 2. Trafalgar Square, 1998.

Scanlan, Lawrence. *Wild About Horses.* HarperCollins, 1998.

Scott, Naomi. *Special Needs, Special Horses*. University of North Texas Press, 2005.

Seunig, Waldemar. *Horsemanship*. Garden City, NY: Doubleday & Company Inc., 1958.

Sharp, Jan. *Trick Training Your Horse to Success*. Eclipse Press, 2004.

Sharp, John. *Knots, Hitches and Their Uses*. Tribune Publishing, 1966.

Smith, Bradford P. *Large Animal Internal Medicine*, 4th ed. Mosby, 2009.

Soren, Ingrid. *Zen and Horses: Lessons from a Year of Riding*. Rodale, 2002.

Spurling, Emma Crosby. *My Kingdom is a Horse*. Branden Publishing, 1999.

Squires, Edward L. *Understanding the Stallion*. The Blood-Horse Inc., 1999.

Stanton, Paul. *The Duckboy Way, or, Quack in the Saddle Again*. Duckboy Cards, 1997.

Stone, Lynn M. *Lipizzans*. Rourke Corp., 1998.

Stoneridge, M. A. *Practical Horseman's Book of Horsekeeping*. Doubleday, 1983.

Sumerel, Dan. *Finding the Magic*. Warwick House, 2000.

Swift, Sally. *Centered Riding*. St. Martin's Press, 1985.

Timmons, Bonnie. *Hold Your Horses*. Workman, 2003.

Twelveponies, Mary. *There Are No Problem Horses, Only Problem Riders*. Houghton Mifflin, 1982.

Vereingung, Deutsche Reiterliche. *Advanced Techniques of Riding*, book 2. Translated and illustrated by Gisela Holstein. Half Halt Press, 1987.

Wanless, Mary. *The Natural Rider: A Right-Brain Approach to Riding*. Trafalgar Square, 1996.

———. *Ride with Your Mind Essentials*. Trafalgar Square, 2002.

Waring, George H. *Horse Behavior*, 2nd ed. Noyes Publications, 2003.

Watson, J. N. P. *Through Fifteen Reigns*. Spellmount, 1997.

Webb, Wyatt and Cindy Pearlman. *It's Not About the Horse: It's About Overcoming Fear and Self-Doubt*. Hay House, 2002.

Wilcox, Charlotte. *The Lipizzaner Horse*. Capstone Press, 1997.

Williams, Marta. *Learning Their Language*. New World Library, 2003.

Windisch-Graetz, Mathilde. *The Spanish Riding School*, 5th ed. Cassell, 1964.

Witter, Rebekah Ferran. *Winning with Horsepower!* Trafalgar Square, 1999.

Wright, Ed, Martha Wright, and Glory Ann Kurtz. *Barrel Racing: Training the Wright Way*. Equimedia, 1999.

Wright, Maurice Delpratt. *The Jeffery Method of Horse Handling*. R. M. Williams Pty., 1973

Xenophon. *The Art of Horsemanship*. Feather Trail Press, 2009.

INDEX

OTHER STOREY TITLES
YOU WILL ENJOY

Among Wild Horses, by Lynne Pomeranz.
An extraordinary photographic journal of three years in the lives of the
Pryor Mountain Mustangs of Montana and Wyoming.
144 pages. Hardcover with jacket. ISBN 978-1-58017-633-0.

The Horse Behavior Problem Solver, by Jessica Jahiel.
A friendly, question-and-answer sourcebook to teach readers how to
interpret problems and develop workable solutions.
352 pages. Paper. ISBN 978-1-58017-524-1.

How to Think Like a Horse, by Cherry Hill.
Detailed discussions of how horses think, learn, respond to stimuli, and
interpret human behavior — in short, a light on the equine mind.
192 pages. Paper. ISBN 978-1-58017-835-8.

Ride the Right Horse, by Yvonne Barteau.
The key to learning the personality of your horse and
working with his strengths.
312 pages. Hardcover with jacket. ISBN 978-1-58017-662-0.

Storey's Guide to Raising Horses, 2nd edition,
by Heather Smith Thomas.
The complete guide to intelligent horsekeeping: how to
keep a horse healthy in body and spirit.
528 pages. Paper. ISBN 978-1-60342-471-4. Hardcover. 978-1-60342-472-1.

Storey's Guide to Training Horses, 2nd edition,
by Heather Smith Thomas.
Vital information about the training process, written from the standpoint
that each horse is unique and needs to learn at its own pace.
504 pages. Paper. ISBN 978-1-60342-544-5. Hardcover. ISBN 978-1-60342-553-7.

What Every Horse Should Know, by Cherry Hill.
A guide to teaching the skills every horse needs to learn to bring out the
full potential of the horse-human partnership.
192 pages. Paper. ISBN 978-1-60342-713-5. Hardcover. ISBN 978-1-60342-716-6.

These and other books from Storey Publishing are available
wherever quality books are sold or by calling 1-800-441-5700.
Visit us at *www.storey.com*.